GARDEN CITY: VANCOUVER

Garden City: Vancouver

MARG MEIKLE & DANNIE McARTHUR

POLESTAR
BOOK PUBLISHERS

Polestar Book Publishers acknowledges the ongoing financial support of The
Canada Council; the British Columbia Ministry of Small Business, Tourism and
Culture through the BC Arts Council; and the Government of Canada through the
Book Publishing Industry Development Program (BPIDP).

Cover art by Bernie Lyon
Cover design by Jim Brennan.
Printed and bound in Canada.

CANADIAN CATALOGUING IN PUBLICATION DATA
       Meikle, Margaret, 1956-
       Garden city
       (The city series)
       ISBN 1-896095-53-4
1. Gardening – British Columbia – Vancouver – Guidebooks. 2. Gardening –
British Columbia – Lower Mainland – Guidebooks. 3. Vancouver (B.C.) – Guide-
books. 4. Lower Mainland (B.C.) – Guidebooks. I. McArthur, Dannie, 1948- II.
Title. III. Series: The city series (Victoria, B.C.)
SB451.36.C3M44 1999 635'.09711'33 C99-910214-1

POLESTAR BOOK PUBLISHERS
P.O. Box 5238, Station B
Victoria, British Columbia
Canada
V8R 6N4
http://mypage.direct.ca/p/polestar/

WE WOULD LIKE TO THANK Michelle Benjamin, Lynn Henry and Emiko Morita of Polestar Book Publishers for their patience and support and for holding out for an extra year while Marg had a baby (Mac, a bonny boy).

Thanks to Carolyn Swayze, literary agent, and Noel MacDonald, Marg's husband and an excellent sandwich maker. And a warm thank-you to the amazing Bernie Lyon — what illustrations!

Thanks to sounding boards and information mines: Moira Carlson, Terri Clark, Barbara Fox, Donna Guillemin, Thomas Hobbs, Roy Jonsson, Clive Justice, Doug Justice, Michael Luco, Bunny Meikle, Judy Newton, Patricia North, Sharon Shindler, Bill Stephen, Ross Waddell and Nancy Wong.

Thanks to contributors: Lolita Aaron, Mary Allen, Ann Bailey, Dr. Art Bomke, The B.C. Landscape and Nursery Association, Odessa Bromley, Ron Clancy, Terri Clark, Dana Cromie, Spring Gillard, Donna Guillemin, Joette Heuft, Jennifer Jones, Roy Jonsson, Claire Kennedy, Ann Kent, Michael Levenston, Cabot Lyford, Bruce Macdonald, Rachel Mackenzie, Stevie McQueen, Paul Montpellier, Aimee Murrell, Angela Murrills, Mike Nassichuk, Moura Quayle, Richmond Nature Park, Jean Schwartz, Shelagh Smith, The Song Bird Project, David Tarrant, The Universal Garden Society, VanDusen Botanical Garden's Master Gardeners, Edward van Veenendaal, Derry Walsh and Elisabeth Whitelaw.

And thanks for the research help from Karen Fraser, Robert Gray, Donna Guillemin, Suzie McArthur, Kephra Senett, Katherine Watson and Laura Wright.

— *Marg Meikle and Dannie McArthur*

To gardeners everywhere —

an extremely down-to-earth lot.

Garden City: Vancouver

PREFACE

It has finally happened: Gardening is now the Number One outdoor leisure activity in Vancouver and the Lower Mainland. According to the British Columbia Landscape & Nursery Association, the nursery trades generate around $750 million in business annually in this province. Half the population of British Columbia (approximately 1.8 million people) lives in the Greater Vancouver Regional District – and we've got the best gardening weather. A lot of people are out there digging. With all of this interest in gardening, the standard patch of mowed lawn with row on row of six basic flowers is going the way of the dodo bird. The more people learn about gardens and gardening, the more adventurous they become.

Garden City: Vancouver is not intended to be a "how-to" book. There are many excellent how-to references for this region and we've even made a list of them (page 263). This is a "how-to-find" and "who-to-ask" book – in other words, the ultimate resource guide. We've found all the people, plants and places you might like to know about to increase your knowledge and enjoyment of gardening. And it has been a challenge – there is an enormous number of gardening resources in the Lower Mainland. In compiling this book, we have tried very hard to get our facts straight and be inclusive. We are not in the business of rating businesses, people or gardens. We are here to let you know what's available so that you can make your own decisions.

This book is about the whole Lower Mainland of British Columbia – indeed, it ought to be called *Garden City: GVRD* (after the Greater Vancouver Regional District, which is the area encompassing the 2930 square kilometres around the mouth of the Fraser River) but *Garden City: Vancouver* just sounded better. The Greater Vancouver Regional District includes: Bowen Island, Burnaby, Coquitlam, Delta, Ladner, Langley, Maple Ridge, New Westminster, North Vancouver, Port Coquitlam, Port Moody, Richmond, Surrey, Vancouver, West Vancouver and

White Rock. We realize that the gardening world flourishes past this boundary but we had to draw the line somewhere.

We apologize in advance for our mistakes and for people and businesses we may have missed. Please let us know about omissions. For a future edition of *Garden City* we're collecting information on the history of gardening in the Lower Mainland. Got a story? Let us know. Send any additions, deletions or comments for the next edition of *Garden City: Vancouver* to the addresses listed at the back of the book.

Researching and writing *Garden City: Vancouver* has been a massive undertaking, but we can also say that digging up the dirt on gardening has been a consistently fascinating adventure. We hope this book is as informative and interesting for you to read as it was for us to research and write.

INTRODUCTION

by David Tarrant

Vancouver is a city of wonderful gardens both private and public, and it boasts an eclectic gardening population. I first visited the city in the fall of 1968, having spent a summer gardening at Chateau Lake Louise. I remember so well walking down Davie Street in a soft autumn rain, passing some still-remaining private homes with giant magnolias and rhododendrons, two of the latter towering above the upstairs bedroom windows. I wandered on past the Sylvia Hotel, which was shrouded in *Parthenocissus,* and on into Stanley Park, meandering under Horse Chestnut trees and among hardy fuchsias, more rhododendrons and many other familiar plants from my childhood and training in the UK. It was then that I decided I must live here — everything was so lush and beautiful. Better yet, I was still in Canada.

Judy Newton and David Tarrant at the Perennial Plant Sale at UBC Botanical Garden. Photo: June West

In the fall of 1969 I was hired at the UBC Botanical Garden where I have remained to this day. Over the last fifteen years or so gardening has gone through something of a renaissance throughout North America, skyrocketing to become the continent's most popular hobby. Of course, since Vancouver's founding there have been gardening clubs, and in the old days the PNE Fall Fair was where everyone congregated to see the vast displays of vegetables and flowers. Nowadays we can hardly wait for the annual VanDusen Flower and Garden Show each June, or the Fall Apple Festival at UBC Botanical Garden, to discover the very latest plant, gadget or gizmo to be added to our own garden, be it on a balcony or in the backyard.

In a climate such as this city enjoys, gardening resources grow almost faster than new plants. Inexhaustible researchers Marg Meikle and Dannie McArthur have come up with the most useful compendium of resources that any local gardener could ever hope to have. I am sure that even gardening fanatics in other cities across the country will find much of the information, lists and sources included here invaluable.

This book is packed with excellent essays, good lists and down-to-earth, helpful information from experts. Author Marg Meikle reflects her own happy gardening character with useful tips and anecdotes that make one laugh out loud and remind us that gardening should be fun. *Garden City: Vancouver* will be an invaluable addition to my library; I'm sure it will be indispensable in yours too.

STARTING TO GROW

Before you begin gardening, it is useful to know a few basic facts. If you understand the ranges of our climate, the make-up of our soil and the availability of our water, you are well on your way to smart growing. Given our annual rainfall, it does seem ironic that water conservation is an issue in Vancouver, but drought is a reality in our summers. Ecological gardening *is* appropriate to this region. We advocate improving soil, cultivating native plants and using less water.

OUR CLIMATE

Among gardening spots in Canada, Vancouver and the Lower Mainland is almost as good as it gets (only Vancouver Island beats us for warmth). But how good is our climate? Environment Canada has been collecting data since 1937, so we have a pretty accurate idea of what to expect each month. The main thing to remember is that because of the mountains and the ocean, the Lower Mainland has dozens of microclimates. Just how great is the variation? How about this: Pebble Hill in Delta has 849.4 mm of rainfall a year while Seymour Falls in the Upper Seymour Valley gets 3814.2 mm. That's four-and-a-half times as much rain! What does this mean for the average gardener? Keep an eye on your neighbours' gardens and watch for what thrives there. For a good example of the variations in microclimates, just look at the differences in what grows above and below the Upper Levels Highway in North Vancouver.

Our Zone: Where Are We?

The Botanical World is broken into a number of climactic zones, and plants are rated according to their appropriateness for those zones. It seems like a simple idea, but there are a number of different opinions on plant hardiness in this region. Most of the maps are based on minimum temperatures, but they aren't all in agreement. So consider the source when you read a text or catalogue or plant label. And don't be a slave to these numbers — visit our botanical gardens and talk to neighbours, folks at the nurseries and your local garden clubs. They will tell you if something is hardy in our climate. Performance is more telling than a number.

Canadian publications and nursery catalogues tend to use the Agriculture Canada's "Map of Plant Hardiness Zones in Canada". They rate the Vancouver area as 8a or 8b with a few microclimates of 9a. See also:
http://www.connect.ab.ca/~buddy/ngarden.htm

The New Sunset Western Garden Book (1995, Sunset) only refers to the coastal parts of BC and puts them into their ranking as zone 4, extending only slightly north of West Vancouver and Nanaimo.

The U.S. Department of Agriculture breaks North America into 10 zones from half-way up the map of Canada through Florida. They put Vancouver in zone 8 near the coast and zone 7 inland. For more information, see:
http://www.hcs.ohio-state.edu/mg/studentlinks/hzones/hzones.htm

What can you do with your old gardening books and magazines?
Donate them to the VanDusen Botanical Garden Library. They have an annual sale to raise funds for purchasing current volumes.

In the City of Vancouver, 55 percent of land is private and 45 percent of land is public. Here's a breakdown of public land:
- Golf courses and VanDusen Botanical Garden: 2%
- Cemetery and other: 2%
- School Board lands: 2%
- Public streets: 30%
- Parks: 9%

SOIL

Do-It-Yourself Soil Improvement

by Dr. Art Bomke and Jean Schwartz

Urban soils provide the foundation for successful gardening and make an important contribution to the sustainability of our urban landscapes. We often forget that soils play a number of roles in cities dominated by roads, buildings, parking lots and other impermeable surfaces. Obviously, soil is the medium in which trees, grass, shrubs and annual plants grow. Soils also provide the sustenance for the vegetation that beautifies, cools and quiets our urban environment. Less appreciated are the roles played by soils in regulating water flow and reducing the waste streaming from urban watersheds.

By intelligently managing our soils in Greater Vancouver we can create the foundation for a better urban environment. Too often, soil management is mistakenly assumed to require large amounts of purchased inputs. We wish to stress that this is usually not the case. Identifying your soil limitations and assessing the resources on hand to improve soil performance are far more important than purchasing material to add to existing soil. Most of the soils in the Greater Vancouver Regional district fall into two categories: upland and floodplain. Upland soils are generally sandy or gravelly and retain low amounts of available water and nutrients. Floodplain soils are much better for plant growth, but are more subject to soil compaction and poor drainage. Both types of soils acidify in our rainy climate and both benefit from increased organic matter. Except where acid-loving plants are being grown, regular liming is recommended for local gardeners. Dolomitic lime is readily available and economical to purchase. Occasional soil testing can verify the need for lime and plant nutrients, and local laboratories can provide this service.

Gardeners can spend a great deal of money on organic amendments and topsoil. Before committing resources to additions to the soil, most of us could benefit from careful thought and expert advice. Two situations demand the purchase of topsoil or the addition of organic matter: where sites exist from which soil has been removed during construction; and where plants are grown in containers. For most gardeners, however, the first priority should be to improve existing soil using your own resources, such as composts and leaf mulch. It is frustrating to see taxes being used to remove garden "wastes" from the city while gardeners in the same urban neighbourhoods buy soil amendments. We think it is important to add organic matter to soils, but this material should come first from the home lot and neighbourhood, then from the region and only as a last resort from outside the region. For example, a home gardener should recycle garden waste before purchasing Fraser Valley mushroom manure or other local agricultural by-products. The latter choice, however, is preferable to importing composted steer manure from out of province. This is simply an application of the principles of sustainability.

Sally Shivers demonstates a compost bin at the Vancouver Compost Demonstation Garden.
Photo: J. Groundwater

It is true that local soil is mostly unsuitable for container gardening and it may be necessary to purchase soil from elsewhere. Remember that container soil should simulate the same conditions of good drainage, available water and nutrient storage and aeration that are required of a garden soil.

In summary, the urban gardener has many local, low-cost choices for improving the ability of soils to function in an urban setting. Before spending large amounts of money on imported soil amendments and fertilizers or truckloads of topsoil, think carefully about whether they are needed. Can you recycle a "waste" material and reduce your contribution to the waste stream and your demands on the environment? Both your garden and your community will benefit.

Safety Always

If you are a gardener, wear gloves and keep your tetanus boosters up to date. Scratches, cuts and insect bites are great incubators for tetanus spores which can be found in soil. Go without gloves and risk *sporotrichosis*, a skin disease caused by handling sphagnum moss infested with the fungus *Sporotrichum schenckii*. Pregnant women need to wear gloves against cat feces which can carry the very dangerous disease *Toxoplasmosis*. Besides, wearing gloves makes clean-up faster and easier.

Topsoil: The Dirt on Dirt

by Roy Jonsson

Every spring, thousands of gardeners and homeowners start looking for topsoil to improve existing gardens or build new ones. Contrary to popular belief, topsoil is not scraped off some Fraser Valley farmer's field and hauled into urban areas for sale. It's against the law to strip topsoil from agricultural land. In fact, all commercial topsoil is manufactured and the quality varies greatly depending on what materials are used in the mix. Good soil is the foundation of any garden or landscaped area and poor quality topsoil will cause problems for years to come. Topsoil prices range from approximately $8 to $28 per cubic yard and generally the price reflects the quality.

Natural soils consist primarily of mineral material in the form of clay, silt and sand. Any combination of these three materials is generally referred to as loam. Clay loams have the smallest particle size. They are sticky when wet and tend to compact, preventing drainage, air movement and root penetration. Silt loams have the next largest particles and behave much like clay loams. Sandy loams have the largest particles, with excellent qualities for drainage, air movement and root penetration but they lack nutrients and dry out too quickly. By adding humus (dead or decaying organic material), soils can be modified and greatly improved. The addition of coarse but well-rotted humus to soil improves aeration and drainage. Clay soils can be loosened up and sandy soils will have more nutrients and better water-holding qualities.

Manufactured topsoils normally fall into three categories. The first type is made primarily from excavation material dug out of construction sites. This sand or clay loam is usually quite deficient in nutrients and has a tendency to compact. It may also contain a variety of weed seeds or roots from noxious weeds such as horsetail and morning glory that were on site. After the material is screened to remove the larger rocks and roots the soil is amended with materials such as manure (mushroom, steer or horse), peat and/or raw sawdust.

A second type of soil is based on sedge peat, dug from a Lower Mainland peat bog and amended with river sand, manure and raw sawdust. The peat and sand may not be contaminated but the fresh manure can be a source of weed seeds. Peat-based soils are very good at holding water but tend to be acidic and short on nutrients unless heavily amended with manure.

The third type of topsoil is manufactured from composted organic waste and manures amended with sedge peat and sand. During the composting process the waste materials heat to 65 to 70 degrees Celsius and this pasteurizes the compost, killing weed seeds, coliform bacteria from animal manures and plant pathogens. For those who are accustomed to using a fine peat soil, you may find compost-based soils slightly coarser in texture. This quality actually improves aeration, drainage and soil structure. Not only is this type of soil rich in nutrients and beneficial microbial life but it is also a very usable recycled material. Organic wastes that are converted into horticultural products and put back on the land complete the environmental loop, a principle that more people need to put into practice.

If you already have an adequate supply of mineral soil in your garden beds but the level has dropped over the years it might make more sense to just add organic matter to the soil and raise the level of the bed. The best and cheapest material is home compost but there never seems to be enough for all the garden beds or planted areas. It is now possible to buy commercial compost as part of the GVRD recycling programs. As with composted topsoil, the compost is coarse in texture but does last longer than manure as a source of nutrients and as a soil conditioner. Mushroom manure (actually spent mushroom compost) has been popular for years but the age and quality is unpredictable. Fresh mushroom manure can be quite alkaline and high in salts. Animal manures are

excellent for amending soil but horse manure does have the potential to be contaminated with undigested weed seeds.

Whatever material you add to your garden, be aware that soil must have large colonies of beneficial microbes to break down the complex fertilizer molecules and make them available to plants. Keeping sufficient organic material in the soil will help to ensure a healthy microbial population. These microbes can also be your first line of defence against some of the plant pathogens and fungi. And remember: Those people with a good sense of humus will be the most successful gardeners.

Sources for Soil

ALDERGROVE:
In Season Farms
27831 Huntingdon Rd. • 857-5781
'Nutri-Rich' composted chicken manure

Otter Co-op
3600 248th St. • 856-2517; fax: 856-2758
Soil amendments: canola seed meal, bone meal, rock phosphate, dolomite lime, kelp meal.

ABBOTSFORD:
Envirowaste Garden Products
27715 Huntingdon Rd. • 856-6221
Pro-mix: compost, peat, sand and mushroom manure. Many depots for pick up throughout Lower Mainland. Price based on quantity and pick up location. Delivery available.

BURNABY:
Northwest Landscape Supply
5883 Byrne Rd. • 435-4842; fax: 436-9443
Topsoil and fill soil. Delivery or pick up.

Western Garden and Lawn Supplies Ltd.
7625 Meadow Ave. • 435-2266
A 36-year-old family business. Sells soil, bark and manure. Makes a mushroom manure/topsoil/sand and peat mix they are very proud of.

DELTA:

Pineland Peat and Soils
5224-88th St. • 946-6873
Peat harvested on site. Topsoil mix, top dressing mix, sand mix, mushroom manure, bark mulch. Custom blends on large orders. Minimum one yard.

Sandy's Soil & Stuff Landscaping Products Inc.
9568 Burns Dr. • 594-5333
(see also: Vancouver)
Many mixtures available. One of their custom mixes is compost, chicken manure, wood mulch and sand. Double screened topsoil. Carry the Answer Garden's Bulk Pro-Mix. Delivery available.

Vancouver Landfill – Burns Bog
5400-72nd St. • 323-7737
Screened compost for residential use. Bring your own shovel. Minimum sale: 1/2 cubic metre. Orders of 5 cubic metres or more will be delivered for $6 per cubic metre plus delivery costs.

LANGLEY:

Stiglich Enterprises
2934-224th St. • 534-8452 or 533-2017
Mushroom manure.

Super Soil Inc.
22-19695 96th Ave. • 888-8881
Double screened topsoil. Laboratory tested. Garden loam, planter mixes, sand-based lawn mix, screened bark mulch, mushroom manure. Delivery only: two yard minimum.

NORTH VANCOUVER:

Capilano Topsoils
100 Bridge Rd. • 341-8020 or 985-8782
Topsoil, manure, compost, peat. Pick up or delivery.

Fraser Richmond Bio-Cycle Ltd.
924-0261
Compost soil amendments and bark mulch. Pro-mix, garden and lawn blends, hemlock and fir bark mulch. Laboratory tested products. Pick up and delivery.

Roberge Trucking
100 McKeen Ave. (Foot of Pemberton Ave.)
• 980-5413
Topsoil, mushroom manure, gravels, rocks. Retail landscaping supplier. Pick up and delivery.

Jim Wiles & Son Ltd.
2121 Front St. • 924-1174
Screened topsoil mix. Sand, gravel and fir bark mulch and manure. Pick up or delivery.

MAPLE RIDGE:
Meadows FeedLot
18211 Dewdney Trunk Rd. • 465-5000

PITT MEADOWS:
Meadows Landscape Supply
18020 Kennedy Pitt Meadows • 465-1311
Composted potting bark. Pick up or delivery.

RICHMOND:
Delta Topsoil Ltd.
215-10451 Shellbridge Way • 276-9522
Screened compost material. Double screened topsoil. Laboratory tested Blended mix, garden mix and sand mix. Custom blending for large orders. Minimum order one yard. Delivery only. Open seven days a week.

VANCOUVER:
Haberlin Soil Supplies Ltd.
8700 Barnard St. • 263-6911
Screened topsoil, garden mix, sand mix. Minimum 1/2 yard for pick up. Delivery available.

Sandy's Soil & Stuff Landscaping Products Inc.
8655 Cambie St. • 324-2212
(See also: Delta)

SURREY:
Scott Road Top Soil Supplies
10175-120th St. • 588-6564
Lawn and garden mix, bark mulch, sand, gravel. Deliver or pick up.

How to meet interesting gardeners and learn more about gardening

There is a club for almost every plant in your garden. Check out our club section (chapter three). Visit a Botanical Garden. Volunteer. You could start by helping out at one of the plant sales. Call them. Check out the volunteer section of this book — there are hundreds of opportunities to work with children, seniors, other gardeners in your community … you name it. Hang out at a nursery, ask questions. And you will never stop learning.

Sources for Growing Mixes

VANCOUVER:

VanDusen Botanical Garden
5251 Oak St. • 878-6700
Annual manure sale: late February (no regular date).
Annual compost sale: last Saturday of September. Pre-orders accepted. Note: VanDusen's information line (878-9274) has a recorded message of upcoming events.

Sources for Turf

DELTA:

Westcoast Instant Lawns Turf Farm
4295-72nd St. • 946-0201 or 878-0763
Topsoil and fill soil.

LANGLEY:

Select Sand Sod Ltd.
23945 River Rd. • 888-2810

Western Turf Farms Ltd.
7897 240th St. • 888-7072

MISSION:

Anderson's Sod Farm
36422 Hyde Baker Rd.
888-8873 (Mission); 462-7717 (Whonock)
Turf, sod or seed.

PITT MEADOWS:

Highland Redi-Green Turf Farm
16897 Windsor Rd. • 465-9812

RICHMOND:

Richmond Country Turf
12900 Steveston Hwy. • 274-0522

Are you a Brian Minter fan?
Look for him monthly in:
American Nursery and
    Landscape Association
    Magazine
Cut and Dried Magazine
    (Florist Industry)
Garden's West Magazine
Plant and Garden Magazine

Slugs are natural garbage collectors. In their own environment they are part of the recycling crew that ensures that the nutrients contained in dead plant material, animal waste or animal remains gets recycled. Recycling makes the environment go 'round and slugs are part of that process. As such, they deserve our respect.

Soil Testing in BC

Not all soils are the same. To get the dirt on your dirt — and to find out whether that stucco falling off your house is affecting your rhododendrons or if all that seaweed is making a difference — test your soil.

Most labs test for basic fertility, measuring for major nutrients, micronutrients and overall soil quality. These basic tests can run anywhere from $22 to $45. From the basic package you can often opt for more elaborate package testing (up to $150) or specify particulars: calcium, magnesium, sodium, buffer pH, percent of base saturation, zinc, copper, iron, manganese, boron, lime requirement, ammonium, chloride, percentage of sand, silt, clay and texture, hand texture and organic matter. Fertilizer recommendations are usually given with results. Some labs can also test the soil for physical properties including particle size, conductivity and retention. These tests range in cost from $67 to $190 depending on which physical properties you are testing for.

To test your soil, take a soil sample that represents your garden. Sample to a depth of six to eight inches from at least 10 spots, mix, and extract the sample to submit to the lab. When you call for further information the lab will tell you the best way to send in your soil and how much they want. It is important to stick with the same lab from year to year to be able to compare results — testing procedures may vary from lab to lab.

LANGLEY:
Nor-West Labs
203-20771 Langley Bypass • 530-4344; fax: 534-9996

RICHMOND:
Pacific Soil Analysis
5-11720 Voyager Way • 273-8226; fax: 273-8082
This lab does much of the area's soil analysis for home gardeners.

Soilcon Laboratories
275-11780 River Rd. • 278-5535
Contact: Sandy

Handling and Disposal of Contaminated Soil

ABBOTSFORD:

Sumas Soil Recycling Inc. (Environmental & Ecological Services)
3092 Sumas Mountain • 556-5464

VANCOUVER:

Sumas Soil Recycling Inc. (Environmental & Ecological Services)
790-1500 W. Georgia • 682-6678

COMPOSTING...
Because a Rind is a Terrible Thing to Waste

Composting is the original recycling effort — garbage turns into black gold — and it's free to boot. Set up your system properly and it will provide your beds with nutritious organic matter that pays off in bigger, healthier and more gorgeous flowers and vegetables, trees and shrubs. The GVRD is ripe with resources to encourage everyone to compost.

The trick is in the layering. The best formula for good healthy compost is two parts nitrogen-rich materials like grass clippings, manure, plant trimmings and chopped up kitchen scraps to one part carbon-rich material like dry fall leaves, straw and newspaper. Leave out plant materials that are diseased or have been sprayed with herbicides or insecticides. Stay away from meat, bones, grease, evergreen boughs and pet wastes. Rodent resistant systems are advised, attainable and afford-able — there are a huge variety of bins on the market and lots of designs for making one your-self. The best ways to learn about composting and to find a set-up

Wes Barrett and Tyleen Katz gathering foodstuffs from the Vancouver Compost Demonstration Garden for May's Place Hospice.
Photo: City Farmer

to meet your needs (and determine whether your municipality subsidizes and sells compost bins) is to call the Compost Hotline operated by City Farmer at 736-2250, and to visit one of the 10 Compost Demonstration Gardens in the Lower Mainland.

Compost Demonstration Gardens

BURNABY:
GVRD Compost Demonstration Garden
4856 Still Creek • 299-0659 (garden) and 436-6803 (November-February)
Staffed from 8 a.m.-3 p.m., Tuesday-Saturday. Mondays available for group tour bookings March 21-October 31. Workshops available at the garden. Service available for all member municipalities.

DELTA:
Delta Recycling Society Compost Demonstration Garden
7046 Brown St. • 946-9828
Open daily 9 a.m.-5 p.m.; staffed from April-October, Wednesday-Sunday, 9 a.m.-1 p.m.

LANGLEY:
Municipal Hall
4914-221st St. • 533-6160
Open May-August 31. Staffed Tuesday-Saturday, 8:30 a.m.-4:30 p.m. Call for workshop information. Operated by Langley Environmental Partners.

MAPLE RIDGE:
Port Haney Compost Education and Urban Organic Garden
11739–223rd St. • 463-5545
Open April-October, Wednesday-Sunday, 10 a.m.-4 p.m. Call for workshop information.

NORTH VANCOUVER:
Park and Tilford Gardens
333 Brooksbank • 984-9730
Self-guided tours from 9:30 a.m.-dusk. Staffed mid-May-October, 8:30 a.m.-4 p.m., Monday-Friday, and weekends 10 a.m.-6 p.m. Call for workshop information.

Did you know? Ninety-three percent of Vancouver area residents who compost do so because it is good for the environment and reduces waste.

RICHMOND:
Richmond Compost Demonstration Garden
5555 Lynas Lane • 270-3257
Staffed Wednesday-Sunday, 9:30 a.m.-6 p.m. year round. For workshop information, call 276-4010 (press 0).

SURREY:
Crescent Beach Compost Demonstration Garden
2916 McBride Ave. • 535-4158
Garden is off McKenzie at Sullivan. Open daily for self-service and staffed on Sundays from 10 a.m.-3 p.m., April-October. Call for workshop schedule.

Kwantlen College Garden
12666-72nd Ave. • 535-4158 (fax also)
Staffed Saturdays from 10 a.m.-3 p.m., April-October. Call for workshop schedule.

VANCOUVER:
Vancouver Compost Demonstration Garden
2150 Maple St. • 736-2250
From April-November, staffed Wednesday-Saturday from 9 a.m.-4 p.m. From December-March, staffed Friday and Saturday 9 a.m.-4 p.m. Worm workshops available at garden or in classroom. $25.00 for materials. There is a composting toilet too. Call for hours of workshops and tours. City Farmer, a non-profit urban agriculture group, operates the garden for the City of Vancouver.

WEST VANCOUVER:
West Vancouver Compost Demonstration Garden
15th and Argyle (Beachside) • 984-9730
Not staffed. Self-guided tours from dawn to dusk. Call for workshop information.

For further information on composting call the Compost Hotline at 736-2250. It is operated by City Farmer. For more information and home pages (with pictures) for many of the compost demonstration gardens, see: http://www.gvrd.bc.ca/waste/bro/swcomp2.html

What is "organic" gardening? "Organic" is an odd term, as everything in a garden is organic. "Organic Gardening" means gardening without using poisons to kill pests or weeds, and fertilizing with compost, fish fertilizer, seaweed, blood and bonemeal and other natural products. Of course, there is even more to it, like crop rotation and planting crops near appropriate other crops. To find out more, visit a compost demonstration garden, especially the Vancouver garden at 6th and Maple streets. Talk to Wes, a fount of information.

Problems with fungus gnats or thrips or whitefly? You need some beneficial insects in your life. For a little biological control, Solar Hydroponic Supply (4752 Imperial St., Burnaby; call: 438-7244) will sell you 50 million Nemasys (to get those fungus gnats) for $72 or 3000 ladybugs (to get your aphids) for $30. They order on a Monday for pick up on a Wednesday.

City Farmer, Canada's Office of Urban Agriculture

Celebrating Twenty Years of Service: 1978-1998
by Michael Levenston, Executive Director, City Farmer

Twenty years ago, a group of environmentalists working at the Vancouver Energy Conservation Centre began to research and promote backyard food production. Bob Woodsworth, who now owns the Naam Restaurant, picked up an inspirational book by William and Helga Olkowski called *The City People's Book of Raising Food* (Rodale Press, 1975). It described everything from raising rabbits for meat to entomophobia. In August 1978 we published the first issue of *City Farmer Newspaper*, an eight-page tabloid that investigated gardens along the back lanes of Vancouver. Its modern descendant is our web publication *Urban Agriculture Notes*, now read by people in 133 countries (Papua New Guinea joined us recently). Writers from around the world submit stories and readers request information. This is a long way from delivering a few thin newspapers to corner stores. In the early years we invited international speakers, held workshops, spoke to the media and developed our library. In 1981 we dug the first bed at our site at the corner of 6th and Maple streets. This became Vancouver's Demonstration Food Garden. Throughout the 1980s, we taught people to garden organically and researched new techniques for growing food. We also worked on a variety of projects that included starting the Strathcona Community Garden, developing a school garden project at Lord Roberts Elementary School in the West End, helping build a rooftop garden at the Manhattan Co-op, and running a horticulture therapy program at Pearson Hospital. Learning from this hands-on experience, we published material about our work and continued to promote it in the media. Our experience grew and we were asked to act as consultants on hundreds of projects.

In the Fall of 1989 the GVRD approached us to rewrite their compost brochure. Their previous one had featured a photo of our three-bin composter at the Demonstration Food Garden. In 1990, with funding from the City of Vancouver, the Vancouver Compost Demonstration Garden and the Compost Hotline were born at the 6th and Maple site. For almost 10 years now our main focus has been composting, which in our minds is the core of urban agriculture. We must develop good fertile soil in the city in order to grow food — and what better way to do so than by using our food waste and garden debris? Issues such as food, waste and water conservation are becoming more important and are now discussed by many people. In 1978 only a handful of people even considered the term "urban agriculture" meaningful. Now it is discussed at the United Nations, the World Bank and at the Food and Agriculture Organization in Rome. City Farmer is involved in this international effort through its work with the "Global Facility on Urban Agriculture" and the "Resource Centre on Urban Agriculture and Forestry." We look forward with great enthusiasm to our next twenty years.

Michael Levenston runs the City Farmer Web site
Photo: J. Groundwater

City Farmer
801-318 Homer St. • 685-5832; fax: 685-0431
e-mail: cityfarm@unixg.ubc.ca
website: http://www.cityfarmer.org
cityfarm@interchange.ubc.ca

Diary Of A Compost Hotline Operator

by Spring Gillard,
City Farmer Compost Hotline Operator

JUNE: June Bug Shop

This week we had a visit from a very beneficial guest, Ursula the Bug Lady. Holy sowbug Batman, does this woman know her pupae! During an hour-and-a-half tour of the underside of our garden, we identified the masses of white things plaguing the worm bins (springtails) and found out that centipedes are not really worm predators after all. When I mentioned my theory that sowbugs are taking over the world, Wes, our head gardener, urged me to pass around our pictures of *Actual Squash-Eating Sowbugs*. I reluctantly showed my sa-squash photos around, but they're quite hazy and few were convinced.

JULY: Hot in the City

We're in the middle of a heat wave and I'm on the compost hotline in my greenhouse office. Once again, I'm divulging our compost recipe to a caller. I wish I had a recorded message I could punch in — or better yet, a rhyming ditty, sung by the Nylons maybe. "No meat, no fish, no po-ohl-tree; no grains, no fats they're bad for yee. Just greens and browns, alternate-ly. Plus egg shells, tea bags and caw-awf-fee."

Spring Gillard on the Compost Hotline.
Photo: J. Groundwater

I take a break from my "de-composition" to wring out the sweat and garden grime. As I drip through the building on my way to the facilities, I hear, "*Psst*. Spring, can I see you for a minute?" It's one of the building "enviroguys." Sweating like a soaker hose, I dart into a dark corner with him, primed for intrigue. "Phew, it's hot eh?" I spray at him. And we both dribble on about the heat. Then without transition, enviroguy says: "The CPR Police have been patrolling the area." He points out the window to a row of community garden plots wilting in the sun.

"Really?" I reply. "Are people dropping like flies then?" I picture the railway tracks outside our building strewn with collapsed, heat-exhausted gardeners and dog walkers waiting for brave uniformed heroes ready to risk their own lives to perform cardio-pulmonary resuscitation. E-Guy looks at me as if I've spontaneously combusted. "CPR, Spring — Canadian Pacific Railway police. They're patrolling the tracks, probably plotting their next pesticide spraying of the line." Oh yes, I remember: weed patrol. Flushed with foolishness, I retreat back to my little oven office and pick up my rottin' refrain.

AUGUST: Calling All Rats

Another day in the hot-as-Hades greenhouse and I'm consoling a caller who has had a rat invasion. It's almost like she was trying to attract rats – she had committed every no-no in the book. She has a bird feeder which generously drops grain all over the ground (grain is a wonderful rat attractant). Her compost bin backs onto a lovely, dense blackberry thicket (all the better to tunnel from, my dear). She left her dog's food dish outside as a midnight snack. Finally, she was just dumping food waste into her compost bin without sprinkling it first with a bit of soil (if they can smell it, they'll find it), then burying it well in a layer of brown material (dry fall leaves, straw or ripped-up newspaper). After telling her to stop feeding the bin until she "relocates" the rats, I break into song once again.

The "Compost Diary" is published regularly on City Farmer's website: www.cityfarmer.org.

Rat Riddance

Got a Rat? City Farmer recommends calling the Health Department in your municipality. Each environmental health office in the Greater Vancouver Region and throughout the Province of BC has a slightly different way of dealing with the problem. In Vancouver, if the officer determines that the problem is neighbourhood-wide he or she will bait the whole area. If the officer feels it is site specific, the caller will be asked to deal with it either by trapping/ baiting on his or her own or by calling a private pest control company. (You want to use a baited trap that keeps the rat inside – the stench of an inaccessible dead rat inside a wall is horrific.)

Other recommendations include keeping your garden areas clean, avoiding large piles of garden refuse and wood, and keeping wood piles away from the house. Never put food waste into an open compost bin and always cover organic material with generous scoops of tired garden soil (keep a container next to your compost bin). Use a "rodent-resistant" bin, like a metal Speedibin or a wood-and-wire mesh West Coast Cedar bin. Alternatively, for less money you can fix up your plastic bin by reinforcing all sides plus top and bottom with 1/4 inch, strong wire mesh. Talk to the Compost Hotline at 736-2250.

Using Your Black Gold

IN CONTAINERS:
Mix the following for potting soil:
1/3 compost
1/3 soil
1/3 vermiculite

IN THE GARDEN:
Dig compost into the vegetable garden and spread it 5 centimetres deep around perennials.

ON THE LAWN:
Aerate the lawn and rake four centimetres of compost over the surface.

FOR MULCH:
Place compost around plants, shrubs and trees to conserve moisture, control weeds and provide nutrients.

Worm Compost: Worms Away

Worm "castings" is a fancy name for worm manure. It is great for your garden and another environmentally friendly way to get rid of your kitchen waste. Apartment dwellers, households and classrooms have discovered that two pounds of red wiggler worms (or 2000 worms) can munch through one pound of food scraps a day. Put it all in a covered bin (like a Rubbermaid Roughneck) with a bed of shredded newspaper, and you've got a marvelous clean and contained mini-composter. For more information on composting methods and where to buy worms (as well as "wormshops" or worm composting work-

shops), call the Compost Hotline: 736-2250 or check out the GVRD website at:
http://www.gvrd.bc.ca/waste/bro/swcomp1.html

Suppliers both local and international can be found at the City Farmer website:
http://www.cityfarmer.org/wormsupl79.html
#wormsupplies

For even more information, contact:
The Composting Council of Canada
16 Northumberland Street
Toronto, Ontario
M6H 1P7
(416) 535-0240
e-mail: ccc@compost.org
website: http://www.compost.org

WATER

Water Conservation Landscaping: Water Wisdom

by City of Vancouver Waterworks Design

Two hundred years ago, Captain George Vancouver's ship *Discovery* sailed towards a land of towering coniferous trees, flowing streams and leaping salmon. The city of Vancouver was founded in the midst of this place – the Pacific Coastal Temperate Rainforest – where trees grow large through typically cool, wet winters. Much of the forest and streams that once were found in Vancouver have since been lost. The rain endures, however, and sometimes it seems to Vancouverites that it will never end .·

The Pacific Coast, however, is not always wet. Summers are often extremely dry and then one is reminded that water is an essential element of life. Homeowners often place great demands on the city water supply

Sally Shivers demonstrates a variety of compost bins at the Vancouver Compost Demonstration Garden.
Photo: J. Groundwater

at these times. By tending the land in a more sensitive, water-conserving manner, Vancouverites can ensure that fresh water will continue to flow well into the future. As part of its Water Conservation Program, the City of Vancouver has developed an initiative to educate citizens about the principles and practices of natural cultivation of the land that conserves water. These methods include contouring of the ground, soil conditioning using compost, collection of rain water, the use of native plants, and passive watering. Rediscovering the importance of water to life in Vancouver will help us to cultivate a society that is water-conserving ... and water wise.

PRINCIPLES OF WATER-WISE GARDENING

Follow the Land by watching the rain as it falls onto the ground. The contours of the land can be changed to catch the rainwater and speed or slow its flow, holding it in the ground for use by plants.

Care for the Soil by adding compost or decomposed organic matter. Compost helps the soil hold water and adds nutrients needed for plant growth. Mulches prevent the soil from overheating and drying out.

Gather the Rain by catching it in rainbarrels when it falls and holding it for later use. The rainwater costs nothing and it can be used in the garden during the summer when the ground is dry.

Plant Naturally by layering plants to make shade and using species that are native to this land. These plants are naturally rain-watered and are adapted to wet winter and dry summer conditions. Plant only those that have been grown in the nursery from collected seeds or cuttings ... leave wild plants in place in their natural habitat.

Water Wisely with a gentle hand and simple tools such as a soaker hose that softly and slowly drips

Did you know? GVRD's water consumption increases 40 percent over the four summer months.

Ross Waddell showing off a City of Vancouver rain barrel at City Farmer's Water-Wise Demonstration Garden.
Photo: J. Groundwater

34

water into the ground. Many plants adapted to dry summers do not need much water a few years after planting.

Tend Patiently with a sparing hand and keeping in mind that plants will grow larger. Plants use nutrients found naturally in the soil and in the added compost. They do not need synthetic chemicals to make them grow better.

Spread the Seeds by sharing the fruits of the garden within the community. Developing wisdom of the land ensures that the city will be a healthy one with food and water for all.

For more information on the Water Conservation Program, contact:
City of Vancouver Engineering Services Waterworks Design Branch
City Hall, 453 West 12th Ave.,
Vancouver, BC,
V5Y 1V4
Water Conservation Hotline: 873-7350

Public Native Plant and Water Conservation Gardens in Vancouver and Regional District

DELTA:
Delta Compost Demonstration Garden
7046 Brown St. (off River Rd.), Tilbury Industrial Park
• 946-9828
A project of the Delta Recycling Society.

NORTH VANCOUVER:
Compost and Water Conservation Demonstration Garden
14th St. at Lonsdale (City Hall grounds)
They took an old concrete fountain from the roof of the council chambers and planted meadow plants, grasses, daisies and *Echinacea*. There are also bumpout planters in the street with similar plants. And they never need to water these gardens.

The irony of gardening in rainy Vancouver is that, come summer, we tend to run out of water. Sprinkling regulations for lawns are advertised every year. (Relax — if your lawn turns brown, the green will come back in the fall when the rain starts again). Rainbarrels are an excellent solution. The City of Vancouver sells them at a subsidized cost (in 1999: $58.06). These flat-backed designs go right up against your house under a downspout and collect 340 litres (75 gallons) of rainwater. There is a tap at the base for use in gardening. Call 871-6144 or 873-7350 for more information. You can see rainbarrels in action at the Vancouver Water-wise Garden Compost Demonstration Garden at 6th Avenue and Maple Street. Or check out the website at:
www.city.vancouver.bc.ca/engsvcswaterworks/conserve/barrelprogram.htm

Other municipalities with rainbarrel programs: Delta; and North Vancouver has a pilot program. Call for information: 990-3862.

VANCOUVER:

City of Vancouver/City Farmer Water-Wise Demonstration Garden
2150 Maple St. (at 6th Ave.)
website: http://www.cityfarmer.org

VanDusen Botanical Garden
Located on the City Pilot Greenway ("Ridgeway")
5251 Oak St. at 37th Ave. • 878-9274
Canadian Heritage garden. Water conservation demonstration garden (in development).

University of British Columbia Botanical Garden
6804 SW Marine Dr. (at 16th Ave.) • 822-9666
BC native garden (8 acres); plant introduction scheme at southwest end of perennial border.

Native Education Centre/Mount Pleasant Walkway
285 East 5th Ave. (at Scotia St.) • 873-3761
Ethnobotanical garden using native plants and BC Indian technology.

Plants in the City of Vancouver's Water-Wise Garden

NATIVE PLANTS, TREES AND SHRUBS

Rhamnus purshiana CASCARA • *Vaccinium ovatum* EVERGREEN HUCKLEBERRY • *Ribes sanguineum* 'King Edward VII' FLOWERING CURRANT • *Ribes sanguineum* 'White Icicle' FLOWERING CURRANT • *Ribes lobbii* GUMMY GOOSEBERRY • *Rosa woodsii* WOOD'S ROSE • *Rosa nutkana* NOOTKA ROSE • *Paxistima myrsinites* FALSEBOX • *Ceanothus velutinus* SNOWBRUSH • *Potentilla fruticosa* 'Yellow Gem' SHRUBBY CINQUEFOIL • *Gaultheria shallon* SALAL • *Mahonia nervosa* DULL OR LOW OREGON-GRAPE • *Arctostaphylos* x *media* MEDIA MANZANITA • *Symphoricarpos mollis var. hesperius* TRAILING SNOWBERRY • *Arctostaphylos uva-ursi* 'Vancouver Jade' KINNIKINNICK OR COMMON BEARBERRY

PERENNIALS

Achillea millefolium YARROW • *Allium cernuum* NODDING ONION • *Allium acuminatum* HOOK-

ER'S ONION • *Allium acuminatum* var. alba
HOOKER'S ONION • *Anaphalis margaritacea*
PEARLY EVERLASTING • *Antennaria microphylla*
WOOLY PUSSYTOES • *Brodiaea coronaria* HAR-
VEST BRODIAEA • *Camassia quamash* COMMON
CAMAS • *Camassia leichtlinii* GREAT CAMAS •
Camassia leichtlinii var. alba GREAT WHITE CAMAS
• *Camassia cusickii* CUSICK'S CAMAS • *Dicentra
formosa* PACIFIC BLEEDING HEART •
Dodecatheon cusickii CUSICK'S SHOOTING STAR
• *Dodecatheon hendersonii* BROAD-LEAVED
SHOOTING STAR • *Dodecatheon pulchellum* FEW-
FLOWERED SHOOTING STAR • *Dodecatheon
pulchellum* 'Sooke' *Dryas drummondi* YELLOW
MOUNTAIN AVENS • *Dryas octopetala* 'Mount
Washington' WHITE MOUNTAIN AVENS •
Epilobium angustifolium FIREWEED • *Erythronium
oregonum* WHITE FAWN LILY • *Erythronium
oregonum* 'White Beauty' *Fragaria chiloensis*
COASTAL STRAWBERRY • *Fragaria vesca* WOOD
STRAWBERRY • *Fragaria virginiana* WILD STRAW-
BERRY • *Fritillaria camschatcensis* NORTHERN
RICE ROOT • *Fritillaria lanceolata/affinis*
CHOCOLATE LILY • *Heuchera micrantha*
SMALL-FLOWERED ALUMROOT •
Lilium columbianum TIGER LILY •
Linnaea borealis TWINFLOWER •
Penstemon cardwellii CARDWELL'S
PENSTEMON • *Penstemon cardwellii*
var. rosea *Penstemon davidsonii*
DAVIDSON'S PENSTEMON •
Penstemon fruticosus 'Purple Haze'
SHRUBBY PENSTEMON • *Penstemon
richardsonii* RICHARDSON'S
PENSTEMON • *Satureja douglasii* YERBA
BUENA • *Sisyrinchium littorale* SHORE
BLUE-EYED GRASS • *Sisyrinchium
littorale* var. alba WHITE-FLOWERED
FORM • *Smilacina stellata* STAR-FLOW-
ERED FALSE SOLOMON'S-SEAL • *Triteleia
hyacinthina* FOOL'S OR FALSE ONIONS •
Triteleia laxa GRASS NUT • *Viola sempervirens*
EVERGREEN YELLOW VIOLET

Native Plants and Water-Conservation Related Organizations

NORTH VANCOUVER:
North American Wildflower Society
5229 Sonora Dr. • 985-2758
Contact: Jim Rainer, Field Editor
Publication: "Wildflower";
Free native wildflower seed list to members.

VANCOUVER:
VanDusen Botanical Garden
5251 Oak St. (at 37th Ave.) • 878-9274
Check out "Seedy Saturday" in February – includes lectures, educational exhibits, seed list and sale. There's also a plant sale in April/May.

University of British Columbia Botanical Garden
6804 SW Marine Dr. (at 16th Ave.) • 822-9666
Native plant celebration and sale (March); perennial sale (May). Seed lists, plant list and sale.

Vancouver Natural History Society, Botany Group
Box 3021, Main Post Office, V6B 3X5
• 738-3177 (information line)
Botany lectures; field trips and tours.

OUT OF TOWN:
Naturescape British Columbia
P.O. Box 9354
Stn. Prov. Govt.
Victoria, BC
V8W 9M1
Phone: 1-800-387-9853; in Victoria, call: 387-9369
Public Education Program and publications available. Membership $20.

See also the Garden Club section of this book for information on:
Alpine Garden Club of BC
Canadian Herb Society
Native Plant Society of British Columbia (NPSBC)
Vancouver Mycological Society

"There is a real need for people to understand their own native landscape — and integrate that into their gardens. There is a very strong British influence here — because you can grow everything here, you will. But there is an irony in that a lot of the native plants that we ignore are regarded as important parts of gardens in other regions of the world — *Ribes sanguineum* (red flowering currant) is a good example."
— Ross Waddell, consultant in Ecological Landscaping

Water-Wise Reading

For further information on water-wise and native plants, read:

Hortus West: A Western North America Native Plant Directory and Journal
P.O. Box 2870
Wilsonville, OR, USA   97070-2870
Phone: (503) 570-0859 or 1-800-704-7927
Fax: (503) 570-0855
Contact: Dale Shank
Biannual Journal, $12.00 US per year. Lists professional services, vendors and plants and seeds directories.

Waterwise Gardening: A Guide for British Columbia's Lower Mainland
Contact: Greater Vancouver Regional District Communications and Education Department
3rd Floor, 4330 Kingsway
Burnaby, BC, V5H 4G8
phone: 436-6795
fax: 432-6399
e-mail: comm_ed@gvrd.bc.ca
web site: http://www.gvrd.bc.ca
Shows how to create water-thrifty gardens through the use of drought-resistant plants. An excellent (and free) booklet on the principles of waterwise gardening with lots of tips and plant lists.

Note: Vancouver Watering Regulations
From June 1-September 30
Even Addresses: Wednesday and Saturday 4 a.m.-9 a.m. and 7 p.m.-10 p.m.
Odd Addresses: Thursday and Sunday 4 a.m.-9 a.m. and 7 p.m.-10 p.m.

Slugs are simultaneous hermaphrodites. Each slug has both male and female organs and during copulation it is possible for both slugs to get pregnant. Copulation takes several hours and may culminate when the enlarged penis of one individual is gnawed off because it is too big to disengage.

URBAN FARMING

Growing Veggies Around Here

by Ron Clancy

How do you get fresh organic produce whenever you want? Grow your own. Wander down any lane in Vancouver and you will find evidence of urban farming. Vegetable gardening in the city promotes exercise, low cost produce, year round enjoyment and ultimate control over your food supply. The secret of vegetable gardening in the Lower Mainland is to adapt common techniques used elsewhere in Canada to our unique climate and growing conditions. While we do have a long growing season, we don't get much heat. Think cool, slow-growing crops. Select varieties developed for northern growers. Don't plant heat lovers until the soil warms up. Garden all year by starting winter crops in late summer to double the productivity of limited space.

Where to start? Observe and ask those neighbours down the lane who are already gardening. Search out the right varieties from local seed companies such as West Coast Seeds. Get locally written books from your library like *Growing Vegetables West of the Cascades* (by Steve Soloman, Sasquatch Books, 1989). Think of our soil as a giant sieve constantly being rinsed out by rain. This means adding back nutrients and organic matter regularly. Never leave your soil bare. Either grow a crop suitable to the season (replace your summer corn with winter kale) or plant a cover crop of green manure such as winter rye. When you run out of your own compost (there is never enough), add easily available sources of organic material such as mushroom manure or well-rotted animal manures.

How do you start? Grow the stuff you like to eat. Plant easy crops first. In early spring plant peas, lettuce, chard and Chinese greens. Follow them up with beets, carrots, leeks, onions and your favourite herbs. When it really warms up try cucumbers, squash and basil. Build up your confidence with these crops and then move on to the more exotic. Artichokes thrive in our climate. Peppers and eggplants require the warmest spot you have and lots of coddling but they will produce if the conditions are right. As August passes into September, plant winter kale, collards and hardy Chinese greens along with your cover crops to see you through to spring again.

A slug has a hole in its side that opens directly into its lung cavity. The hole is always on the right side of the body.

Too shy to meet the neighbours? There are public demonstration gardens to visit for ideas and inspiration. The UBC Botanical Garden has a huge kitchen garden where you can see in real life just about any vegetable we can grow here. VanDusen Botanical Garden has a tidy kitchen garden just inside the entrance which combines the edible with the ornamental. West Coast Seeds (formerly Territorial) has just opened trial and demonstration plots next to Richmond's London Farm at the foot of No. 2 Road. There you can see what most of the varieties in their extensive catalogue look like in real life. A trip along Marine Way in Burnaby reveals rows of fields behind Marine Drive's produce stands, showing you how much can be grown year round in a small space. If you are concerned about what you eat, what better way to control your food supply than by growing it yourself? We're lucky: We live in a place that makes it possible.

GARDEN ETIQUETTE

Importing and Exporting Plants

Canadian Food Inspection Agency (CFIA) regulates plants, plant products and other things to prevent the entry and spread of plant pests and diseases. Imported plants and plant products are capable of introducing new pests into Canada that could threaten Canadian agriculture and forestry. CFIA's Plant Health and Production Division is responsible for develop-

The Banana Slug (*Ariolimax columbianis*) is the largest slug on the Pacific coast. It is a native species that grows up to nine inches. It can travel up to 40 feet a night and consumes 30 to 40 times its body weight daily (or nightly — most slugs are active during the cool dark hours).

ing programs to protect plant life and the agricultural and forestry sectors of the Canadian economy. The regulatory authority to carry out this mandate is provided under the Plant Protection Act and Regulations.

Canadian Plant Quarantine Import Requirements (PQIR) are outlined in this document. Import requirements are listed in a chart format for all commodities regulated under the Plant Protection Act and Regulations.

Import requirements depend on the degree to which the commodity poses a pest risk. Some commodities are prohibited entry into Canada. Others require import permits and/or must be accompanied by a phytosanitary certificate at the time of entry. Import permits, issued by CFIA, authorize the importation of commodities in accordance with specified requirements. The plant protection agency in the exporting country issues the phytosanitary certificate, a document which certifies that the requirements of the importing country, such as inspection or treatment, have been met.

Plants that require these certificates are:
Chrysanthemums
Onions
Perennial geraniums
Annual geraniums
Peppers
Aquatic plants
Most woody plants

For more information, contact:
The Permit Office
Plant Protection Division
Canadian Food Inspection Agency
Room 103, 620 Royal Ave. • 666-9283 or 666-8577
New Westminster
website: http://www.cfia-acia.agr.ca/

PESTS AND DISEASES

Pests and Diseases That Love Your Garden

by Mike Nassichuk

The very conditions that make gardening in the Vancouver area so rewarding, such as our mild winters and abundant precipitation, are the same ones "loved" by a host of plant pests and diseases (Ps & Ds). At one time, the sight of Ps & Ds in our gardens would initiate the launch of an arsenal of highly toxic and environmentally disruptive synthetic pesticides. Now, gardeners can apply a range of biological, cultural and other practices — an integrated pest-management approach — to keep Ps & Ds under control while safeguarding the environment.

Here is my short list of favourite Ps & Ds to watch out for and some basic control strategies to consider.

PESTS IN GENERAL

Slugs and Snails

No Vancouver garden would be complete without these slithering terrestrial mollusks on the prowl (escargots anyone?). These grazers enjoy munching on many different plants; their populations, even in relatively small gardens, can reach the hundreds or thousands. Their size, habitat preferences and slow speed make them ideal candidates for hand picking and removal. Small boards, overturned grapefruit halves or loose piles of cabbage leaves placed on the soil throughout and around garden beds, or on garden paths, provide ideal refuges for snails and slugs. Leave these items in place for 48 hours or more, turn them over and you will find a veritable feast of slugs and snails that can readily be destroyed. Gardening books and magazines will suggest many more chemical-free techniques for keeping these critters under control.

Aphids

These soft-bodied insects, winged or wingless, with colours ranging from light green to black, attack a variety of plants. They are sap-sucking insects with cell-piercing mouth parts. They love new growth on

Slug Trivia

The fastest slug in the Pacific Northwest is the introduced species *Limax maximus*, known as the Great Slug of Europe. It is a cannibal (yes, it will take a bite out of other slugs) and can move at a rate of 10.5 inches/minute. In comparison, the average slug moves about 5 inches/minute.

The word slug is derived from the Norse word "slugga," meaning slow.

plants such as roses and apples and secrete a sticky honeydew substance loved by ants. Colonies of aphids can easily be squished between thumb and forefinger. A jet of water from a hose can effectively remove aphids, leaving their mouthparts behind (ugh! but you won't have to worry about those aphids anymore). If you wish to use a chemical spray, try an insecticidal soap mixed with water according to label instructions.

IN THE VEGETABLE PATCH
Tomato: Late Blight

Who can resist the sweet juiciness of a home-grown tomato? Not me. But seeing these delicious beauties reach the stage where they can be picked has become a frustrating challenge. A common fungal disease called "late blight" affects potatoes and tomatoes and has become increasingly problematic in our cool, coastal environment. Fungal spores, spread by rain and overhead watering, flourish on tomatoes, leading to purple, discoloured stems and leaves, and rotting fruit in mid-summer. To avoid this problem, grow early-ripening varieties in large containers under an overhead shelter such as a roof overhang, an enclosed patio or greenhouse. Water the soil only, not the vegetation, and don't over-fertilize. Practise scrupulous garden sanitation. Any infected leaves, stems or fruit must be destroyed — don't place this material in your compost where spores may overwinter. In a garden bed, try growing plants under a temporary plastic roof. Don't despair, late blight can be beaten.

Carrot: Carrot Rust Fly

Many a Vancouver carrot-lover has concluded that its impossible to grow carrots because of the damage caused by the pesky larvae, or grubs, of a small fly called the carrot rust fly. Eggs laid by the adult fly near newly growing carrots hatch into larvae which tunnel into the carrot roots leaving them unsightly and unappetizing. The solution to growing carrots larvae-free is to keep adult flies away from the carrot plants. This is best accomplished by growing carrots under a floating row cover such as Remay®, which is designed to let ample light and water in, but prevents the fly from accessing the plants. After the seeds are

Betty Hunter Dunning says she "came to Deep cove in 1943. At that time there were a number of garter snakes but there were no slugs or snails at all. Now we are so built up that there are no snakes and loads of snails and slugs."

sown, a piece of row cover is placed loosely over the entire carrot patch so that the carrot can grow up under it but the flies cannot reach the plants. Try it — it works!

In the Shrubbery

Rose: Black Spot

There are thousands of varieties of rose, but only some that will do well in our cool and moist summers. Black spot, a fungal disease, is a common problem confronting the rose grower. Circular brown spots develop on leaves. Eventually the spots turn black and the leaves will often prematurely drop from the plant. Some roses display some resistance to black spot and otherwise perform well in our growing area and these should be selected wherever possible. Where to find them? The Vancouver Rose Society (see page 143) produces a list of roses known to grow well in our area. Ensure your roses are grown in full sun and receive proper feeding and pruning. Remove and destroy all infected leaves that fall from the plants. A fungicidal spray, made by mixing one tablespoon of baking soda with a teaspoon of vegetable oil and one gallon of water, can be tried as a homemade remedy. Synthetic fungicides are also available. Check with a pesticide specialist at your favourite nursery or with a Certified Master Gardener and be sure to follow label instructions when mixing and applying any fungicide. Remember, fungicides you spray on your roses will not "cure" any existing black spot problems; they will help prevent the spread of the disease and new outbreaks.

Rhododendron: Root Weevils

Root weevils, in their adult form, are nocturnal beetle-like pests with snout noses. They spend their days hidden at soil level under rhododendrons and many other shrubs, and pass most of their evenings chewing on leaves. Notched or "chewed" leaves are signs that root weevils are living happily among your rhodos. The larvae or grubs of the weevil compound the damage by feeding on the plant's roots. Two good, non-chemical control strategies involve a) a flashlight and b) those boards described above when not being used for snail and slug control. Because the adults

After years of trial and error with deer resistant plants, Elaine McLeod of Meadowbrook Corner on Bowen Island thinks she has figured out that deer stay away from anything medicinal (e.g. Artemesia, Echinacea, Shasta Daisy, Yarrow and Lavender).

only emerge at night, evening patrols with a flash-light (tell your neighbours) with a hand-picking technique is quite effective. Fortunately, the adult weevil is a rather slow moving creature and can be easily nabbed. The boards, laid around the base of the shrub, serve as refuge for the adults. After a few days in place, the boards can be overturned and the exposed adults summarily dismissed.

IN THE FRUIT TREES
Apple: Apple Scab
A common fungal disease of coastal apple trees is apple scab. Infections on leaves begin as greenish spots that become black. Entire leaves turn yellow and fall prematurely. Fruit can be stunted and marred by large brown spots and cracks in the fruit surface. To en-sure scab isn't an overwhelming problem, begin by avoiding highly susceptible varieties such as Golden Delicious. Plant more resistant varieties like Jonagold and Transparent. Rake up and destroy fallen, infected leaves and prune off infected twigs. If scab is present but the fruit is not severely affected, chemical sprays won't be necessary — the fruit can still be eaten. Where scab is a severe problem on prized trees, chemical fungicides can be used. As the timing of application is critical for optimum control, the reader should con-sult a guide like *A Gardener's Guide to Pest Prevention and Control in the Home and Garden* (Province of British Columbia, Ministry of Agriculture and Fisher-ies, 1995) for further information and advice on control products.

OTHER PS & DS
Yes, there are many other Ps & Ds that might find your plants irresistible. But there are numerous sources of information to help you identify the problem and decide on an appropriate control strategy. Ask the experts at your garden nursery, consult a Certified Master Gardener, check out *A Gardener's Guide to Pest Prevention and Control in the Home and Gar-den*. Have a look at the gardening books and magazines in your local library or surf the Internet for gardening information. Happy pest- and disease-free gardening.

Most garden or agriculture damage done by slugs is courtesy of introduced species (usually European in origin). Our native species seldom venture out of their natural habit as they don't like our "man-made" places.

SONGBIRDS

Songbirds are pleasant to the eye and ear, but there are also very practical reasons to encourage them into your garden. Provide them with a good habitat and food and they will thank you by cleaning out pests and insects.

Vancouver Area Songbirds

by The SongBird Project

Songbirds you'll see in this area include:

Common resident songbirds: House Sparrow (introduced); House Finch; Black-capped Chickadee; Song Sparrow; American Robin; Red-winged Black Bird; Golden-crowned Kinglet; White-crowned Sparrow; Starling (introduced)

Common migrant songbirds: Yellow-rumped Warbler; Orange-crowned Warbler; Tree Swallow; Violet-green Swallow; Barn Swallow; Dark-eyed Junco; Savannah Sparrow; Rufous Hummingbird; American Pipet (common bird, difficult to find)

Endangered songbirds: Chipping Sparrow; Crested Mynah (introduced); Swainson's Thrush; Brewer's Blackbird; All Flycatchers (Olive-sided, Western Wood Pewee, Pacific Slope, Hammond's)

Rare and at-risk songbirds: Grey Catbird (rare); Yellow-headed Black Bird; House Wren; Eastern and Western Kingbird; Chipping Sparrow; Meadow Lark; Bullock's Oriole; Lazuli Bunting; Common Nighthawk; Hammond's Flycatcher; Olive-sided Flycatcher; Hutton's Vireo; Brown Creeper (any cavity nester); Nuthatch; Wilson's Warbler; Winter Wren; American Dipper; Townsend's Warbler; Varied Thrush; Cedar Waxwing (common only in some areas)

Slug slime defies washing. The role of slime is to absorb moisture and help keep the slug hydrated. If you have slime on your hands and try to wash it off, it will only get worse as it absorbs water! The trick to getting rid of slime is to rub your hands together while dry, as if you were rolling a glue ball. The slime will roll up into a sticky little ball that you can easily remove with a tissue. Once you've rolled it all up then you can wash your hands.

Attracting Songbirds: What Songbirds Need

Songbirds need water, food and shelter. Whatever size your property — and your budget — you can help meet their needs and enliven your yard or outdoor living space.

Water: Songbirds need water for drinking and bathing. If your resources are unlimited, you can add a pond to your landscape. Short of that, buy a bird bath or put a shallow dish of water out. A large plastic plant saucer works well. Here are some things to remember. The water should be less than two inches deep, at least in part, so the birds can bathe. Birds will drink at ground level, but putting their water up on a pedestal or stump, or hanging it from a tree limb, gives them a better view of predators. A quick escape route from predators — such as an overhanging branch or a nearby bush — is essential. The water should always be clean; regular scrubbing is required. Ponds should be placed in sunny locations, bird baths in shady ones. Birds are attracted to running water. If you can, hang a dripping hose or bucket over the water source, and conserve water with a recirculating pump. A thermostatically controlled bird bath heater provides water during subfreezing weather when the need for water is critical.

Food: Songbirds need a variety of foods depending on the season. Migratory birds arrive at the same time as the first spring caterpillars and find them a succulent source of protein. Berries provide carbohydrates and fats, especially in the late summer and fall. Try to: plant a wide variety of fruiting and flowering plants — plants that bloom or bear fruit from early spring through late fall; include plants that attract insects. Oaks, hickories and maples are good choices, as well as any type of rotting wood; go native — native plants are well adapted to local soils and climates and require less water, fertilizer and pest control. They also offer the best overall food sources and birds will help to disperse their seeds.

Shelter: Shelter includes nesting places that protect birds from predators such as hawks and cats, and from harsh weather. Evergreen trees, shrubs and thick brush piles provide good cover.

Threats to Songbirds

Habitat loss is the biggest concern for songbirds and the key to preserving songbirds is to preserve habitat. An ideal songbird habitat is safe from predators, has plants and water, and contains a place to feed (on insects and seeds), nest and rest during migration. Any human activity that reduces songbird habitat reduces biodiversity; on the other hand, human activity in an urban area that improves habitat increases the opportunity for biodiversity. Every wildlife-friendly environment made by an individual, group or community in a balcony, backyard, park space or office tower counts. These yards, balconies or green spaces could become the living rooms, nesting or feeding areas for some of Vancouver's disappearing songbirds.

Urban threats to songbirds:
- Parks with reduced shrub areas that could provide cover and insects for birds.
- Development with no trees, shrubs or plants that provide food and shelter for birds.
- Free running dogs; uncontrolled cats.
- Housing without cavities where birds can nest.
- Replacing gravel roofs with torch-on material. These new materials attract heat and kill the eggs of birds that nest on these roofs.
- Highly reflective, large windows, especially on migration routes. Any glass can be lethal, as most birds just do not perceive it as a barrier.
- Feeding birds (cheap) seed with too high cereal-grain content ... this sustains starlings and the rodent population and is attractive to a limited range of songbirds.
- Mounting improperly designed nestboxes (predators love perches and certain hole sizes attract less desirable birds, like starlings and the house sparrow). Nestboxes also need to be cleaned out (not destroyed) at the end of the

If we can't respect them for their environmental role, maybe we can grudgingly respect them for their role in medical science. Slug slime production and composition is an area of study for researchers seeking a cure for cystic fibrosis. It seems the slime has a lot in common with the mucus produced in the lungs of cystic fibrosis sufferers. If we could learn to regulate the quality or quantity of that mucus (as a slug quite naturally does) maybe we could cure or treat the disease. Research is also being done on the optic nerves of slugs. They have a huge optic nerve (even though they have minimal vision) that lends itself very well to research. The lowly slug may someday be a medical hero.

Slug slime is an amazing compound that serves many functions. It provides a moist and slippery "frictionless" surface for the animal to glide over dry or rough areas (slugs can safely flow over crushed glass or razor blades); it acts as glue to enable slugs to cling to vertical surfaces for hours or days; it prevents dehydration by coating the body in a moist layer that can absorb water directly from the atmosphere; it aids in self-defense — the sticky slime tastes very bad and causes most predators to spit slugs out; it is an aid to navigation since slugs can smell their way along an old slime trail of their own, locate a potential mate by following their slime trail or perhaps even finding a meal by following the slime trail of a potential cannibalized meal.

breeding season or once a nest is abandoned.

- Poor placement of bird feeders can put birds at increased risk of window collisions. The best place to put feeders is within one metre of a window. This may seem counter-intuitive, but it means they do not build up enough speed to injure themselves against a window if they are startled and fly in the direction of the feeder. Placing a feeder four to 10 metres from a window creates a hazardous zone in which 70 percent of window strikes are likely to be fatal. The same applies to birdbath placement. The best thing homeowners or tenants can do to reduce window mortality of birds is to install exterior blinds. There is no convincing evidence that hawk silhouettes are effective, despite their wide use.

Easy Songbird-Friendly Things To Do:

- Create a songbird-friendly habitat and the birds will come. Provide food, water, plant shelter or nestboxes.
- Control cats and dogs by sectioning off their yard area and leashing them in parks.
- Drink only organic, shade-grown coffee. Coffee is traditionally grown using shade canopies (habitats for birds), but the current trend in coffee plantations is to strip the area, causing soil erosion and devastation of mammals, insects and bird life. CoDevelopment Canada in Vancouver imports and distributes organic, shade-grown coffee called Cafe Etico, selling directly to individuals and businesses. They can be contacted by calling 708-1495.
- Take visitors to local birding areas like Queen Elizabeth Park, Iona Island, Boundary Bay, UBC's Pacific Spirit Park, Reifel Bird Sanctuary, Stanley Park or Jericho Park.
- Encourage the city and the people you know to establish bird and wildlife-friendly parks, boulevards and streetscapes. Support community-led initiatives like The SongBird Project – the False Creek southeast shoreline reclamation and

community gardens to save bird habitat.
- Learn more: Get a Naturescape kit by calling 1-800-387-9853, join a birdwatching group, participate in continuing education programs, become a member of the Vancouver Natural History Society or the Wildbird Trust, participate in the SongBird Project. Go on a neighbourhood nature walk. Buy and study "Birds of Vancouver: Where to go birding in Vancouver." Organize your family and neighbours to make your neighbourhood bird-friendly.

The SongBird Project
Directors: Beth Carruthers and Nelson Gray
(250) 247-7290 (Bowen Island)
voice mail: (604) 813-1134; (604) 657-5598
website: http://www.songbirdproject.org/

GENERAL GARDENING ORGANIZATIONS AND TELEPHONE HELP LINES

BC Horticultural Coalition
phone: 588-1958
Has information on business and trade organizations.

BC Hydro
phone: 540-8883
A guide to trees recommended for planting and growing near power lines; Vegetation Management Program.

City Farmer
phone: 736-2250 (Compost Hot-Line) • 685-5832 (Office)
Open Wednesday to Saturday, 9 a.m. to 4 p.m. Compost and organic gardening information.

Delta Farmland & Wildlife Trust
phone: 940-3392
Has information regarding agriculture conservation programs.

The Richmond Nature Park stages a Slug Fest which usually happens during the first weekend of June at 11851 Westminster Hwy. It's a day of fun and games for slugs and their owners, culminating in the Great Richmond Slug Race. Call 273-7015 for more information.

BC Hydro puts out a large glossy brochure called "Planting Near Power Lines" which lists recommended trees for this potentially dangerous situation. They encourage tree planting, as long as the tree choice is appropriate for the location. For a copy call: 528-1555.

Master Gardener Plant Information
phone: 257-8662
Open Monday, Wednesday and Thursday, 1 to 3 p.m.

Naturescape British Columbia
phone: 1-800-387-9853
Phone for provincial guide for homeowners on caring for wildlife habitat as well as a guide to native plants. Three-booklet kit available for $20.

Poison Control Centre
phone: 682-5050
Provides information on poison, including plants and pesticides, and treatments.

Talking Yellow Pages
phone: 299-9000 (3535)
A source of gardening tips.

UBC Botanical Garden
Friends of the Garden Society (FOGS)
phone: 822-5858 (HortLine)
Open Tuesdays and Wednesdays, 12 to 3 p.m. Pest and disease information; answers to general horticultural queries.

Vancouver Board of Parks & Recreation
phone: 257-8438
Has information regarding garden tours.

Water Conservation Hot-Line
phone: 873-7350
Information on rain barrel program for gardens (for Vancouver residents only). Water-wise gardening information and general water conservation information.

Waterwise Gardening
GVRD
phone: 436-6795
How to create water-thrifty gardens through the use of drought-resistant plants.

MUNICIPALITIES: EVENTS AND SERVICES

(See also: Community Gardens, page 178 and
Compost Demonstration Gardens, page 26)

BURNABY:

Burnaby has an annual contest and garden tour where
the public is invited to participate. In late July or early
August there is a tour of the short-listed gardens. The
contest is advertised in local newspapers and applications are available at city hall and through the
community centres. Contact Dorothy at 294-7450 for
more information.

COQUITLAM:

Coquitlam has their community beautification awards
program. Nomination forms are distributed between
mid May and early June with the judging occurring
in the last week of July. Call: 933-6224, for more information. The municipality also participates in the
Communities in Bloom competition and more information is available at the same number.
• Subsidized compost bins are available to residents
of Coquitlam for $25. They have a one-day event each
year in the spring (April/May). Watch newspapers
for information or call: 927-3500.

DELTA:

Delta has a rain barrel program and a compost program for residents. For more information, call Don
Daily: 946-4141, local 4350.

LANGLEY:

Solid Waste-Operations (532-7301) of the Langley
Community Garden has a demonstration garden set
up as an educational facility with an emphasis on conservation and waste reduction. For visitors it is a place
to "get away" while learning. Workshops are offered
to the public, schools and special interest groups. The
garden is run from compost awareness week (the end
of April or beginning of May) to mid September. The
garden is staffed by students and young people.
  The garden also offers a "Grow a Row" program.
There is a designated vegetable bed where members

Burnaby has an annual contest
put on by the Burnaby
Beautification Committee. The
contest is advertised in local
newspapers and applications
are available at city hall, the
libraries, garden centres and
community centres. Call
Burnaby Parks and Recreation
at 294-7450 for more
information.

Call Before you Dig

"What did I do? I turned off everything I could find, ran like mad, called everyone I could think of and hoped like heck that no one was smoking anywhere nearby." That was the panicky response of an embarrassed landscape designer who hit an underground gas line while digging a new garden bed. He'll only do that once. A better idea? BC Gas'"Call Before You Dig" program is there to help contractors and homeowners avoid a calamity. They will supply plans showing where the underground gas pipes are located. It's free and can save you time, embarrassment, and a possibly dangerous and costly situation. Call 298-1400.

of the public can grow plants. A portion of the vegetables harvested are donated to the food bank. There is also an open house in the spring or early summer, often in conjunction with compost awareness week.

Finally, the garden offers advice on worm composting and backyard composting. And the summer talk series covers a wide range of topics: beneficial insects; water wise gardening; crafts like hanging baskets. There is an associated program of compost bin distribution — the cost is variable so call the above number for more information.

MAPLE RIDGE:

For information on the community garden, call Sharon at 463-0663 (see page 178).

NEW WESTMINSTER:

The Parks Department in New Westminster can be reached at 527-4567. Gardeners who want to compost their green waste should take it to the recycling centre at 6th Avenue and McBride Boulevard. There the material is composted and then recycled for repurchase. In the fall, the city has a leaf pickup program where all the material goes to the parks department compost. Watch local papers for notices on this program or call the above number. The Parks Department itself composts all their own materials for their own reuse.

The municipality is in the process of developing a community garden. Those interested are encouraged to call City Hall for more information.

Around the municipality there are several extraordinary gardens to visit. Queens Park has an exceptional rose garden and gazebo with a beautiful display of summer annuals and roses. This location can be used for weddings and other functions for a set fee. Call Queen's Park Arena at 524-9796 for more information.

The newest and latest addition to New Westminster's parks is the Fort Royal Development in Queensborough. With its naturalized planting and river's edge walk it's a must-see.

New Westminster's waterfront lock along the river is the finest example of a garden esplanade. Visitors come from everywhere to see the displays. The esplanade is divided into two parts, with a wooden walk on one side of the river and a brick walk on the other. The activity along the river makes the place scenic.

The municipality grows all of their own plant material in the greenhouse operation they've had for about 105 years — it's the oldest park system in BC. New Westminster was the original capital and so there is a lot of beautiful Victorian architecture and quaint gardens. A real mix of exotic tropicals, annuals and perennials to feast upon. Call Parks and Recreation at the above phone number for a complete map if you want to tour the many smaller parks in New Westminster.

There's a friendship garden behind City Hall that is a joint project of New Westminster and their sister city in Japan. Lots of cherry trees bloom there in the spring.

NORTH VANCOUVER:

For the annual North Shore Garden Contest, entries must be received sometime in April. Application forms are available at City Hall, with the judging occurring in the 3rd week of July. Call Jan Bednarczyk at 985-9783 for more information. The municipality also enters Communities in Bloom.

There is a composting program with subsidized compost bins available for $45 including taxes. Call the recycling office at 984-9730.

A pilot rain-barrel program has been running for the last three years in North Vancouver. Three types of barrels are being tested: 1) City-of-Vancouver style; 2) a couple of commercial types; 3) a couple of recycled do-it-yourself barrels that are assembled and used by volunteers. The city will be making their decision after this irrigation season. Call 990-3862 for more information.

PITT MEADOWS:

Compost dumping is free for Pitt Meadows residents. There's a no-charge dump site for grass as well as tree trimming, and they do the composting. Compost is sold as topsoil blend. It's a high-end product:

Communities in Bloom
People, Plants and Pride ...
Growing Together
Communities in Bloom is an all-Canadian venture. It's a non-profit program designed to foster civic pride, environmental responsibility and beautification through community participation and the challenge of national competition. Launched in 1995, municipalities who choose to participate are evaluated on topics such as Tidiness effort, Urban forestry development, Turf areas, and Heritage conservation and Community involvement.

Lower Mainland participants:
City of Burnaby, 1996 National Winner
District of West Vancouver, 1997 National Winner
City of Richmond, 1998 National Winner
City of Vancouver
City of Surrey
City of Port Coquitlam
District of Pitt Meadows
District of North Vancouver
City of North Vancouver

For information, write: Communities in Bloom, 112 Terry Fox, Kirkland, Quebec, H9H 4M3.
Phone tolll-free: 1-888-532-5666, or fax: 514-694-3725. To reach the BC contact, call Martin Thomas at 250-387-4090. The e-mail address is: bloom.fleur@sympatico.ca

$20 a yard; very high grade. Compost: 35%. Concrete, dirt, gravel and sod accepted; $5 a minute or $9 a cubic yard. No garbage please.

For questions about what is acceptable or any other questions call for information:
Meadows Landscaping
18020 Kennedy Rd.
465-1311; 465-1312 (fax)

PORT MOODY:

Encourages home composting, but there's also curbside pick up. No bin distribution.

The municipality is reviewing the potential of allotment gardens and looking into rain barrels. For more information call the Operations Department at 469-4555.

RICHMOND:

There is an annual garden contest held with the co-operation of the Richmond Garden Club to encourage people to garden and develop their skills. There is competition in a wide range of categories, in including back/front gardens and natural gardens. Prizes are given for the top three entries and the contest helps beautify the city and encourages gardening. Check local newspapers for deadlines in the spring. Judging takes place in July. Call Mike Redpath at 244-1275 for more information.

Mike Redpath is also in charge of the Partners in Beautification Program and the community gardens project, which is just in the process of selecting a site.

For courses and events, check the Richmond Community Service Leisure Guide, available through the Leisure Services Department at 276-4107.

SURREY:

Surrey has compost education centres. For more information call Louise Robertson at 535-4158.

Want to be a VIP? In Surrey that stands for Volunteer Involvement in Parks. Gardeners can volunteer at places like Darts Hill Garden Park where they can garden and possibly lead tours. There are a few native-plant gardens and volunteers in the city are building more. The volunteer parks program puts on free workshops on a variety of subjects like "building wildlife gardens" or "pruning." Through these workshops and talks volunteers share their skills with the rest of the community. The VIP people say, "If you do not have gardens and you want to add more to the city, then your ideas contributions and suggestions are always welcome." For volunteer possibilities or information call the Volunteer in Parks co-ordinator Carmel Jorgensen at: 501-5173.

The Leader newspaper sponsors a gardening competition called "Surrey's Greatest Gardens" and the municipality also participates in the Communities in Bloom competition.

WEST VANCOUVER:

Gardeners can participate in the North Shore Garden Contest. West Vancouver also participates in Communities in Bloom, both provincially and nationally — they were the national winners last year in their category. As a result, they've been entered in Nations in Bloom this year.

Parks and Recreation offers courses, and information can be found in their leisure guide. Courses include a spring moss hanging-basket course, plant identification tours, "All About Bulbs," garden tours, neighbourhood walk-throughs, herbal gift making and patioscaping with seasonal plants. Call the community centre at 925-7270 for more information.

WHITE ROCK:

White Rock sponsors a gardening contest in co-operation with South Surrey. Leisure Services offers courses as well. Call: 541-2161 for information.

The North Shore Gardens Contest Society runs an annual garden competition for North Shore residents and businesses. Find entry forms in the libraries, any of the three municipal halls, local nurseries and *Avant Gardener.*

SUPPLIES AND ACCESSORIES

Whether you are a gardening novice looking for a splash of seasonal colour or a fanatic plant collector who has to have every *Hosta* or *Hebe* known to humankind, the Lower Mainland is a haven. We realize that many hardware, drug and grocery stores are selling plants, but we've chosen to stick with folks who are in the gardening business. Why? Because there are plenty of remarkable specialists around here, and there is an incredible range of nurseries and garden centres — everything from tiny mom-and-pop shops to large sophisticated operations.

We hope that this section will encourage you to carry this book in your car because no matter where you are, there is a nursery nearby. But we heartily recommend that you call ahead. Most of these places have seasonal hours and some are by appointment only. We don't want you to be disappointed when you have your heart set on a plant fix. We are not ranking or endorsing these 100 businesses, just letting you know that they're out there for you to discover.

Credit for this section goes to avid gardener, writer and photographer Donna Guillemin, who spent long hours chatting with plants people (owners or managers) discussing services and checking Latin plant names. Thanks, Donna.

Here is what our nurseries and plants people have to say about themselves — and why they think you should come out and visit them!

NURSERIES AND GARDEN CENTRES IN THE LOWER MAINLAND

BOWEN ISLAND:

Bowen Island Nursery
Plant Picks:

Impatiens

Leucanthemum x superbum
  SHASTA DAISY

Jasminum nudiflorum
  WINTER JASMINE

Bowen Island Nursery
Owner: Clement and Johanna Van Strien
Trout Lake Rd. • 947-2016
Plants and garden tools, stepping stones made by Clement.
Courses: No
Catalogue: No
Specialty: General garden centre
Wheelchair Access: Yes

Meadowbrook Corner
Plant Picks:

Echinacea purpurea
  CONEFLOWER

Echinacea angustifolia
  CONEFLOWER

Echinacea pallida
  CONEFLOWER

Meadowbrook Corner
Owner: Don and Elaine McLeod
1125 Grafton Rd. • 947-9988
Full service garden centre – open almost year round
Courses: Ask about workshops
Catalogue: No
Specialty: Deer resistant plants. Also growing medicinal herbs. Sells tinctures called "Bowen Island Botanicals"
Wheelchair Access: Yes

BURNABY:

Art Knapp in the Heights
Plant Picks:

Lithodora diffusa 'Grace Ward'

Lavatera thuringiaca 'Barnsley'

Sarcococca confusa SWEET
  BOX

Art Knapp in the Heights
Owner: Wim Vander Zalm
Manager: Jenny Fehr
4362 Hastings St. • 299-1777
website: www.artknapp.com
Full service nursery offers a European neighbourhood flavour with a relaxing courtyard setting.
Courses: Seasonal displays
Catalogue: No
Specialty: Serving all gardening needs as well as ideas for small spaces and patio gardens. Unique container plants and European favourites
Wheelchair Access: Yes

GardenWorks
Owner: John Zaplatynsky
6250 Lougheed Hwy. • 299-0621; fax: 299-4403
website: www.icangarden.com/gw.htm

Check website for class schedules, nursery location information, newsletter archive on-line.

Five acres with three acres devoted to a diverse and beautiful selection of well-known as well as hard to find plant material

Courses: Many classes and workshops offered.

Catalogue: Quarterly newsletter

Specialty: One of the largest horticultural selections in BC

Wheelchair Access: Yes

GardenWorks Plant Picks:
Viburnum plicatum 'Summer Snowflake'
Hostas
Cosmos bipinnatus COSMOS

Mandeville Gardens Centre

Owner: Summer Winds

4746 Marine Dr. • 434-4111; fax: 434-0240

Pottery, garden accessories, furniture, gifts and floral service. Café. 50th anniversary in 1998

Courses: Bi-monthly newsletter for courses and workshop information

Catalogue: Yes (free)

Specialty: Five acres. A diversified, quality-driven destination garden centre

Wheelchair Access: Yes

Mandeville Gardens Centre Plant Picks:
Acer palmatum dissectum 'Crimson Queen' JAPANESE MAPLE
Artemesia stelleriana 'Silver Brocade' DUSTY MILLER
Clematis armandii

Sunny Bonsai and Orchid Greenhouse

Owner: Sam Law

316-4820 Kingsway, MetroTown Centre • 437-3828

Bonsai and orchid plants/pots/books

Courses: Sam offers courses through other organizations such as Hon. David Lam Garden Society

Catalogue: No

Specialty: Bonsai

Wheelchair Access: Yes

Sunny Bonsai and Orchid Greenhouse favourite bonsai plant: *Azalea*

COQUITLAM:

Como Lake Garden Centre

Owner: Bill Pastorek

1649 Como Lake Rd. • 939-0539; fax: 939-0535

Garden supplies, bedding plants, perennials, annuals, soil, terracotta, and fresh flowers. A neighbourhood shop with great community feeling. Offers good service and the best quality plants available

Courses: No

Catalogue: No

Specialty: Good selection of roses, Japanese maples,

Como Lake Garden Centre Plant Picks:
Adiantum capillus-veneris MAIDENHAIR FERN
Viola sororia 'Freckles' VIOLET
Acer palmatum 'Shishigashira' JAPANESE MAPLE

custom-made hanging baskets and planters. Poinsettias and 14 varieties of cut Christmas trees
Wheelchair Access: Yes

Delta:

Bakerview Nursery & Gardens

Bakerview Nursery & Gardens
Plant Picks:

Lavatera thuringiaca
 'Barnsley'
Musa basjoo JAPANESE
 BANANA
Passiflora caerulea BLUE
 PASSION FLOWER

Owner: Keith Baker
7234 No. 10 Hwy. (access from 72nd St.) • 946-6575
General outdoor landscape shrubs, perennials, water plants and hardy exotics
Courses: No
Catalogue: Yes
Wheelchair Access: Yes

Harris Nurseryland and Florist

Harris Nurseryland and Florist
Plant Picks:

Acer japonica JAPANESE
 MAPLE
Calluna vulgaris SCOTCH
 HEATHER
Pieris japonica LILY OF THE
 VALLEY BUSH

Owner: Vernette Harris
5456 12th Ave. (located in Tsawwassen) • 943-2984; fax: 943-6816
Nursery/full florist/gift items
Courses: Christmas/pruning/hanging baskets
Catalogue: No
Specialty: Friendly knowledgeable staff offers a wide selection of great plants
Wheelchair Access: Yes

Harris Nurseryland and Florist

Owner: Vernette Harris
6508 Ladner Trunk Rd. (located in E. Ladner) • 946-5986
Nurserystock, cut flowers
Courses: Hanging baskets
Catalogue: No
Specialty: Four acres of selling space dedicated to quality hedging, shrubs, trees.
Wheelchair Access: Yes

Plants Plus Garden Centre

Plants Plus Garden Centre
Plant Picks:

Ceanothus CALIFORNIA LILAC
Styrax japonicum JAPANESE
 SNOWBELL TREE
Corydalis flexuosa 'Blue
 Panda'

Owner: Lori McLeod
11941 80 Ave. (at Scott Rd.) • 572-7231; fax: 502-8896
Full service with outdoor and indoor plants, giftware and a floral department. Bulk soils by the bag
Courses: No

Catalogue: No
Specialty:
Wheelchair Access: Yes

Sanderson & Sons Nursery
Owner: Bernie and Steve Sanderson
4635-60B St. (located in E. Ladner)
• 946-6210; fax: 946-6361
Friendly service and knowledgeable staff combined with a large selection including unusual plants and trees, outstanding summer annuals and hanging baskets. Pond equipment, aquatic plants and Christmas trees (cut and live) too
Courses: No
Catalogue: No
Specialty: Creatively planted hanging baskets and planters (silver medal winner 1997/98 VanDusen Garden show). Also many unusual perennials
Wheelchair Access: Yes

Sanderson & Sons Nursery
Plant Picks:

Hydrangea macrophylla
'Lemon Wave' (tri-colour)
Petunia 'Marco Polo' (double
trailing)
Zantedeschia aethiopica
'Crowborough' CALLA LILY

Sunnyside Nursery Ltd.
Owner: Van Vliet Family
2300-56th St. (located in Tsawwassen) • 943-9712; fax: 943-1879
Bedding plants, perennials, shrubs, terra cotta, garden soil (delivery available)
Courses: Complimentary hanging basket courses; Fall "pumpkin patch" tours for schools
Catalogue: No
Specialty: Custom made hanging baskets/planters. Good quality plants at good prices. In-house landscaping advice
Wheelchair Access: Yes

Sunnyside Nursery
Plant Picks:

Calibracoa Million Bells Series
Acer rubrum 'Fireglow' RED
MAPLE
Ornamental grasses

Sutton Orchids
Owner: Bob Sutton
6106-28th Ave. (located in E. Ladner) • 946-7370
Selection of most genera
Courses: No
Catalogue: No
Specialty: One of the few and one of the largest orchid growers in the Lower Mainland
Wheelchair Access: Yes

Tropic to Tropic
Plant Picks:
___
Bambusa phyllostachys vivax
Eucalyptus debeuzevillei
Hedychium densiflorum
 "Assam Orange" FLOWERING
 GINGER

Tropic to Tropic Plants

Owner: Ray Mattei

1170-53A St. (located in Tsawwassen) • 943-6562; fax: 948-1996

Hardy exotics. Mail order and by appointment

Courses: No

Catalogue: List of hardy exotics, $2

Specialty: Known as "Canada's Only Outdoor Banana Plantation". Specialty is introducing new species to North America from all over the world (Zone 8 U.S.D.A.). Look for *Musa basjoo*, as well as many varieties of *Eucalyptus*, *Hedychium* and Bamboo

Wheelchair Access: Yes

FORT LANGLEY:

Buds 'n Petals
Plant Picks:
___
Amaranthus hypochondriacus
 'Pygmy Torch'
Artemesia annua SWEET
 ANNIE
Nigella orientalis

Buds 'n Petals

Owner: Lisa Blair

23124 96th Ave. • 513-1522

Specialty: Fresh and dried flowers, herbs, grasses, seedheads, pressed flowers and leaves. Specialty plant sale

Wheelchair Access: Yes

The Cottage Garden
Plant Picks:
___
Clematis armandii
Clematis jackmanii
Clematis montana

The Cottage Garden (Garden Centre & Nursery)

Owner: Pam/Gord Davies

23170 96th Ave. • 888-0223

Nursery stock, ponds/lawns and garden supplies. Tropical and house plants/gifts for the gardener

Courses: No

Catalogue: No

Specialty: Unique perennials and nursery stock

Wheelchair Access: Yes

LANGLEY:

Aarts Nursery
Plant Picks:
___
Culluna vulgaris SCOTCH
 HEATHER
Hibiscus syriacus
Tilia cordata LINDEN

Aarts Nursery Ltd.

Owner: Leo and Mary Aarts

7200-216th St. • 888-3555; fax: 888-3566

25 acres with wide selection of perennials, shrubs and large trees

Courses: No

Catalogue: No

Specialty: Ornamental trees and shrubs

Wheelchair Access: Yes. Paved parking lot, cement floor in store, packed gravel pathway

Arbor Vita Nursery
Owners: Dave and Sheila Ormrod
5910 216th St. • 534-9979; fax: 534-0919
Nursery stock
Courses: Dave teaches pruning occasionally.
Catalogue: No
Specialty: Cedar hedgings and fruit trees. Propogating apple trees. Farm tours
Wheelchair Access: Yes

Art Knapp Plantland
Owner: Wim Vander Zalm
22454- 48th Ave. • 533-0388; fax: 533-8238
e-mail: www.artknapp.com
Nursery indoors/outdoors. Full florist, giftware
Courses: Seasonal centerpieces, pruning, moss baskets
Catalogue: No, but see website
Specialty: Full floral (weddings), Christmas greens/accessories/collectibles
Wheelchair Access: Yes

Beier Nursery
Owners: Elmer and Janice Beier
27374 40th Ave. • 856-2183
Hanging baskets, living wreaths, live topiary
Courses: No
Catalogue: No
Specialty: Victorian Moss or Ecomat (for windy, hot locations) baskets. All plants grown on site
Wheelchair Access: Yes, partial

Brookside Orchid Garden
Owners: Will and Marlene Van Baalen
23779-32nd Ave. • 533-8286; fax: 533-0498
website: www.brooksideorchids.com
On-farm specialty shop for orchids/cyclamen. Four acres under glass (two designated for orchids)
Courses: Yes. Call ahead. Tours also available (book two months ahead)
Catalogue: Yes. Costs $3, but info. also available on website. See also free electronic greeting cards
Specialty: 12 different genera of orchids, 600 varieties. Working within the genera of *Zygopetulum* also

Arbor Vita Nursery
Apple Picks:
Gravenstein
Northern Spy
MacCoun

Art Knapp Plantland
Plant Picks:
Chamaecyparis obtusa 'Gracilus obtusa' GOLD HINOKI CYPRESS
Heuchera micrantha 'Bressingham Bronze'
Oxydendrum arboreum SOURWOOD

Beier Nursery
Plant Picks:
Calibracoa Million Bells series
Sutera cordata 'Snowstorm' (often called Bacopa)
Verbena Temari Group

Brookside Orchard Garden
Plant Picks:
Calypso bulbosa
Cypripedium LADY'S SLIPPER ORCHID
Paphiopedilum VENUS SLIPPER

of *Odontoglossum* to create new orchid introductions that will thrive in the low light and cool conditions of the West Coast
Wheelchair Access: Yes

Brookswood Nursery
Plant Picks:

Citrus
Gardenia
Serissa foetida TREE OF 1000
  STARS

Brookswood Nursery and Garden Centre
Owner: Lucille Pinette
3497-205th St. • 530-8029; fax: 530-3457
Landscape plants, bonsai, books, pottery
Courses: Bonsai courses, baskets etc.
Catalogue: No
Specialty: Bonsai, and bonsai "sitting service" for 50 cents a day. "Village Gardener" concept that promotes BC grown plants and great hands-on service in an organic environment
Wheelchair Access: Limited

Cedar Lane Farm
Plant Picks:

Lavatera thuringiaca 'Barnsley'
Osteospermum 'Pink Polar
  Star'
Petunia Madness Series

Cedar Lane Farm
Owner: George and Brenda Foerster
2367 250th St. • 856-1578 (fax also)
Farmgate sales offer homegrown bedding plants, trailing basket stuffers and Victorian style moss baskets. Small selection of perennials
Courses: Hanging-moss basket classes
Catalogue: Call and they will fax a flyer
Specialty: Offer a wide selection of classic basket stuffers, unusual and hard to find varieties, and new and upcoming selections
Wheelchair Access: No

Cedar Rim Nursery
Plant Picks:

Acer griseum PAPERBARK
  MAPLE
Hibiscus syriacus 'Bluebird'
  ROSE OF SHARON
Hydrangea aspera

Cedar Rim Nursery
Owner: Russ Bruce
7024 Glover Rd. • 888-4491; fax: 532-1009
website: www.cedar-rim-nursery.com
28-acre site with over 500,000 plants; water garden supplies
Courses: Spring/Fall lecture series/seasonal displays
Catalogue: No
Specialty: Good selection of uncommon vines and perennials. Many varieties of *Magnolias*, Japanese maples, fruit trees and other specimen trees
Wheelchair Access: Yes

Elizabeth Cottage Perennials
Owner: Elizabeth Sheppard
24980 56th Ave. • 856-5279 (fax also)
e-mail: esds@uniserve.com
Small nursery garden offers "cottage-style" perennials as well as companion plants for roses
Courses: No
Catalogue: Plant list available
Specialty: An intimate garden experience
Wheelchair Access: No

Elizabeth Cottage Perennials
Plant Picks:
Campanula alliariifolia
Geranium versicolor
Pulmonaria rubra

Erikson's Daylily Gardens
Owner: Pam Erikson
24642-51st Ave. • 856-5758
Tours for local/worldwide groups
Courses: No
Catalogue: Yes: $2
Specialty: Largest collection of daylilies in Canada — over 1300 varieties
Wheelchair Access: Yes

Erikson's Daylily Gardens
Plant Picks:
Hemerocallis 'Janice Brown'
Hemerocallis 'Langley Pink Greeting'
Hemerocallis 'Sandalwood Sister' (a great companion to Brad Jalbert's miniature rose 'Sandalwood')

Foxglove Farm
Owner: Rebecca Black
6741-224th St. • 888-4140; fax: 888-0740
e-mail: foxglove_farm@compuserve.com
Gatehouse and conservatory shop
Courses: Call ahead for class descriptions
Catalogue: Price list on request
Specialty: Dried-flower display gardens and custom arrangements
Wheelchair Access: Yes (in the gardens)

Foxglove Farm
Plant Picks:
Carlina aucalis CARLINE THISTLE
Echninops GLOBE THISTLE
Hydrangea macrophylla

Free Spirit Nursery
20405-32nd Ave. • 533-7373; fax: 530-3776
Owner: Lambert and Marjanne Vrijmoed
website: www.plantlovers.com
General Info: Grows and offers choice selection of perennials, ornamental grasses, vines and woodland plants
Courses: No
Catalogue: Price list available
Specialty: The unique instructional garden shows the specific behaviour of perennials and woodland plants
Wheelchair Access: Yes

Free Spirit Nursery
Plant Picks:
Digitalis lanata GRECIAN FOXGLOVE
Epimedium x perralchicum 'Frohnleiten' BARRENWORT or FAIRY FLOWER
Thalictrum rochebruneanum MEADOW RUE

Gibbs Nurseryland
Plant Picks:

Ceanothus CALIFORNIA LILAC
Davidia involucrata DOVE TREE
or HANKERCHIEF TREE
Zantedeschia aethiopica
CALLA LILY

Gibbs Nurseryland and Florist
Owner: Dave and Sharon Preston
7950-200th St. • 888-2121
Three acres of garden delights including nursery stock,
floral shop, bedding plants (one acre under glass)
Courses: Call ahead
Catalogue: No
Specialty: Unique topiary, Mexican giftware, wrought
iron and statuary
Wheelchair Access: Yes

Glads Nursery
Plant Picks:

Astilbe
Fuchsia (hardy types)
Hosta 'Sum & Substance'

Glads Nursery
Owner: Gladys Bayer
23859 14A Ave. • 530-5298
Retail: Plants, bird houses, planters
Courses: No
Catalogue: Plant list available
Specialty: "Small shrubs for small places" (Container
stock)
Wheelchair Access: Yes

Gracious Gardens
Plant Picks:

Monarda didyma 'Blue
Stocking' BEE BALM
Geranium psilostemon
Verbena 'Homestead Purple'

Gracious Gardens
Owner: Rod and Grace Bruer
22051 56th Ave. • 530-2168
Large selection of perennials including top sellers as
well as unusual selections
Courses: No
Catalogue: No
Specialty: Creating a destination nursery that offers
the chance to see (labelled) perennials grown in a
gracious garden setting
Wheelchair Access: Yes

Killara Farm
Plant Picks:

Rosa mulliganii
'Ghislaine de Féligonde'
'Madame Alfred Carriére'

Killara Farm
Owner: Christine Allen
21733-8th Ave., RR No. 14 • 532-9831
Outdoor nursery offers roses
Courses: No
Catalogue: $2
Specialty: Old garden roses and shrub roses on own
roots. Half-acre display garden
Wheelchair Access: Yes

Lunzmann, Mrs. Valle
Owner: Mrs. Valle Lunzmann
4549-220th St. • 530-8440
Courses: Owner gives demonstrations on grafting to Master Gardeners as well as to small groups. Also "budding" classes available in August
Catalogue: No
Specialty: 100 varieties of apple scionwood and pears
Wheelchair Access: Limited

Mrs Valle Lunzmann's
Apple Picks:
Lord Lambourne
Bramley's
Scab Free Varieties PIR
  Introductions

Made in the Shade Nursery
Owner: Dyann Goodfellow
4586 Saddlehorn Cres. • 856-2010; fax: 856-0049
Retail nursery on 2.5 acres which includes display gardens
Courses: No
Catalogue: No
Specialty: Growing plants for shade and plants that thrive in our West Coast gardens. Cultivating a greater awareness about the extraordinary world of ferns
Wheelchair Access: For nursery only

Made in the Shade
Plant Picks:
Hosta 'Patriot'
Dryopteris x *complexa*
  'Robusta' ROBUST HOLLY
  FERN
Cyrtomium macrophyllum BIG
  LEAF HOLLY FERN

Marvellous Mushrooms (Western Biologicals Ltd.)
Owner: Bill Chalmers
25059-50th Ave. • 856-3339
e-mail: western@prismnet.bc.ca
Mushroom spawn, mushroom kits, mushrooms, herbs such as Stevia and limited quantities of sweet-scented plants including different Night-Blooming Cereus
Courses: Mushroom cultivation and plant tissue culture workshops
Catalogue: Yes: $3 (mushrooms)
Specialty: Specialty mushrooms including medicinal varieties, mushroom growing kits. Also Asian Pear varieties
Wheelchair Access: Yes

Marvellous Mushrooms
Plant Picks:
Cucurbita pepo 'Styriaca'
Lentirius edodes SHITAKE
  MUSHROOM
Stevia rebaudiana

Meadowsweet Farms
Owner: Randal Atkinson
23900-16th Ave. • 530-2611
e-mail: meadowsweet@pacificgroup.net
Retail: perennials
Courses: No
Catalogue: Yes: $3

Meadowsweet Farms
Plant Picks:
Deschampsia caepitosa
  'Northern Lights'
Euphorbia amygdaloides var.
  robbiae
Stachys byzantina 'Primrose
  Heron'

Specialty: Unusual perennials, *Hostas,* ornamental grasses
Wheelchair Access: No

Misty Creek Nurseries
Plant Picks:

Argyranthemum 'Butterfly'
  MARGUERITE
Diascia barberae 'Ruby Fields'
  TWINSPUR
Nemesia 'Bluebird'

Misty Creek Nurseries

Owner: Lynn and Gary Spaan
22996 56th Ave. • 534-7048 (fax also)
Hanging baskets, annuals, perennials
Courses: No
Catalogue: No
Specialty: Custom plantings of your favourite plants/colours/combinations
Wheelchair Access: Yes

P&J Greenhouses
Plant Picks:

Pelargonium 'Mr. H. Cox' (a tri-colour Zonal GERANIUM)
Pelargonium 'P.J. Miranda' (a P&J Greenhouse Regal introduction)
Pelargonium 'Vancouver Centennial' (Gold Steller)

P&J Greenhouses

Owner: Jean Hauserman
20265-82nd Ave., RR No. 11 • 888-3274; fax: 888-3211
Large selection of *Fuchsias* and *Pelargoniums*
Courses: No
Catalogue: Yes: $2
Specialty: *Pelargoniums:* fancy leaf and scented ivy, minis, dwarfs, regals and zonals
Wheelchair Access: No

Ponds Beautiful
Plant Picks:

Ceratophylum demersum
Elodea canadensis CANADIAN PONDWATER
Pontederia cordata PICKEREL WEED

Ponds Beautiful

Owner: Roger Pinette
21797-61st Ave. • 534-9133; fax: 534-3133
Aquatic plants, hardware, pumps, liners, filters, accessories
Courses: Yes, seminars on Saturdays.
Catalogue: No
Specialty: Water plants, koi, water stabilizing materials, hard goods
Wheelchair Access: Yes

Rainforest Nurseries
Plant Picks:

Anthemis tinctoria 'Sauce Hollandaise'
Artemesia latifolius 'Silver Frost'
Leucanthemella serotina (Gertrude Jekyll's signature plant)

Rainforest Nurseries

Owner: Tony Milbradt
Manager: Barry Bélec
1470-227 St. • 530-3499; fax: 530-3499
Perennials, grasses, trees, shrubs, selected annuals and containers. Design and display gardens
Courses: Free public workshops. Lectures also available through garden clubs and societies

Catalogue: Free newsletter. Descriptive catalogue: $4
Specialty: More than a business, Rainforest suggests a sense of refreshment for body, mind and spirit as well an expansive vision of garden-worthy plants and people
Wheelchair Access: Yes

Select Roses
Owner: Brad Jalbert
22771-38th Ave. • 530-5786 (fax also)
e-mail: bjalbert@uniserve.com
Roses – garden and miniature/patio
Courses: Spring pruning and demonstrations
Catalogue: Plant list available at nursery.
Specialty: Large selection of "own root" miniature/patio roses. Also many varieties of Canadian grown garden roses. Display garden features over 600 roses
Wheelchair Access: No

Sunshine Garden Centre
Owners: Al and Diana Lesack
23166 Fraser Hwy. • 534-2228
Seasonal plants, animal feed, garden ornaments, crafts, woodworking
Courses: No
Catalogue: No
Specialty: Concrete seagulls
Wheelchair Access: Yes

Turner Trees
Owner: Alan Turner
1437-212th St. • 532-9262
Courses: No (provides on-site information)
Catalogue: Plant list free with self-addressed stamped envelope (SASE)
Specialty: Rare and unusual trees and shrubs. Many different pine species and cultivars. Five-acre display garden has over 350 conifers and broad-leaved trees. Will do plant search for hard to come by trees/shrubs (or their seeds)
Wheelchair Access: Yes

Barry Bélec at the cutting bench at Rainforest Nurseries in Langley.
Photo: Rainforest Nurseries

Select Roses
Plant Picks:
Rosa centifolia 'Fantin Latour' (Old Garden Rose)
Rosa 'Fellowship' (Floribunda)
Rosa 'New Dawn'

Sunshine Garden Centre
Plant Picks:
Fuschias
Impatiens
Pelargonium

Turner Trees
Plant Picks:
Chamaecyparis nootkatensis 'Pendula' WEEPING NOOTKA CYPRESS
Pinus densiflora 'Tanyosho' TANYOSHO PINE
Pinus thunbergii 'Yatsubusa' DWARF JAPANESE BLACK PINE

Valley Garden Centre and Florist
Owner: Russ Bruce
20811 Fraser Hwy. • 534-3813 for garden centre; 533-1551 for florist; fax: 530-8406
Large outdoor nursery for year round gardening needs. Also full service florist and indoor tropical selections
Courses: Yes. Call for details
Catalogue: Monthly newsletter, free to club members
Specialty: Perennials and roses
Wheelchair Access: In store, yes; outdoor is gravel

MAPLE RIDGE:

Hansi's Nursery
Plant picks:
Anemone nemorosa'Vestal'
  WINDFLOWER
Campanula cochleariifolia
  'Alba'
Dianthus glacialis

Hansi's Nursery
Owner: Hansi Pitzer
27810 112th Ave. • 462-8799; fax: 462-8042
Five-acre nursery offers demonstration garden, perennials, shrubs, trees as well as top information from experienced gardener
Courses: No
Catalogue: No
Specialty: Growing unique perennials
Wheelchair Access: Yes

Rainforest Gardens
Plant Picks:
Geranium x oxianum'Phoebe
  Noble'
Hosta'Canadian Shield'
Pulmonaria'David Ward'

Rainforest Gardens
Owner: Elke & Ken Knechtel
13139-224th St. • 467-4218; fax: 467-3181
e-mail: info@rainforest-gardens.com
Herbaceous perennials, native flora (nursery propogated!)
Courses: Yes, see catalogue
Catalogue: $4 for a two-year subscription
Specialty: Two acres of mature display gardens. _Hosta, Geranium, Astilbe, Primula_, ferns and ornamental grasses
Wheelchair Access: Yes

Triple Tree Nurseryland
Plant Picks:
Kalmia latifolia MOUNTAIN
  LAUREL
Picea orientalis'Aurea' GOLDEN
  ORIENTAL SPRUCE
Salix integra'Itakuro Nishiki'

Triple Tree Nurseryland
Owner: Tom Van Der Pauw
20503 Lougheed Hwy. • 465-9313; fax: 465-0898
Total garden supplies (plants, soil, pots, fertilizer, etc.), water gardening and hydroponics
Courses: No
Catalogue: No

Specialty: Trees (including a large selection of fruit trees), ponds, hydroponics
Wheelchair Access: Yes (very wheelchair-friendly)

NORTH VANCOUVER:

Capilano Nurseryland
Owner: Warren Whyte
705 West 3rd Ave. • 988-8082
Complete indoor/outdoor garden supplies
Courses: No
Catalogue: No
Specialty: Serving the North Shore for 50 years. Good selection of ground covers, shrubs and containers
Wheelchair Access: Yes

Dykhof Nurseries and Florist
Owner: Ineke Milligan and Henry Dykhof
460 Mountain Hwy. • Florist Shop: 985-1292; Nursery: 985-1914
Full nursery plus hardware, giftware, florist, pots, clay, tropical plants
Courses: No
Catalogue: No
Wheelchair Access: Yes

GardenWorks
Owner: John Zaplatynski
3147 Woodbine Dr. • 980-6340; fax: 980-6399
Full selection at this indoor/outdoor garden centre including giftware
Courses: Periodically
Catalogue: Newsletter (free)
Specialty: Shade plants for local environments
Wheelchair Access: Yes

GardenWorks Plant Picks:
Hosta 'June'
Hosta 'On Stage'
Miscanthus floridulus

Maple Leaf Garden Centre
Owner: Duynstee Family
1343 Lynn Valley Rd. • 985-1784
Nursery and garden centre with trees, perennials, shrubs and tropical plants
Courses: No
Catalogue: Yes (free)
Specialty: Shrubs, trees, perennials
Wheelchair Access: Yes

Valley Orchid Partners
Plant Picks:

Bulbophyllum
Coelogyne
Phalaenopsis MOTH ORCHID

Art Knapp Plantland (Port
Coquitlam) Plant Picks:

Choisya ternata'Sundance'
 MEXICAN ORANGE
Hakonechloa macra'Aureola'
Nandina domestica'Plum
 Passion'

Art Knapp Plantland (Port
Moody) Plant Picks:

Diospyros kaki'Fuyugaki'
 JAPANESE PERSIMMON
Hibiscus syriacus'Blue Bird'
 ROSE OF SHARON
Iris germanica BEARDED IRIS

PITT MEADOWS:
Amsterdam Greenhouses & Garden Centre
Owner: Ronald/Lidy Kok
19100 Dewdney Trunk Rd. • 465-6073; fax: 465-6768
Courses: Pruning, bonsai, propagation, hanging and
moss baskets, water gardens, design, etc.
Catalogue: No
Specialty: Specialty bedding plants, hanging baskets
as well as custom orders, fuschias, including specialty
standards and hardy varieties. Large selection of
Datura
Wheelchair Access: Yes

Valley Orchid Partners
Owner: Betty Berthiaume
12621 Woolridge Rd. • 465-8664; fax: 465-8374
Orchid Greenhouse
Courses: No
Catalogue: No
Specialty: Orchids – species and hybrids
Wheelchair Access: Yes

PORT COQUITLAM:
Art Knapp Plantland
Owner: Wim Vander Zalm
1300 Dominion St. • 942-7518; fax: 942-1859
website: www.artknapp.com
An innovative and upscale "home and garden" shop-
ping experience.
Courses: Spring and Christmas courses.
Catalogue: No
Specialty: Fabulous Christmas theme display.
Wheelchair Access: Yes

PORT MOODY:
Art Knapp Plantland
Owner: Wim Vander Zalm
3150 Saint John St. • 461-0004; fax: 461-0708
website: www.artknapp.com
An open market feel as you stroll along terra cotta
walkways throughout the store for all your nursery
needs, including a full florist and a unique gift area
Courses: Seasonal demonstrations
Catalogue: No

Specialty: Great service and everything you need for your garden from balcony-sized plants to backyard specimens
Wheelchair Access: Yes

RICHMOND:

Art Knapp Plantland (Fantasy Garden World)
Owner: Frank Van Hest
10840 No. 5 Rd. • 271-9581; fax: 271-4151
website: www.artknapp.com
Perennials, shrubs, trees, tropicals, seeds, soil, bulbs, fertilizer, pottery, etc.
Courses: From gardening to crafts
Catalogue: No
Specialty: New and improved varieties. Knowledgeable service. "No question too small!"
Wheelchair Access: Yes

Art Knapp Plantland
(Richmond) Plant Picks:
Cryptomeria japonica 'Cristata'
JAPANESE CEDAR
Eunoymus alatus WINGED
SPINDLE TREE
Nandina domestica HEAVENLY
BAMBOO

Garden City Greenhouses
Owners: Bing Chin and Dave Kosiur
9240 Cambie Rd. • 278-0722; fax: 278-0723
Year round seasonal plants and tropicals
Courses: In store advice
Specialty: Bedding plants, tree peonies. Also special plants for celebrations and other occasions
Wheelchair Access: Yes

Green Acres Tree Farm
Owner: Sam Cho
5440 No. 6 Rd. • 273-1553
Ornamental trees, shrubs and perennials
Courses: No
Catalogue: No
Specialty: Large selection of the above
Wheelchair Access: Yes

Green Acres Tree Farm
Plant Picks
Azalea
Camellia
Rhododendron

Hawaiian Botanicals & Water Gardens
Owner: Jack and Jeanie Wootton
6011 No. 7 Rd. • 270-7712; fax:271-2443
Water plants. Unusual tropicals for conservatories/ hardy exotics
Courses: No
Catalogue: Plant list/cultural information available on site

Hawaiian Botanicals
Plant Picks:
Bromelia
Nelumbo nucifera 'Shiroman'
Costus barbatus SPIRAL
GINGER

Specialty: *Bromelia, Hedychium, Nelumbo, Plumeria,*
and *Passiflora* species
Wheelchair Access: Yes

Jones Garden Centre
Plant Picks:

Cotula squalida NEW ZEALAND
BRASS BUTTONS
Magnolia grandiflora
EVERGREEN MAGNOLIA
Trachycarpus fortunei
WINDMILL PALM

Jones Garden Centre
Owner: Bill and Jackie Jones
Manager: Brenda Crockett
16880 Westminster Hwy. • 278-8671; fax: 273-0650
Full service garden centre for annuals, perennials,
bulbs, seeds, roses, shrubs and trees including fruit
as well as berry bushes. Also ceramics, pottery and
hard goods
Courses: Yes. Call about short seminars
Catalogue: Free newsletter available at nursery
Specialty: Specimen shade and ornamental large
caliper trees. Custom container plantings and landscape design
Wheelchair Access: Yes for store but not for nursery
grounds

Keefer Farms and Greenhouses
Owner: Dan Keefer
17080 Cambie Rd. • 278-8943
Hanging baskets and containers
Courses: No
Catalogue: No
Specialty: Beautiful hanging baskets and containers
Wheelchair Access: No

Phoenix Perennials Nursery
Plant Picks:

Euphorbia x *martinii* SPURGE
Geranium wallichianum
Penstemon gloxiniodes
'Midnight'

Phoenix Perennials Nursery
Owner: Clare Philips
3380 No. 6 Rd. • 270-4133
website: www.phoenixperennials.com
Working nursery with greenhouse and sun/shade
stock beds. Plants are grouped alphabetically within
respective growing requirements. Also shrubs, vines,
grasses and silver foliage plants
Courses: Call ahead about educational seminars
Catalogue: Yes — $3.00
Specialty: Hardy perennial stock always gwowing with
new and viable plant selections. Look for *Campanula
primulifolia*. Design work also available
Wheelchair Access: Partial

Prickly Pear Garden Centre
Owner: Allan Surette, Brian Gilmore and Patti Maskall
12311 No. 1 Rd. (located in Steveston) • 241-4717
(fax also)
Retail: plants, fertilizer, soil, gifts
Courses: Yes, crafts and moss hanging baskets
Catalogue: No
Specialty: Custom planting and potting. Also wide
selection of succulents
Wheelchair Access: Limited

Tai Koon Yuen Nursery
Owner: Alex Shiu
13480 Westminster Hwy. • 821-0131; fax: 821-0191
Trees, shrubs, perennials, annuals and tropical plants
including orchids
Courses: Occasional seminars
Catalogue: No
Specialty: Large variety of the above
Wheelchair Access: Yes

Wong's Greenhouse & Nursery
Owner: Yuen and Dorothy Wong
Manager: Paul Wong
9360 Cambie Rd. • 278-1028; fax: 278-1268
Grower/retail: bedding plants, hanging baskets,
shrubs, trees, tropicals, poinsettias and garden supplies
Courses: No
Catalogue: No
Specialty: Plants grown on site. Custom-made hang-
ing baskets
Wheelchair Access: Yes

SURREY:

Art's Nursery Ltd.
Owners: Art Vander Zalm
Manager: Sandra Blieberger
8940-192nd St. • 882-1201; fax: 882-5969
e-mail: arts@direct.ca
Family business offers 10 acres of nursery stock including outdoor trees and shrubs. Design and
gardening advice
Courses: Seasonal demonstrations scheduled – bonsai,
moleman etc.

Prickly Pear GardenCentre
Plant Picks:

Delosperma nubigenum ICE
PLANT
Lithodora diffusa 'Grace Ward'
Sedum oreganum

Wong's Greenhouse
Plant Picks:

Osmanthus fragrans
FRAGRANT OLIVE
ASIAN PEAR
Cyperus papyrus EGYPTIAN
PAPER REED

Art's Nursery
Plant Picks:

Cornus mas CORNELIAN
CHERRY
Hamamelis vernalis pendula
WEEPING VERNAL WITCH
HAZEL
Syringa reticulata 'Ivory Silk'
JAPANESE TREE LILAC

Catalogue: Call for weekly specials
Specialty: Shop in a golf cart, grower direct, grow 50% of what they sell. Cantonese and Mandarin translators available during the spring. Great service
Wheelchair Access: Yes

Art Knapp Plantland
Owner: Kerry, Lonnie, Jamie and Marty Vander Zalm
4391 King George Hwy. • 596 – 9201; fax: 596-9240
website: www.artknapp.com
Retail: Big selection of water-gardening supplies, tropical plants and a nursery
Courses: No
Catalogue: No, see website at www.artknapp.com
Specialty:
Wheelchair Access: Limited

Art Knapp Plantland Fleetwood
Owner: Kerry, Lonnie, Jamie and Marty Vander Zalm
Manager: Jamie Vander Zalm
16287 Fraser Hwy. • 597-9701; fax: 597-9784
website: www.artknapp.com
Garden centre plus giftware, bird food, feeders, fish, ponds and water-gardening needs
Courses: No
Catalogue: No
Specialty: Great community service. Field trips to garden centre for primary grades
Wheelchair Access: Yes

Ben's Farm
Owner: Mrs. Chu
18341 Fraser Hwy., at rear • 574-4135 (fax also)
Bedding plants, shrubs, trees, plus produce
Courses: No
Catalogue: No
Specialty: Good all around selection including hardy banana trees
Wheelchair Access: Yes

David Hunter Garden Centre
Owner: Ron Hunter
15175-72nd Ave. • 590-2431; fax: 590-1281
Full service community garden centre and florist with

Art Knapp Plantland
Fleetwood Plant Picks:
Araucaria araucana MONKEY
  PUZZLE TREE
Gunnera manicata GIANT
  RHUBARB
Wisteria

exclusive giftware, ceramic/stoneware containers/bird-houses and tools. Top notch perennials, shrubs, trees, good seed selection and 250 rose varieties
Courses: Some gardening seminars
Catalogue: No
Specialty: Longtime employees who take pride in offering the best service possible. In-house landscaping consultations. Customer "want" list
Wheelchair Access: Yes

Easy Acres Herb Farm
Owner: Steve Hoffman
12063-64th Ave. • 596-8485
Retail and wholesale: Herbs only. Main retail outlet is at Granville Island from March until July
Courses: No
Catalogue: Weekly list available
Specialty: 350 varieties of potted herbs and scented geraniums. Main herb supplier for VanDusen spring plant sale
Wheelchair Access: No for nursery. Yes for Granville Island

Gramma's Farm
Owner: Elisa Lin
4793 176th St. • 576-8958; fax: 576-8990
Annuals, hanging baskets, perennials, shrubs, trees (including fruit). Poinsettias at Christmas
Courses: No
Catalogue: No
Specialty: Oriental trees, shrubs, and flowers
Wheelchair Access: Yes

Hi-Knoll Nursery and Garden Centre
Owner: Kevin Kim
4947 192 St. • 576-7733; fax: 576-7764
"Old barn" atmosphere with gravel paths. Trees, shrubs, bedding plants, pottery, cut flowers, hanging baskets
Courses: Occasionally – call for details
Catalogue: Yes (free)
Specialty: Imported pottery, hanging baskets/Christmas plants
Wheelchair Access: Yes

David Hunter Garden Centre
Plant Picks:

Ceanothus 'Victoria'
CALIFORNIA LILAC
Ginkgo biloba MAIDENHAIR TREE
Salvia verticillata 'Purple Rain'

Easy Acres Herb Farm
Plant Picks:

Agastache 'Tutti Frutti' GIANT MEXICAN LEMON HYSSOP
Hyssopus officinalis HYSSOP
Monarda astromontana MEXICAN BERGAMOT

Hi-Knoll Nursery
Plant Picks:

Osteospermum
Primula auricula
Salix integra 'Itakuro Nishiki'

Holland Nursery
Plant Picks:
_____
Buxus BOXWOOD
Canna generalis CANNA LILY
Primula species and hybrids

Holland Nursery
Owner: Len Warmedan
16170-84th Ave. • 572-7666; for delivery: 572-4145
Retail: perennials, fertilizer, pond plants and fish
Courses: No
Catalogue: No
Specialty: Hedging material
Wheelchair Access: Yes

Hong's Nursery
Plant Picks:
_____
Impatiens'Super Elfin'
  IMPATIENS
Pelargonium GERANIUM
Petunia Supertunia Series

Hong's Nursery
Owner: Jerry Hong
10582 120th St. • 588-3734; fax: 588-8836
Floral department, basic garden tools, plants, shrubs, Japanese Koi fish, perennials, hanging baskets
Courses: Yes. Seasonal, spring clean-up, hanging baskets (incl. moss). Fall clean-up
Catalogue: No
Specialty: Large selection of annuals, bedding plants, and hanging baskets, including moss baskets
Wheelchair Access: Yes

Huckleberry Farm
Plant Picks:
_____
Solenostemon scutellarioides
  COLEUS
Tibouchina PRINCESS FLOWER
Zinnia angustifolia'Crystal
  White'

Huckleberry Farm and Garden Centre
Owner: Randy and Leslie Buhr
19100 16th Ave. • 536-9001; fax: 535-5567
"A most unusual place," includes garden antiques, fine hand-made BC crafts, gardening gifts and paraphernalia
Courses: Craft fairs held Valentine's weekend and the last weekend in November
Catalogue: No
Specialty: Growing unusual perennials, annuals. Large collection (23 varieties) of Bougainvillea
Wheelchair Access: Yes

Japan Bonsai
Plant Picks:
_____
Acer palmatum JAPANESE
  MAPLE
Juniperus chinesis CHINESE
  JUNIPER
Pinus thunbergii JAPANESE
  BLACK PINE

Japan Bonsai
Owner: Tak Yamaura
2337 140th St. • 536-9220; fax: 536-8799
Bonsai and Japanese garden-style plants
Courses: Spring and fall classes
Catalogue: No
Specialty: Bonsai and specially trained Japanese black pine
Wheelchair Access: Yes

Jenray Gardens Nursery
Owner: Ray Beckhurst
19429 62A Ave. • 530-8226
Home-based nursery. Offers mainly helleborus, also some interesting perennials
Courses: On site information/advice
Catalogue: Plant list available on request
Specialty: Helleborus specialist. Look for future release of Helleborus argutifolius 'Jenray Gold'
Wheelchair Access: No

Jenray Gardens
Plant Picks:
Helleborus foetidus
Helleborus x *sternii*
Helleborus x *hybridus*

Knotts Nurseries & Produce Centre Ltd
Owner: Sam Jeerh
4490 152 St. • 576-3144 (fax also)
Full nursery, garden, landscape supplies including bedding plants, hanging baskets, florist, tropical plants, pottery, gift items. Wholesale: terra-cotta
Courses: No
Catalogue: No
Specialty: Hanging baskets made on site including custom orders. Large selection of bedding geraniums. Great Christmas selection of poinsettias
Wheelchair Access: Yes

Knotts Nurseries
Plant Picks:
Nymphaea WATERLILY
Pelargonium GERANIUM
Petunia Supertunia Series

Koco Garden Centre
Owner: Danny Ng
13589 16th Ave. • 536-6828; fax: 536-2285
Full service nursery with knowledgeable and creative staff
Courses: No
Catalogue: No
Specialty: Inspiring display of foliage — texture and colour of rare and unusual plants
Wheelchair Access: Yes

Koco Garden Centre
Plant Picks:
Cimicifuga ramosa 'Brunette'
Hakonechloa macra 'Aureola'
Polemonium caeruleum 'Brise d'Anjou'

Ninety-Nine Nursery & Florist
Owner: Lin Hui
9376 King George Hwy. • 584-6555; fax: 589-8636
Indoor-outdoor, tropical plants, wicker, giftware, ceramic, floral shop, flowers
Courses: No
Catalogue: Brochure for floral department
Specialty: Bedding plants and florist
Wheelchair Access: Yes

Ocean Park Nurseries
Owner: Paul Johnson
2124 128 St. • 535-8853; fax: 538-4626
Retail: trees, shrubs, perennials, pottery, fountains, pools
Courses: Yes — pruning, planting, waterplants, hanging baskets and seasonal classes
Catalogue: No
Specialty: Knowledgeable, long-term staff
Wheelchair Access: Yes

Port Kells Nurseries
Plant Picks:

Canna x generalis

Hosta

Acer palmatum JAPANESE
  MAPLE

Port Kells Nurseries
Owners: Rene and Joanne Duineveld
18730 88 Ave. • 882-1344; fax: 882-1323
28 acres of stock including annuals, perennials, bulbs, shrubs, trees, as well as lava rock, soil, mulch, etc.
Courses: Hanging basket demonstrations
Catalogue: No
Specialty: Hedging cedar, hanging baskets, bedding plants, and a petting zoo. Display garden of *Canna* and *Hosta* varieties (available on site or by special order)
Wheelchair Access: Yes

Torii Nursery
Plant Picks:

Calceolaria 'Gold Fever'

Pelargonium Swiss Balcony
  Series GERANIUM

Petunia 'Purple Wave' PETUNIA

Torii Nursery
Owner: Rick Tsuyuki
9082-140 St. • 591-1528 (fax also)
Retail: bedding plants and hanging baskets; family farm. Everything grown on-site
Courses: No
Catalogue: No
Specialty: Moss hanging baskets
Wheelchair Access: Yes

Wrenhaven Nursery
Plant Picks:

Rhododendron 'Bouqueta'

Rhododendron 'Golden Ruby'

Rhododendron yak 'Ken
  Janeck'

Wrenhaven Nursery
Owner: Hart Wellmeier and Tiina Turu
16651-20th Ave. • 536-7283
Courses: No
Catalogue: Yes (free)
Specialty: Field grown *Rhododendron* and *Azaleas*. Peak bloom time April/May. Also bonsai
Wheelchair Access: Yes, but limited

Art Knapp The Urban Garden

Owner: Wim Vander Zalm
1401 Hornby St. • 662-3303; fax: 662-8268
website: www.artknapp.com
Indoor/outdoor plants, books, gifts and pottery
Courses: No
Catalogue: No
Specialty: Wide selection of herbs and pottery
Wheelchair Access: Yes

Art Knapp The Urban Garden
Plant Picks:
Eucalyptus viminalis RIBBON GUM
Prostanthera rotundifolia AUSTRALIAN MINT BUSH
Osmanthus fragrans SWEET OLIVE

Art Knapp Figaro's

Owner: Wim Vander Zalm
1896 Victoria Dr. • 253-1696
website: www.artknapp.com
A garden centre with community flavour. Offers annuals, perennials, herbs, shrubs, seeds, indoor house plants, trees and climbers
Courses: Sometimes – call for details
Catalogue: Newsletter (free)
Specialty: Unusual shrubs, trees, and vines
Wheelchair Access: Store, yes; nursery, no

Art Knapp Figaro's
Plant Picks:
5 in 1 Apple
Hebe 'Patty's Purple'
Nandina domestica 'Gulf Stream' HEAVENLY BAMBOO

Balconies Beautiful Ltd.

Owner: Steve Hackett
1035 West 67th Ave. • 266-4104; fax: 264-9453
A shop for container gardeners (indoor/outdoor)
Courses: Free in-store advice
Catalogue: No
Specialty: Container plants and plantings for small space gardening. From custom work to helping self-starters get off the ground. Consultations available
Wheelchair Access: Yes

Balconies Beautiful
Plant Picks:
Clematis x jackmanii
Narcissus 'Cheerfulness' DAFFODIL
Osmanthus x burkwoodii

David Hunter Garden Centre

Owner: Ron Hunter
2084 West Broadway • 733-1534; florist: 733-5811
Local garden centre and florist offers seeds, annuals, perennials, shrubs, trees, 250 rose varieties, bulbs
Courses: In-store seasonal demonstrations.
Catalogue: No
Specialty: Specialty perennials and nursery stock. Customer "want" list
Wheelchair Access: Yes

David Hunter Garden Centre
Plant Picks:
Choisya ternata 'Sundance' MEXICAN ORANGE
Euonymus fortunei 'Blondy'
Rudbeckia fulgida 'Goldsturm' CONEFLOWER

Earthrise Garden Store
Plant Picks:

Old Roses
Styrax japonica SNOWBELL
Species Rhododendrons

Earthrise Garden Store
Owner: Michael Luco
2954 West 4th Ave. • 736-8404
Good selection of books and antique garden orna-
ments. Specialty trees, shrubs, perennials. Also
selection of seeds including Bolton's Sweet Peas
Courses: No
Catalogue: No
Specialty: English roses, peonies, *Clematis* and other
climbers. Fall bulbs. Fresh flowers every Thursday.
Will also seek unusual plants for customers. Residen-
tial garden design and consultation.
Wheelchair Access: No

Ford's Flowers & Nursery
Owner: Erin Froese
4445 West 10th Ave. • 224-1341; fax: 224-1467
English garden bouquets, baskets, pots. Spring and
summer: selected nursery stock/bulbs
Courses: No
Catalogue: Newsletter (free)
Specialty: English garden bouquets, French country
baskets
Wheelchair Access: Yes

Gardenworks Plant Picks:

Coreopsis verticillata
 'Moonbeam'
Helleborus orientalis
Heuchera varieties

GardenWorks
Owner: John Zaplatynski
8697 Granville St. • 266-9313
"Everything to make your garden work"
Courses:
Catalogue: Quarterly newsletter, "Garden Notes"
Specialty: Good selection of prime, high-quality plants
Wheelchair Access: Yes

Murray Nurseries
Plant Picks:

Aquilegia vulgaris
 Vervaeneana group
 'Woodside' COLUMBINE
Euphorbia myrsinites
Heuchera 'Chocolate Ruffles'

Murray Nurseries
Owner: John Murray
Manager: Betty Murray
3140 West 57th Ave. • 261-2151; fax: 266-8514
"Down to earth" Garden Centre serving Vancouver
gardeners since 1916
Courses: Seminars on hanging baskets. Note: Betty
Murray has a radio gardening show from 11 to 12
a.m. on AM-1040 called "Greenleaf's BC Gardening
Show with Betty Murray"

Catalogue: No
Specialty: Perennials. Also roses and varieties. Well-informed and educated staff available
Wheelchair Access: Yes

Shop-in-the-Garden
UBC Botanical Garden
6804 S.W. Marine Dr. • 822-4529
Good selection of books, tools and accessories. Perennials, shrubs, native plants and UBC Introductions. Look for UBC Botanical Garden Seeds and others
Courses: Call UBC at 688-8404
Catalogue: List available of UBC Plant Introductions
Specialty: Good value for garden worthy classics as well as for many unusual and eclectic surprises from diverse sources
Wheelchair Access: Yes

Shop-in-the-Garden
Plant Picks:
Geranium species
Meconopsis betonicifolia BLUE POPPY
Primula species

Somerville Orchids
Owner: Norm Dorosh
5138 Somerville St. • 327-4248
By appointment only
Courses: Hands-on special care for orchid planting, re-potting
Catalogue: See Norm's handbook for beginners: "Cultural Basics for Orchid Growing" (also available at Mandeville's)
Specialty: Orchid presentation for home/office/weddings. Offers specially designed clear plexiglass orchid containers. Also custom indoor/outdoor topiary
Wheelchair Access: No

Somerville Orchids
Plant Picks:
Phalaenopsis MOTH ORCHID
Cattleya
Encyclia

Southlands Nursery
Owners: Thomas Hobbs and Brent Beattie
6550 Balaclava St. • 261-6411; fax: 261-6429
website: www.southlandsnursery.com
Conservatory built in 1901. Imported terra-cotta planters, rare plants including orchids, garden furniture, tools, seeds, bulbs and pottery from England
Courses: Call for courses offered by Thomas Hobbs
Catalogue: No
Specialty: Unusual plants. "New plants usually appear here first!"
Wheelchair Access: Yes

Southlands Nursery
Plant Picks:
Colocasia esculenta "Black Magic'
Cornus controversa 'Variegata'
Magnolia sargentiana var. 'Robusta'

Southside Gardens
Plant Picks:

Aster novae-angliae and *Aster
   novi-belgii* FALL ASTERS
Fragaria 'Everbearing Tri-Star'
   STRAWBERRY
Nepeta x *faasseni*

Brambles and Blooms
Plant Picks:

Cimicifuga ramosa 'Brunette'
Euphorbia characias ssp.
   wulfenii
Lysimachia clethroides
   GOOSENECK LOOSESTRIFE

Southside Gardens
Owner: Odessa Bromley
3250 West 55th Ave. • 261-7665; fax: 261-4200
Perennials
Courses: Advice on environmentally friendly alternatives for plant and garden care
Catalogue: Free plant list by request
Specialty: Large selection of well-grown hardy perennials, ground covers, potted bulbs, vines, hardy herbs and berries. Mostly on-site propagated
Wheelchair Access: Yes

WEST VANCOUVER:

Brambles and Blooms
Owner: Shelly Sorenson
2474 Marine Dr. (in rear lane) • 925-1082
A neighbourhood plant shop offers an impressive selection of perennials, shrubs, topiary and organic goods. Helpful service and knowledgeable staff
Courses: Yes. Call ahead
Catalogue: No
Specialty: Unusual shrubs and perennials in a practising organic setting. Will source plants
Wheelchair Access: Yes

Maple Leaf Garden Centre
Owner: Duynstee Family
2558 Haywood Ave. • 922-2613; fax: 926-7631
Outdoor supplies. Trees, shrubs, bedding plants, ceramic pots
Courses: No
Catalogue: Newsletter
Specialty: Colour, perennials, bedding plants
Wheelchair Access: Yes

West Van Florist Ltd.
Owners: Rob and Wendy Harrington
1821 Marine Dr. • 922-4171; fax: 922-9735
Full customer service garden centre and florist shop
Courses: Yes (via municipality plus in-house demos)
Catalogue: Several flyers per year
Specialty: Large specialty; perennials, colour for garden, annuals, pots, containers, accessory items
Wheelchair Access: Limited

UBC Botanical Garden Plant Introduction Scheme

by Bruce Macdonald,
Director of the UBC Botanical Garden

Botanical gardens are sometimes referred to as "museums" of living plants. The UBC Garden now has over 12,000 plants from many continents around the world and countries such as China, Japan, Nepal, Switzerland, New Zealand and Chile.

In the past, visitors to the UBC Botanical Garden would often ask "Where can I buy that plant?" only to be told it was not available — it was growing only at UBC. The UBC Botanical Garden wanted to change this very traditional and conservative approach. So during the early 1980s they met with BC growers, retailers and landscapers to formulate a program that would make these plants available. The UBC Botanical Garden Plant Introduction Scheme was born.

To implement this scheme, a knowledgeable group of horticulturists meet at regular intervals during the different seasons to evaluate plants within the Garden. This panel is made up of garden retailers, growers, landscape architects and representatives from the Parks Boards. Among the important criteria that the plants must meet before being selected for introduction are the following:

Bruce Macdonald, Director of the UBC Botanical Garden.
Photo:

- Flowering and foliage: length of flowering period; are the flowers hidden by the foliage?; is the attractiveness of the foliage relative to the flower colour?;
- Pest and disease susceptibility;
- Cold hardiness and tolerance of summer heat;
- Plant size, particularly considering the need for plants for small gardens and patios;
- Good growth under a wide range of soil types;
- Is the plant significantly different or an improve-

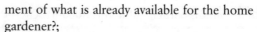

Saint Fiacre is the Patron Saint of Gardening.

ment of what is already available for the home gardener?;

- Ease of propagation and sales appeal at retail outlets.

When a plant has been selected, it is carefully propagated and grown at the Botanical Garden's nursery until sufficient numbers have been produced for distribution. Currently there are 42 participants in the BC nursery industry as well as growers in many areas of the world. To ensure the new plants can withstand the vagaries of the Canadian climate they are sent to various test sites across North America. To date, over 16 million plants have been produced throughout the world from the 19 different introductions.

In order to ensure that the program continues in the future, the Garden is planning an active role in plant breeding and international collecting. This will be greatly assisted by the Garden's recent twinning with the Nanjing Botanical Garden in China and the Hokkaido Botanical Garden in Japan. As well, J. Henry Eddie and his family made a major gift to UBC to establish a foundation named after his father, Henry M. Eddie. The goal of this foundation is to produce new plants for decades to come. The BC nursery industry have also made significant contributions. The funds from the foundation are used for plant breeding and plant exploration with the intent of developing new and improved garden plants.

Among the most successful of the introductions to date are the following:

Arctostaphylos uva-ursi 'Vancouver Jade'
KINNIKINNICK
Now the most popular evergreen ground cover for the Pacific Northwest. Rapidly spreads, resulting in a thick carpet of green foliage. Has darker pink flowers than the other forms of this native plant. Also considerably more tolerant of leaf spot diseases. Well over 1.5 million plants produced annually in BC.

Aronia melanocarpa 'Autumn Magic' CHOKEBERRY
An attractive deciduous shrub growing up to two metres. Native to the eastern United States. White

flowers in the spring are followed by exceptional autumn colour with the leaves turning to shades of red, orange and plum. An added attraction are the shining black berries, which are a favourite food for many wild birds.

Artemisia stellariana 'Silver Brocade' DUSTY MILLER

This was the program's first perennial to be introduced. Its intense, silver, attractive leaves make it a wonderful contrast plant with other perennials. This hardy plant is ideal to site in the front of borders. Also provides a good addition to baskets and containers on garden patios.

In 1898 the Georgia Street Nursery was opened at the corner of Georgia and Burrard.

Clematis 'Blue Ravine'

This outstanding clematis has received international acclaim. It is a hybrid between 'Nelly Moser' and 'Ramona.' Its large flowers, which grow up to 18 centimetres in diameter, are an intense silver blue with a pale pink bar down the centre of each petal. It has a long flowering season and is ideal for containers, as it flowers low down on the previous season's wood.

Genista pilosa 'Vancouver Gold' BROOM

Along with 'Vancouver Jade,' this was the first introduction from the program. This hardy evergreen is an excellent ground cover for sunny well-drained sites. In the spring a mass of golden yellow flowers are produced. After flowering, 'Vancouver Gold' does not produce seed like other plants in this genus.

Lonicera 'Mandarin' HONEYSUCKLE

This outstanding new vine was bred by Wilf Nichols at the UBC Botanical Garden. It is a hybrid between the large flowering Chinese species *Lonicera tragophylla* and the famous hardy Canadian red flowering hybrid 'Dropmore Scarlet.' Combined with the attractive new foliage of *Lonicera tragophylla*, its very large orange-red flowers make it a must for the home garden. Grows in full sun or partial shade.

A tip: when you are plant shopping in Southlands at Murrays, Southlands or Southside Nurseries, try the McCleery Golf Course café. Thomas Hobbs says it's great for lunch.

Penstemon fruticosus 'Purple Haze' PENSTEMON
This low-growing native penstemon produces intense purple flowers during the spring. It is an evergreen but does need a very sunny well-drained site to grow successfully.

Potentilla fruticosa 'Yellow Gem' SHRUBBY CINQUEFOIL
This is a very hardy selection of this low growing native plant. Growing to around one metre, it produces a continuous mass of yellow flowers during the summer months. An ideal deciduous shrub for small gardens.

Sorbus hupehensis 'Pink Pagoda' MOUNTAIN ASH
This was the program's first shade tree. The foliage is an attractive glaucous blue. It is noted for its bright pink berries, which form in late summer. These are retained into December and eventually turn a pinkish-white. For some reason this is the only Mountain Ash with fruits that are not eaten by wild birds.

Viburnum plicatum 'Summer Snowflake' VIBURNUM
This viburnum has the longest flowering period of any deciduous shrub within the Botanical Garden. It has many good qualities, which include its intense white flowers, reddish-purple autumn colour, reddish brown berries and tolerance to many soil types in full sun or partial shade. Grows between two and three metres in height.

Clematis chiisanensis 'Lemon Bells' CLEMATIS
This very new introduction arose from seed sent by the Chollipo Arboretum in South Korea. Its 2.5-centimetre pendulous flowers are yellow with a reddish tinge at the base of each petal. The foliage is excellent. Additional merits are its black stems and silvery seed heads which last into the autumn. 'Lemon Bells' is the earliest flowering yellow cultivar of all the small flowered clematis. This is an ideal plant for a trellis or wall in sun or partial shade. Grows to around three metres in height.

GARDEN FURNITURE, TOOLS AND ACCESSORIES

While many nurseries and garden centres have shops that sell tools and accessories, the shops in this section specialize in those items and, for the most part, don't sell plants at all. We recognize that the big drug, grocery and hardware stores also are into gardening accessories, furniture and landscape supplies, but in the interest of space we've chosen to focus on the smaller specialty businesses. These are the places where you know you will always find the perfect gift for your gardening friend, or the perfect tool or book for yourself. You'll get ideas and inspiration – and you'll likely come away with a fistful of seed packets (or maybe a load of gravel).

"What is a weed? A plant whose virtues have not been discovered."
—Ralph Waldo Emerson

ALDERGROVE:
Otter Co-Op
3600 248th St. • 856-2517; fax: 856-2758
Garden shop, general store and cafeteria with weekly specials. Wide selection of tools. Canola seed meal, bone meal, rock phosphate, dolomite lime, kelp meal. Bulbs and seeds, lawn fertilizers and grass seed. Functions like a small community. Check out the Saturday Special. Breakfast for $2. West Coast Seeds.

DELTA:
Multiturf Specialists Ltd.
6455-64th St. • 946-0446; fax: 946-5547
Plastic picnic tables and benches.

LANGLEY:
Classic Stone Products
20167 Industrial • 533-6793; fax: 530-2955
Picnic tables, planters, benches, garbage receptacles, bird baths.

Fraser Valley Cement Gardens Ltd.
23664 Fraser Hwy. • 534-5558; fax: 530-1397
Fountains, planters, bird baths, patio tables, benches, statues, plaster mouldings, columns and stepping stones. Over 1500 items. Concrete fencing also available.

Two great teas are served at garden centres around here: *Red Rose* by the vat load at Earthrise Garden Store in Vancouver; *Tazo* tea at Rainforest Nurseries in Langley.

SURREY:

The Potting Shed
1706 152 St. • 541-6100
Garden ornaments, gifts, garden furniture and antiques, plants.

VANCOUVER:

The Avant Gardener
2235 West 4th Ave. • 736-0404
Garden ornaments and accessories including seeds, bulbs, gift items, composters and an excellent selection of garden tools. Seeds: Seeds of Change; West Coast Seeds; and McKenzie.

Chintz and Company
950 Homer St. • 689-2022; 689-2055
European garden statuary, umbrellas, hammocks and outdoor furniture. A lot of teak, glassware and picnic baskets to use in any garden.

Dig This Garden Shop
10-1551 Johnston St., Granville Island • 688-2929; fax: 688-2999
Everything for the garden except the plants. Tools, accessories, gifts, gear, statues, seeds and books. Known for their selection of garden clothing and unusual garden gimmicks. Seeds: Richter's Herbs; West Coast Seeds; Father Gills; Seeds of Change (organic); Suttons.

Hewer Home Hardware
4459 West 10th Ave. • 224-4934
Indoor and outdoor pots, soil, gardening tools, huge basket collection. Seeds: MacKenzie.

Hobbs
2129 West 41st Ave. • 261-5998; fax: 261-5979
Owned by the same people as Southland's Nursery. Specializing in home and garden accessories including terracotta pots, outdoor furniture, wrought iron arches and unusual imported and local gardening gifts. Good book selection.

Lee Valley Tools

1098 SW Marine Dr. • 261-2262

Local showroom for national mail order company. Large selection of gardening hand tools, accessories, clothing and gifts. Kitchen and garden composters.

Pacific Northwest Garden Supply

2137 E. Hastings • 254-4765; 254-4724

Pots and soil, books, fertilizers and insecticides. Seeds: Rainforest; Herbal (Terra Flora).

Pinks: A Gift Shop for Gardeners

4235 Dunbar St. • 222-3772; fax: 222-3775

Lanterns, oil lamps, garden chimes, small garden furniture, bird baths, stepping stones, lanterns, pots, tools, soil and books. Seeds: Cedar Creek. Also carry bulbs.

Primatif Imports Ltd.

1425 Odlum Dr. • 254-2774; fax: 254-8801

Importers of fine pottery and garden ornaments. Manufacture their own line of iron home and garden accessories. Canadian distributor for "Stoneworks." Open to the trade.

Shop-in-the-Garden

6804 SW Marine Dr. (at 16th Ave.) • 822-4529; fax: 822-1514

Best garden book selection in town. Very good plant centre with many perennials. Statuary, fountains, pots. At Christmas they have fresh Christmas wreaths. Seeds from the Botanical garden on the premises and Cedar Creek Seeds.

Suquet Interiors Inc.

1211 East 6th Ave. • 872-3155 (fax also)

Imported Mexican, Spanish and Italian garden furniture, pots, containers, ornaments and statues made of wrought iron, bronze and quarry stone, concrete. Columns, fountains, sidewalk and stairway stones and wrought-iron gates also available.

Check out:
Ital Décor Canada Classic Arts
6886 Hastings, Burnaby
• 291-7571
Columns, statues, lanterns, birdbaths, planters, and architectural ornaments.

Thomas Hobbs Florists by Maureen Sullivan
2127 West 41st Ave. • 263-2601 fax 263-0822
Mainly fresh flowers, but they also carry gifts for gardeners, outdoor pots, birdhouses, benches and indoor and outdoor water fountains.

VanDusen Botanical Garden Gift Shop
5251 Oak St. • 257-8665; 266-4236
Gifts, some unusual tools and an excellent selection of books. Seeds: West Coast Seeds; seed collectors sell seeds on the deck by the shop. Plant material propagated from the garden and other stuff.

Weatherstone
3067 West Broadway • 733-7001
Giftware and garden accessories.

West Coast Gardeners Co-op of BC
4289 Slocan • 430-4117; fax: 430-1528
Garden tools, clothing and supplies, in-season plants wholesale by the flat. Vancouver Japanese Gardeners Association owns the store and sometimes has courses.

WEST VANCOUVER:
The Avant Gardener
1460 Marine Dr. • 926-8784
Garden ornaments and accessories including seeds, bulbs, gift items, composters and an excellent selection of garden tools. Seeds: Seeds of Change; West Coast Seeds; and McKenzie

"What wondrous life is this I
   lead!
Ripe apples drop about my
   head;
The luscious clusters of the
   vine
Upon my mouth do crush
   their wine;
The nectarine, and curious
   peach
Into my hands themselves do
   reach;
Stumbling on melons, as I pass
Ensnarled with flowers, I fall
   on grass."
—Andrew Marvell,
"The Garden"

Landscape Supplies

These specialty landscape supply companies carry a range of brick and concrete pavers, interlocking building tiles and patio slabs. Some carry used bricks and clay pavers; many carry planters, lanterns, ponds, rock, gravel and sand, garden ornaments and furniture. Call around, or better yet — go visit and get inspired.

When you plant a perennial, the first year it sleeps, the second it creeps and the third it leaps.

BURNABY:
Northwest Landscape Supply Co.
5883 Byrne Rd. • 435-4842; fax: 436-9443

Steel Industrial Products
3455 Bainbridge Ave. • 415-3800; fax: 421-0448

DELTA:
Sandy's Soil & Stuff
9568 Burns Dr. • 594-5333; fax: 594-8911

LANGLEY:
Fraser Valley Cement Gardens Ltd.
23664 Fraser Hwy. • 534-5558; fax: 530-1397

NORTH VANCOUVER:
Bricks 'N' Blocks
1371 McKeen Ave. • 984-3008; fax: 984-3358

Capilano Topsoils
100 Bridge Rd. • 341-8020; 985-8782

Deerwood Garden and Landscape Supplies
825 West 1st St. • 987-1221; fax: 986-5279

Roberge Trucking
100 McKeen Ave. (foot of Pemberton Ave.) • 980-5413

United Landscape Supplies
125 Riverside Dr. • 929-4555 (fax also)

RICHMOND:
Steel Industrial Products
10780 Cambie St. • 278-5567; fax: 278-6969

Why isn't it safe to tell a secret in a garden? Because the corn have ears and the beans talk.

SURREY:

Fraser Valley Brick and Block Supplies
13240 Comber Way • 591-7377; fax: 591-7002

Sanderson Concrete Inc.
12665 116 Ave. • 580-4108; fax: 580-4111

Steel Industrial Products
15050–54A Ave. • 576-9131; fax: 576-3154

VANCOUVER:

Fraser Valley Brick and Block Supplies
3595 East 1st Ave. • 299-0270

Water Garden and Fountain Supplies

BURNABY:

Northwest Landscape Supply Co.
5883 Byrne Rd. • 435-4842; fax: 436-9443

DELTA:

Sandy's Soil & Stuff
9568 Burns Dr. • 594-5333; fax: 594-8911

MAPLE RIDGE:

Unique Koi and Water Gardens
11761 272nd St. • 462-9925
Open by appointment. Set in a false-front town circa 1934. Sells water plants, koi, custom made statuary.

SURREY:

Nature's Choice Waterfalls and Ponds
14832-96th Ave. • 618-4126; fax: 589-2985 (press 51)
Installations of ponds and waterfalls — they have all the necessary supplies, pumps etc. They do not have a showroom, but just call for brochures.

VANCOUVER:

Trasolini E. Pool Construction
1351 Adanac St. • 255-8551; fax: 255-6681
Ponds and fountains, supplies and installation.

Greenhouses and Related Supplies

BURNABY:

BC Greenhouse Builders and Easy Living Conservatories
7425 Hedley • 433-4220; fax: 433-1285
toll-free: 1-888-391-4433
e-mail: bc-green@direct.ca
Hobby greenhouses built with aluminum frames and glass or twin wall polycarbonite sheets in all sizes. $1000 and up.

Solar Greenhouse and Hydroponic Supply
4752 Imperial • 438-7244; 436-1540
Predominantly hydroponics and a lot of biological controls for greenhouses. Automatic watering systems and fans, timers. They do not carry actual greenhouses but mostly supplies, pots, soil, fertilizer, books and accessories.

Jon's Plant Factory
3951 E. Hastings • 294-3000; fax: 294-3055
Hydroponic and greenhouse supplies. Home of green-gro hydroponic food (fertilizer).

DELTA:

California Hydroponic Warehouse
9509 120th St. • 930-0565; fax: 930-0592

RICHMOND:

Advanced Greenhouse Manufacturing Ltd.
120-12820 Clarke Place • 276-8060; fax: 276-2944
website: www.greenhouse.bc.ca
Greenhouse coverings available for hobby or residential gardeners; they do not carry commercial greenhouses. Heaters, fans and accessories available in the showroom.

Home Greenhouse Supplies Ltd.
2960 Olafson • 270-6788; fax: 270-6094
toll-free: 1-800-668-1556
website: www.homegreenhouse.com

Dickson's Gardening Rule:
When weeding, the best way to make sure you are removing a weed and not a valuable plant is to pull on it. If it comes out of the ground easily, it is a valuable plant.

Best bets for buying
gardening books:
New:
UBC Shop-in-the-Garden
VanDusen Botanical Garden
 Gift Shop
Book Warehouse
Duthies
Chapters
Also, check out Costco (for
about a dozen titles a year).

Used:
McLeod's
Lawrence Books

Greenhouses as well as hydroponics. They carry rare seeds from the rainforest and lights for indoors. Their new aeroponic garden is hot hot hot. Plants are placed in a six-inch pipe and nutrients are misted into the roots so they are very oxygen enriched — a growing method that has become very popular recently.

SURREY:

Coastal Grower Supplies Ltd.
103-12824 Anvil Way • 599-1778; 599-1776
Hydroponics — everything you'd need. There's a store with pots and tools. Sells seeds from spring until August: "Stokes."

VANCOUVER:

False Creek Industries Ltd.
8811 Laurel • 324-4311; fax: 324-4411
Films, ground cover, shade cloth and mulch films.

MAIL ORDER SUPPLIERS

Nothing heralds the New Year like the thump of seed catalogues through the mail slot. They start arriving around Christmas and joyfully keep coming through January. That is, if you ask for them. Do ask, because not only are catalogues great sources of actual seeds and plants, they are also excellent reference material. You can learn a great deal from the folks who toil away, bringing you the best they can by mail. You can also daydream, plan and fantasize about your garden — all for a nominal fee which is often refundable when you order something.

When is a gardener like a mystery writer? When she digs up a plot.

We were so impressed by the resources just outside of our Lower Mainland borders that we decided to start making a list. And then we decided to expand to the entire province of BC but not to include the whole country (because that would be another book). Many of these places have on-site nurseries so if you are travelling around the province, go visit, but call first for hours. Happy reading!

BC MAIL-ORDER COMPANIES:

Alannah's African Violets
Site 640, RR No. 1
Grand Forks, V0H 1H0
phone: (250) 442-2552;
fax: (250) 442-0288
website: http://www.alannahs.com
e-mail: alannah@alannahs.com
Starter plants and fresh-cut leaves of Africa Violets and assorted Gesneriads. Starter plants of specialty geraniums: scented, miniature, and unusual varieties. Catalogue $2 refundable. Visits by appointment.

Alyssa's Garden
Dept. 402, Box 6718
Fort St. John, V1J 4J2
phone: (250) 785-2220; fax: (604) 785-2213
Lilies (martagon and Asiatics), irises, peonies, daylilies and perennials. All hardy to Zone 2. List $2; customers get it free. No visits from public.

To see herb farming operations firsthand, Dr. Allison McCutcheon, botanist and President of the Canadian Herb Society, recommends:

Heather Fair at Tuscan Farms in Langley (530-1997);

Jodi and Estar Lazzarotto at Terra Flora Botanicals in Surrey grow plants, collect seeds and make tinctures. It's a teaching garden with sales by appointment (576-1755);

For medicinal herbs, try Don and Elaine McLeod at Bowen Island Botanicals on Bowen Island (947-2384).

Boni Townsend, Lowland Herb Farms at 5685 Lickman Road, Sardis (call first: 858-4216). Open 10 a.m. to 6 p.m. daily, from April to October (and see her at the East Vancouver Farmer's Market). Ask her about information sessions.

Ambrosia Gardens
PO Box 1135
Vernon, V1T 6N4
phone/fax: (250) 766-1394
e-mail: ambrosia@silk.net
websites: http://www.icangarden.com/catalogue/ambrosia.htm
http://www.silk.net/personal/ambrosia/index.htm
Suppliers of Canadian grown perennials: daylilies, lilies, bearded, species and aril bred iris, Siberian iris and hosta. $2 catalogue. Out of town visitors can make an appointment or visit Saturdays 10 a.m. to 3 p.m., May 15 to July 4 only.

Aurora Farm
3492 Phillips Rd.
Creston, V0B 1G2
phone/fax: (250) 428-4404
e-mail: aurora@kootenay.com
website: http://www.syberspace.com/aurora
Suppliers of heritage and native seeds. Catalogue $3 (non-refundable). A biodynamic farm specializing in open-pollinated and heirloom seeds and herbal alternatives (echinacea, St. John's Wort oil). Currently they run a training program in Biodynamic Agriculture. Open to the public upon phone notification.

Blue Haven Specialty Nursery
2881 Church Way, RR No. 2
Mill Bay, V0R 2P0
phone/fax: (250) 743-3876
website: http://bluehavennursery.com/
Specialize in Cultivars of perennial plants, meconopsis and primulas. Rare, hard-to-find perrenial plants. Visitors welcome February to October. Catalogue $3.

Bluestem Ornamental Grasses
1949 Fife Rd.
Christina Lake, V0H 1E3
phone/fax: (250) 447-6363;
Ornamental grasses, sedges, rushes and willows. Ornamental grasses have a wide range of heartiness. Books available. Catalogue $2, published once a year. Visits by appointment.

Bradner Bulb Gardens
6735 Bradner Rd.
Abbotsford, V4X 2C6
phone/fax: (604) 856-4923
e-mail: bradnerbulb@bc.sympatico.ca
website: http://www3.bc.sympatico.ca/
BradnerBulbGardens/
Daffodils, tulips and other spring bulbs. Catalogue
$2. Visits by appointment.

Brentwood Bay Nurseries
1395 Benvenuto Ave.
Brentwood Bay, V8M 1J5
phone: (250) 652-1507; fax (250) 652-2761
A specialty nursery growing a large selection of rare
and unusual perennials as well as a wide variety of
roses, hard-to-find shrubs, trees, climbers and tropicals.
e-mail: plants@coastnet.com
website: http://www.coastnet.com/~plants
Catalogues: roses $2; perennials etc. $2 (both refundable). Mail order within Canada only. Open for visits
from the public. (Require warning for coach load.)
Hours are: 9 a.m. to 5 p.m., Monday to Saturday; 10
a.m. to 5 p.m., Sundays and holidays. Closed Christmas to New Year's.

The Canadian Gardener is filmed at the UBC Botanical Garden where David Tarrant is the education coordinator. Check it out at: http://tv.cbc.ca/canadiangardener/

British Columbia's Wild Heritage Plants
47330 Extrom Rd.
Sardis, V2R 4V1
phone: (604) 858-5141 or 858-5245
e-mail: bcwild@uniserve.com
Northwest native plants: perennials, bulbs,
groundcovers, trees and shrubs. Catalogue can be
obtained free via e-mail or send $2. Open Saturdays
from April to June, 10 a.m. to 4 p.m.; or visitors welcome anytime with appointment (please phone first).

Brookside Orchid Garden
23711 32nd Ave., RR No. 12
Langley, V2Z 2J2
phone: (604) 533-8286; fax: (604)533-0498
website: http://www.brooksideorchids.com/
Orchid Access, classes and seminars. Custom arrangements.

Butchart Gardens

Box 4010, Stn. A
Victoria, V8X 3X4
phone: (250) 652-4422; fax: (250) 652-1475
e-mail: @butchartgardens.bc.ca
website: http://butchartgardens.bc.ca/butchart/
Seeds, bulbs and gardening-related gifts. Large selection of annual and perennial seeds available, all hand-packaged at The Butchart Gardens. Special collection packages include annuals, perennials, rock garden, window box, cottage garden and children's. Over 90 different types of premium quality Dutch bulbs. Call or write for a free catalogue.

Campbell Craig Delphiniums

14219 Middlebench Rd.
Oyama, V4V 2B9
phone: (250) 548-9271
e-mail: camcraig@cnx.net
website: www.cnx.net/~camcraig/delphiniums/
Hand-pollinated F1 Hybrids of name varieties and selected seedlings. Very vigorous growth and exciting colours. SASE for list.

Cardinal Gardens Nursery

13050 Cardinal St.
Mission, V2V 5X4
phone: (604) 820-0845
Thirteen acres of display gardens to see. Specialists in perennials, herbs, pondside plants, ornamental plants and bog plants. Catalogue available for $2, refundable with order. Open for visits from March to September. Please call ahead.

Cedar Creek Seed Co.

254 East 1st St.
North Vancouver, V7L 1B3
phone: (604) 984-6594; fax: (604) 984-6558
Catalogue free, full colour. All seed packets come with full-colour plant stake information on the back with UV protection to keep it from fading. More seeds per pack than most companies. Specializing in wild flowers. Seeds, Everlastings, Herbs.

Copperbush Seeds
Box 61
Port Alberni, V9Y 7M6
phone: (250) 724-6241
website: http://www.webquay.com/copperbush/
Wholesale and retail. Wildflowers and other plants for decorative purposes and to help with environmental approaches to things like soil stabilization. Seeds for small trees, shrubs, sages, brushes. This year shifted to Native Northwest wildflowers. Species list $1. No showroom, but the owner says that if you want to see his product, go for a walk in the forest.

Cusheon Creek Nursery
175 Stewart Rd.
Salt Spring Island, V8K 2C4
phone: (250) 537-9334; fax: (250) 537-9354
e-mail: cusheoncreek@saltspring.com
website: http://vvv.com/~amdigest/cusheon.htm
We grow cacti and succulents, alpines, perennials, trees and shrubs, with an emphasis on unusual and drought-resistant species. Plant list available and catalogue available in 1999 for $2. Visits Thusday, Friday from 10 a.m. to 5 p.m., Saturday from 12 a.m. to 5 p.m., March 1 to October 15. Otherwise by appointment.

Dacha Barinka
46232 Strathcona Rd.
Chilliwack, V2P 3T2
phone: (604)792-0957
Seeds for everlasting flowers, vegetables, herbs, Chinese vegetables, wine grapes and nuts. Free catalogue with SASE. Call ahead for visits.

Dahlias Galore
RR No. 1, Legion Site C22
Sechelt, V0N 3A0
(250) 885-9820; fax: (250) 885-4841
More than 300 kinds of dahlias and 50 varieties of Japanese Irises. Price list available with business-size SASE. Visits in June for the Iris and August to October for Dahlias. Open Monday through Saturday, 9 a.m. to 6 p.m.

A Gardener's Creed

I want it.

I want it all.

I want it now.

If everyone else has it, I must have it too.

If it will not grow in my zone or is prohibitively expensive, I want it most of all.

I am perfectly willing to forego any necessities of life in order to have it.

I recognize my horticultural dependency.

I recognize your horticultural dependency.

I will willingly aid and abet your dependency, as you will mine.

This makes us infinitely happy.

Any money saved by virtue of comparison shopping equals money found and therefore is not counted as spending.

If I have planted everything that I have already purchased, I must immediately buy more plants.

(At this point it is customary to recite your VISA number from memory.)

Durand's Nursery
9 Johnson Rd.
Christina Lake, V0H 1E2
phone: (250) 447-6299; fax: (250) 447-9499
Explore the aromatic, culinary and medicinal versatility of these wonderful plants. Small retail nursery with 60 percent of their own propagating. Good variety and a display herb garden. Fourteen-page catalogue, $2 refundable. Open year round for visits.

Erikson's Daylily Gardens
24642 51st Ave.
Langley, V2Z 1H9
phone: (604) 856-5758; fax: (604) 856-0716
e-mail: pamela1@istar.ca
website: http://www.icangarden.com/catalogue/eriksons.htm
Over 1300 varieties. $2 catalogue. Canada's first official daylily display garden. Host the largest collection in the country. The gardens offer ideas for planting and culture, including displays with hundreds of companion plants and trees. Open weekends from April to June, and then daily for the month of July, during peak bloom time.

Ferncliff Gardens
8394 McTaggart St.
Mission, V2V 6S6
phone: (604) 826-2447; fax: (604) 826-4316
Catalogue $3. Visits at certain times of the season. Call ahead. Irises, peonies, daylilies, gladiola and dahlias. New dahlia introduced each year.

Fragrant Flora "Scentsational Plants to Live By"
3741 Sunshine Coast Hwy.
RR No. 5, Site 21, C11, Gibsons, V0N 1V0
phone/fax: (604) 885-6142
e-mail: fragrant_flora@sunshine.net
Fragrant and aromatic plants including Penstemons, Nepetas, Magnolias, Dianthus and hundreds of other special plants. Butterfly, bee and hummingbird plants available. Catalogue $3, deductible from order. Garden visits possible in the spring and fall, Sundays from noon to 5 p.m.

Fragrant Rose Company
8185 Island Hwy.
RR No. 1, Site 19, Dept. 8
Fanny Bay, V0R 1W0
phone: (250) 335-2101; fax: (250) 335-1135
toll-free: 1-888-606-rose
Catalogue $2. Fragrant roses, all imported from England; high quality roots stock from Europe. Display Garden at Island Sun Green Houses. Drop in. Open every day except Christmas and New Year's, from 9 a.m. to 5:30 p.m.

Fraser's Thimble Farms
175 Arbutus Rd.
Salt Spring Island, V8K 1A3
phone/fax: (250) 537-5788
thimble@saltspring.com
Pacific Northwest natives; more than 120 varieties of ferns, 20 varieties of trilliums, 20 varieties of erythroniums and over 1,000 shade perennials. Over 500 species of West Coast natives. Hearty ground orchids. Catalogue $3, refundable. Fall catalogue $2. Open 10 a.m. to 4:30 p.m., Tuesday through Sunday. In spring, open seven days a week.

Gulf Island Seeds
2301 Otter Bay Rd., RR No. 1
Pender Island, V0N 2M1
Contact: Margaret Grimmer
phone: (250) 629-3373
Seeds for untreated and open-pollinated perennials, annuals, wildflowers, herbs and some vegetables. Catalogue $2.

Holt Geraniums
34465 Hallert Rd.
Abbottsford, V3G 1R3
phone: (604) 859-3207
e-mail: mholt@uniserve.com
Unusual pelargoniums such as Stellars, Regals, Angels, Uniques, Scented Leaf, dwarf and miniature zonals, Silver Leaf. Unusual flowered such as rosebud, carnation, tulip and cactus, Species, Frutetorum Hybrids, ivy leaf and hybrid species. Catalogue $2.

The "Fraser Valley Farm Fresh Guide" is produced by the Fraser Valley Farm Direct Marketing Association in co-operation with the BC Ministry of Agriculture and Food. It lists over 60 farms and nurseries. To obtain a copy, check with your local tourism office or Chamber of Commerce. Many of the farmers listed in the guide also give it out. You can also go to their website: http://www.bcfarmfresh.com/

Howe Sound Seeds
Box 109
Bowen Island, V0N 1G0
phone: (604) 947-0016; fax (604) 947-0945
e-mail: jdunster@bigfoot.com
Specializes in open-pollinated vegetable varieties grown in the Howe Sound region of BC during the late Victorian period (1885-1901). For a catalogue, U.S. customers should send $1; Canadians send four first-class stamps.

Inner Coast Nursery
Box 115, Manson's Landing
Cortes Island, V0P 1K0
phone/fax: (250) 935-6384
e-mail: Innersea@oberon.ark.com
website: http://oberon.ark.com/~innersea
Organic growers of disease resistant, coastal adapted, heritage fruit trees.Catalogue available for $5. Includes cultural and historical information about the trees and descriptions of 300 varieties of fruit trees along with detailed planting instructions.

Island Specialty Nursery
8797 Chemainus Road, RR No. 1
Chemainus, V0R 1K0
phone/fax: (250) 246-9355
e-mail: isn@island.net
website: http://www.island.net/~isn/1
Specializes in premium quality, unusual species of trees, shrubs and perennials. New for winter 98/spring 99: many exciting forms and species of flowering hellebores and cyclamen. Open and welcoming every day, 10 a.m. to 5:30 p.m., February through November. Display gardens to browse.

Made in the Shade Nursery
4586 Saddlehorn Cres.
Langley, V2Z 1J7
phone: (604) 856-2010; fax: (604) 856-0049
e-mail: goody@intergate.bc.ca
Ferns and other shade loving plants. Hostas, shade perrenials, shrubs and ground covers.
Call for free catalogue.

Nature's Garden Seed Company
PO Box 32105, 3749 Shelbourne St.
Victoria, V8P 5S2
phone/fax: (250) 595-2062
e-mail: Naturesgarden@bc.sympatico.ca
Native Canadian plants and trees seeds. Gift items
with botanical theme. Free catalogue.

Old Rose Nursery
1020 Central Rd.
Hornby Island, V0R 1Z0
phone: (250) 335-2603; fax: (250) 335-2602
"Own root" old garden roses, ramblers, climbers,
David Austin English roses and cold hearty varieties
Explorer and Rugosa. Large plants, one-gallon pots.
Catalogue $2 with SASE. Display garden open in the
summer. Hours vary throughout the year; call ahead.

PK Growers
22646 48th Ave.
Langley, V2Z 2T6
phone: (604) 530-2035; fax: (604) 530-2022
e-mail: pfitness@uniserve.com
Specializing in Fuchsias – over 300 varieties. Uprights,
trailers, winter hardy triphylla and species. Also an
extensive collection of Pelargoniums including Regals
(also known as Martha Washingtons), Scented Geraniums, and Angel Pelargoniums. Catalogue $2,
refundable. Mail order business, but welcome customers to pick up orders at the greenhouse if they make
an appointment.

Parkside Gardens
251 Demetri Way
Salt Spring Island, V8K 1X3
phone: (250) 653-4917; fax: (250) 653-4918
Bog, aquatic and marginal plants. Water lilies, irises
and other plants. Grown naturally and they are all
hearty. Catalogue $2, refundable. Visits by arrange-
ment.

The Plant Farm
177A Vesuvius Bay Rd.
Salt Spring Island, V8K 1K3

GREAT GARDEN RESTAURANTS:
VanDusen Botanical Garden:
Sprinklers
5251 Oak St.
261-0011

Queen Elizabeth Park:
Seasons in the Park
874-8008

Minter Gardens:
Bloomer's Café
The Trillium Restaurant
2892 Bunker Rd., Rosedale
794-7191

West Vancouver:
Tudor Room
Park Royal Hotel

The "Langley Farm Fresh Guide" is a terrific resource. It's a co-operative project of the Langley Chamber of Commerce, the *Langley Times* and the Township of Langley. Agriculture plays a very important role in the economy of Langley and their local farms and nurseries offer outstanding products. Visitors are always welcome to visit any of the facilities listed in the guide. Visit the Langley Chamber of Commerce Infocentre at No. 1, 5761 Glover Rd., or phone 530-6656.

phone/fax: (250) 537-5995
Specialists in bamboo, hostas, roses, rhododendrons, heathers, ornamental grasses, beardless irises, deciduous azaleas, daylilies and numerous selected exotica. Liners (starter plants) available. $3 for two years' subscription to 50-page descriptive catalogue. Three-acre display garden open to public Thursday to Monday, 10 a.m. to 4 p.m.

Rainforest Gardens
Elke and Ken Knechtel
13139 224th St.
Maple Ridge, V4R2P6
phone: (604) 467-4218; fax: (604) 467-3181
e-mail: info@rainforest-gardens.com
website: http://www.dsoe.com/rainforest/
Grow and sell over 2000 varietes of perennials through mail order and retail walk-in-garden sales. Two acres of mature display gardens. Our mail order and Garden to Garden services offer over 1100 varieties of perennials. Two-year subscription to our catalogue for $4. Visa, MC or cheque. Open for public visits Thursday though Saturday, 10 a.m. to 5 p.m., but call ahead.

Salt Spring Seeds
Box 444
Ganges, Salt Spring Island, V8K 2W1
phone: (250) 537-5269
website: http://www.saltspring.com/ssseeds/
Organically grown seeds, including high-protein beans, amaranth, quinoa, 20 varieties of garlic. Lots of lettuces and tomatoes. $2 for catalogue. Call ahead for visits.

Scents of Time Gardens Co.
PO Box 204, 11948 207th St.
Maple Ridge, V2X 1X7
phone: (604) 467-8588
$10 for catalogue; seed list only for $4. Heritage flower, vegetable and herb seeds. Catalogue is full of historical and botanical information as well as recipes. Seeds date from ancient times through Victorian times.

Sylvan Nursery
848 Stonybrook Rd.
Kelowna, V1W 4P3
phone:(250) 764-4517; fax: (250)764-0166
e-mail: SylvanRoses@bc.sympatico.ca
Sylvan roses grown on their own roots. One of the largest selections of David Austin, Harkness, Agriculture Canada and Antique roses. Satisfaction guaranteed. More varieties each season. Catalogue for $3. Visits by appointment only.

Trillium Herb Farm
Donna and Todd Scheven
8561 Bradner Rd.
Abbotsford, V4H 2X5
phone: (604) 856-2920
Mail order seeds, rootlets, herbs and native plants. Retail and display garden. Catalogue free.

Valley Orchid Partners
12621 Woolridge Rd.
Pitt Meadows, V3Y 1Z1
phone: (604) 465-8664; 465-8374
Orchid hybrids and species. No catalogue. Visits by appointment.

West Coast Seeds (formerly Territorial Seeds)
206-8475 Ontario St.
Vancouver, V5X 3E8
phone: (604) 482-8800; fax: 482-8822
website: http://www.westcoastseeds.com/index3.htm
Vegetable, flower and herb seeds. BC's biggest supplier. Free catalogue. They also run a demonstration garden at London Heritage Farm in Richmond, 6511 Dyke Rd. (website: http://www.steveston.com/heritage.htm).

Western Biologicals Ltd.
Box 283
Aldergrove, V4W 2T8
phone/fax: (604)856-3339
e-mail: Western@prismnet.bc.ca
Wide variety of mushroom spawn for home gardeners, hobbiests and commercial growers. Limited variety

Did you know? The Vancouver Park Board is one of the largest horticulture employers in the province.

of specialized plants including Slevia, a sugar leaf plant, and some herbs. Workshops on growing mushrooms and plant tissue culture available. Catalogue for $3, refundable with purchase. Includes a useful manual. Also available, a free "Mushroom Information" sheet which lists all the better known types.

Wrenhaven Nursery
16651-20th Ave
Surrey, V4P 2R3
phone: (604)536-7283
Specialists in rhododendrons, azaleas, bonsai. Exceptional selection and quality. Field-grown on premises. Free catalogue.

SEED COLLECTING

A Year in the Life of a Seed Collector

by Aimee Murrell,
Chair of the VanDusen Garden Seed Collectors

Did you know that VanDusen Botanical Garden puts out an interesting and extensive Seed List every year? This little catalogue is the culmination of a year's work by the Volunteer Seed Collectors of the Garden. In it you will find annuals, perennials, trees, shrubs, grasses, ferns and herbs, all harvested from the garden plants in the previous year. Many are unusual and hard-to-find varieties.

We seed collectors are an enthusiastic and committed group of volunteers. We are in the garden from early spring to late autumn. The first part of our year is spent in refreshing our memories and in observation. Our anticipation grows as we watch the first blooms emerge. Garden beds may be replanted and new acquisitions appear. We make notes and research new arrivals. At times, we have disappointments: perhaps some of our favourites are not setting seed this year; others may have disappeared. Cold wet springs, hot dry summers, disappointing autumns all take their toll. Seed collectors are like farmers, dependent on the weather.

Aimee Murrell, Chair of the VanDusen Garden Seed Collectors.
Photo: Dannie McArthur

It isn't long before we can be seen with our red collecting boxes, holding secateurs, paper bags, notebooks and pens. As we harvest seeds, each bag is marked with botanical name, garden area and date. Our day's collections are also entered in a special recording book.

As the season progresses, bags quickly pile up in our volunteer classrooms. To cope with this accumulation, around 30 of us meet every Tuesday and start with an hour of seed cleaning. This is a labour of love, for it is painstaking and can be tedious. Nonetheless, the room is full of friendliness and laughter as we work and a coffee break with treats from home adds to the pleasure of the day.

In the autumn, as our year winds down, we see the mountain of seed bags gradually disappear and our storage refrigerator filling up with bottles neatly labelled and ready for packaging. We scramble to make sure our new seed list is correct and complete, for it must go to the printer in mid-November to be ready for mailing with the "VanDusen Garden Christmas Bulletin." That done, with a great sense of relief and achievement we take our Christmas holiday.

The work of The Seed Collectors at VanDusen Botanical Garden.
Photo: Dannie McArthur

The last cycle of our year begins in January. This is packaging time. Mail order requests for seeds pour in from BC as well as other parts of Canada, the United States and other countries. As many as 1500 packages of seeds will be mailed out during the first three months of the year. Seedy Saturday is fast approaching too. This event is VanDusen Garden's Heritage Seed Day. It is always held on the last Saturday of February and is convened by the VanDusen Garden Seed Collectors. Home gardeners, small seed companies and heritage fruit-tree growers come from all parts of the Lower Mainland, Sunshine Coast, Gulf Islands and Vancouver Island to sell their organically grown heritage wares. The "Seed Swap" is an important part of the day where heritage seeds can be traded

or bought for a small donation. The VanDusen Garden Floral Hall is an exciting place to be on Seedy Saturday.

Happily working and learning together, and bound by a deep sense of service, the VanDusen Garden Seed Collectors are a wonderful example of the pleasure and value of volunteering and the enduring fascination of seeds.

The Seed Collectors
VanDusen Botanical Garden
5251 Oak St. • 878-9274
Vancouver, V6M 4H1
Cost of seeds: $1.50 per packet. To request a free seed list, send to the above address or pick one up at the garden. Seeds are available at Seedy Saturday or on the garden deck, daily from 1 to 4 p.m. from Easter until October.

For Italian lettuce seeds (direct from Italy), check out Tosi Italian Food Import Company at 624 Main St. (in the heart of Chinatown).

GARDEN ART AND PHOTOGRAPHY

The botanical world is a natural and appealing subject for those with artistic inclinations. And for fans of gardening, works of botanical art and photographs are a wondrous thing to own.

If you are interested in seeing good botanical art, there are occasional exhibits at both UBC and VanDusen botanical gardens. Both gardens sell reproductions of botanical art in their shops. In addition, courses in painting and botanical drawing are held sporadically at VanDusen and UBC botanical gardens. Call for information.

These are three of the most well-known botanical artists in the Lower Mainland:

Mary Comber Miles is a botanical illustrator and artist. She is VanDusen Garden's artist-in-residence and she is represented by the Harrison Gallery in Vancouver and West Vancouver.

Lyn Noble is a watercolourist who collaborates with the UBC Botanical Garden. She has won three medals for her botanical art from the Royal Horticultural Society in London.

Valerie Pfeiffer also does watercolours. She has shown in galleries, her work has been published widely and it is currently being used on products like mugs, kitchenware and tee-shirts.

There are a number of very talented garden photographers in the Lower Mainland whose work you can see in books and magazines. One of the busiest is **Paddy Wales,** who recently wrote and took the photographs for *Journeys Through the Garden: Inspiration for Gardeners in BC and the Pacific Northwest* (Whitecap Books, 1998). Paddy teaches a popular course on garden photography at VanDusen Botanical Garden. Call 878-9274 for information.

There is an American Society of Botanical Artists: http://huntbot.andrew.cmu.edu/ASBA/ASBotArtists.html or c/o Michele Meyer 18 Lansing Street, No. 101 San Francisco, CA, 94105-2612

Look for: *Plantae Occidentale: Two Hundred Years of Botanical Art in British Columbia,* published by UBC Botanical Garden Technical Bulletin No. 11, 1979.

DESIGNERS, SPECIALISTS AND CLUBS

Pardon the pun, but gardening is a serious growth industry. Sales are booming, services are blooming — in short, there are more and more folks getting involved. We've tried to help you figure out how and where to find qualified help. And we have profiled a few folks with rather interesting gardening-related careers. Finally, in this section we haven't ignored the social side of gardening. We made an enormous list of garden clubs and associations — enough to keep your dance card full forever.

GARDEN SPECIALISTS

Horticulture Professionals

Here's some advice: If you can afford it, concentrate on what you enjoy doing in your garden and hire pros to do the rest. For example, the difference between an amateur pruning job and the work of a professional arborist can make all the difference to the look and the life of a tree. And the ideas of a skilled garden designer can transform a drab lot into a magical and useable space.

But how do you find these people? It can be tricky. For starters, their titles are a tad murky. To use the handle "landscape architect" in BC, one must pass provincial exams regulated by the BC Society of Landscape Architects. The same goes for certified arborists – the International Society of Arboriculture (ISA) sets examinations. But who can call themselves a landscape designer or a garden designer? Anyone can, as there are neither criteria nor professional associations – this is a young business and difficult to police. Then there are garden maintenance workers, gardeners and landscape maintenance people, plant maintenance workers, landscapers, irrigationists and more.

There are lots of talented people working under all of these titles, and there are also some who are simply not good at what they do. Like any service, buyer beware. With gardening, the research to find qualified help can be delightful. Visit the VanDusen Garden Show and the Vancouver and Abbotsford Home and Garden Shows. Check out the displays and see whose work you like. Wander neighbourhoods looking for gardens you admire; if someone is out in their yard, ask them who they use. And when you are considering hiring someone, ask for references and check out their previous work. For work in your home garden, be sure to look for someone with a strong background in horticulture – the person must know plants. Finally, know if you want a quick job or if you wish to build a long-term relationship.

We started to list all of the horticulture professionals, but for reasons noted above as well as the enormous numbers of people involved, we decided against it. We have, however, listed all of the professional and umbrella organizations to make your searching for help much easier. And the following list, gratefully reprinted from the BC Landscape and Nursery Association, should help in hiring a landscape professional too. Good luck. The right match will make your life just that much easier and your garden that much more lush.

HOW YOU CAN IDENTIFY A LANDSCAPE PROFESSIONAL.

QUALIFICATIONS:
·Brother-in-law has a truck...
·Lots of other stuff but I can't remember what.

QUALIFICATIONS:
·Industry certification.
·Horticultural training
·Experience & references
·Environmentally aware & responsible
·Business registration & license
·Follows provincial Landscape Standard
·GST & WCB registration
·Liability insurance
·Member of provincial industry assoc.

Therese d'Monte calls herself a garden coach — she works alongside those who don't have time to take courses and need motivation. She is mad for perennials and specializes in the "flower-arranger's garden." Therese also gives courses at VanDusen Botanical Garden on this topic. For information, call: 738-9927.

Cartoon by Grahame Arnould

How to Hire a Landscape Professional

by the BC Landscape and Nursery Association

1. Be aware of industry classifications for landscape services, including:
- tree care: pruning, transplanting, removal, cabling and bracing, hazard assessment, spraying;
- lawn care: sod installation, hydroseeding, fertilizing, spraying;
- interiorscaping: design, installation, maintenance;
- landscape design: landscape planning;
- grounds maintenance/landscape gardening: all aspects of continuing plant, lawn and yard care;
- landscape installation: construction, grading and drainage, plant and tree installation, irrigation, lighting, water features and so on.

Many companies offer a range of these services while others may specialize.

2. Clearly define the tasks you want done:
- Decide what the job is - even if it's a wish list or will take five years to complete;
- Should you involve a landscape consultant? Early professional advice can give you the results you want - often more economically - whether you plan to do the work yourself or hire a contractor;
- Determine how much you can realistically afford for the project, in total or per year;
- Identify those contractors offering the services you need, including companies from neighbouring municipalities.

3. Select a contractor:
- Contact one or more potential contractors, briefly outline your project and assure yourself their schedule suits your needs;

What did the dirt say when it began to rain?
If this keeps up, my name will be mud.

118

- Verify the contractor's level of professional and business standards;
- When considering more than one contractor, ensure that each is quoting on the same project requirements so that you can make a fair comparison.

4. Sign a contract:
- Review and sign a contract or letter of agreement which details the work to be completed, the fees and expenses, the schedule of work and payments and the standard of work expected. This agreement protects both the client and the contractor and guides the professional relationship throughout.

For more information on the Landscape and Nursery Association, check out their website at: www.canadanursery.com.

Sheila Watkins, a well-known *Gardens West* columnist and teacher of basic gardening skills at VanDusen Botanical Garden and North Shore Continuing Education, makes house calls for garden advice. For information, call: 980-2265.

Related Professional Associations:

ABBOTSFORD:

Irrigation Industry Association of BC
2330 Woodstock Dr. • 859-8222
e-mail: iiabc@home.com

MAPLE RIDGE:

Western Canada Turf Grass Association
22097 Isaac Cres. • 467-2564; fax: 467-0500

RICHMOND:

BC Recreation and Parks Association
No. 30-10551 Shellbridge Way • 273-8055; fax: 273-8059
e-mail: bcrpa@bcrpa.bc.ca

SURREY:

BC Landscape and Nursery Association
101-5830 176A St. • 574-7772; fax: 574-7773

VANCOUVER:

BC Society of Landscape Architects
110-355 Burrard St. • 682-5610

INTERNATIONAL:

Pacific Northwest Chapter,
International Society of Arboriculture
PO Box 4202
Salem, OR, 97302
phone: (503) 585-4285
toll-free: (800) 335-4391
e-mail: pnwisa@teleport.com
website: http://www.teleport.com/~pnwisa/

SUSTAINABLE LANDSCAPES

Cabot Lyford: An Edible-Landscape Consultant

by Marg Meikle

Before energy was cheap and transportation systems were efficient, we had to grow our own food. Today, Cabot Lyford of Vancouver champions the idea of "edible landscaping," a new name for an old art form. It's urban agriculture that looks and tastes good. Lyford consults on designing these productive gardens — what he calls "elegant and functional foodscapes."

Examples of the traditional European "potager," or kitchen garden, range from humble to grand. Rosalind Creasy and Robert Kourik pioneered edible landscaping in California during the 1970s and 1980s and published books on the subject. Vancouver has its share of edible landscapes, though they are perhaps not named as such by their owners: grapevines shading driveways, or front yards full of fruits and vegetables planted side by side with flowers, are not uncommon here.

Edible landscapes can be formal or informal, high or low maintenance and can fit onto a balcony or cover an acreage. Apples, pears, plums, hazelnuts and figs are attractive landscape features for those with enough room. Raspberries and gooseberries can fit into smaller spaces while grapes and kiwis can be trained up buildings, their foliage helping to ward off summer heat. The nooks and corners can be filled with a wide assortment of low-care perennials like salad burnet, Welsh Onion, nine-star broccoli, edible flowers and culinary herbs.

Lyford has tried out a variety of edible "niche" plants suitable to the challenges of Vancouver gardens. Edible perennials such as Mauritian Mallow, Good King Henry and Welsh Onion provide fresh food during some of the hungry gaps in the food production cycle, such as late winter. Fresh herbs and unusual foods such as lovage and Miners' lettuce can provide culinary delight and help supply many

Plant Picks of Don Fraser,
Northwest Landscape Supply:
Pontaderia cordata
'Pickerell Rush'
Waterlily 'Rose Avey'
Caltha palustris
MARSH MARIGOLD

Watch the Guerilla Gardening at a very public location of a privately owned empty lot: 4th and Alma in Vancouver.

health-giving nutrients missing from our modern diets. For balconies and other small spaces, annual vegetables with generous inputs of compost (from your worm composter) may suit you best. Larger gardens can be more adventurous, along with your palette. Miner's lettuce and chickweed can yield fresh February salads. Mallow and campanula provide an abundance of edible summer flowers. It is not practical to meet all of your food needs from an edible landscape, but by selecting the right plants you can replace a significant portion of your California-grown products with food that is interesting, tasty, organic and very fresh.

Vancouver Permaculture Network

The word "Permaculture" comes from the words Permanent Agriculture and Permanent Culture. It is the conscious design and maintenance of ecologically permanent food, energy, housing and non-material systems that meet the needs of people. The Vancouver Permaculture Network (VPN) serves to:

1) Educate about designing for sustainable living through Permaculture workshops, projects and promotions;

2) Provide a social link to those who engage in sustainable living practices.

For more information, contact:
Harold Waldock • 645 9529
e-mail: haroldw@alternatives.com
website: http://www.alternatives.com/vpn

ECOLOGICAL LANDSCAPING

by Angela Murrills

A planner and planter of ecological landscapes, Steve Thompson of Natural Space Design has always viewed nature as an ally — and nature returns the favour. In the top branches of a dogwood tree, waiting for room to land, chickadees are stacked up like 747s. As counterpoint to the birdsong and the drumming of the rain, water gurgles into a small pool. Black pine and maple trees frame a gently rolling landscape planted with shrubs and edged with rocks. It's an idealized piece of wilderness, a small life-affirming miracle, and it measures just 10 metres wide by six metres deep in that part of Kitsilano where the tall Edwardian houses butt up against each other with the snugness of a carpentry joint.

Walls on three sides and a few haphazardly planted shrubs were all that faced Thompson when he first moved into the home he now shares with two other households. "You start by looking at your garden in context," he says, "with the neighbourhood, the house, the site and your lifestyle." Then, before you so much as browse through a seed catalogue, you check out the micro-climate: the rain, wind, light, drainage and — far and away the most important factor — the state of the soil.

In the wild, nature recycles leaves and dead plants into new nutrient-loaded soil. "Living in the city, we have to bring back the ecological balance," says Thompson. "High-quality soil is dark, active and full of life. I renew the soil every year. Mushroom manure is a fast fix but costs money. Compost takes time and is free. Orange peels, tea leaves, vegetable trimmings — it all goes onto the compost heap and eventually turns into something rich and black as treacle, a sort of horticultural super-food." Turn your compost, keep it moist and line your bin with quarter-inch wire mesh to keep rodents out, Thompson advises. Not that you need a bin. Short on space, he simply dug his eggshells and apple cores into the ground. Last year he started a communal composting system on an adjoining property.

When Gardeners Jump the Sidewalk

Here are a few great boulevard plantings.

Vancouver
16th and Sasamat
8th and Sasamat
15th and Camosun
West 40th between Manitoba and Ontario (Palm City)
Trafalgar between 4th and 5th Ave.
2200 block of Trafalgar
Balaclava between 6th and 8th Ave.
18th and Willow
SW corner of North Ingleton and McGill
McLean and Grant
Union between Heatley and Jackson

North Vancouver:
Westview and West 22nd Ave.
Corner of Moody and East 19th Ave.
Larson and just west of Jones

Can you legally plant the boulevard between your sidewalk and the curb? If the garden obstructs access to the sidewalk, or obstructs, say, the view of a car coming, you may hear from City Hall. Sidewalks and streets are city property so it can be a liability risk. The city is also keen on keeping a consistent "look" within the context of each neighbourhood. The City of Vancouver hands out about 3500 encroachment notices a year. They are mostly about keeping sidewalks clear for pedestrians. City inspectors walk each block once a year. Planting annuals around the base of trees is okay.

Neighbourliness is part of this new ecological approach to gardening. Like a potluck supper, everybody brings something to the table — seeds, plant cuttings or ideas — and all enjoy the combined results. Stands of bamboo visually tie Thompson's garden to one next door. He point out a formal "knot" garden he designed for his neighbour on the other side. A view of Lombardy poplars some 50 feet away is woven into his own big picture. "A number of people are looking out or down onto this garden," he says. "Think about your neighbour's point of view."

Gardening ecologically means recycling wherever possible. When the city jack-hammered the corner of his street to install wheelchair ramps, Thompson took the slabs to edge his garden. Rounded granite boulders are transplants from Spanish Banks. There's total harmony everywhere, even in the shed where tools and bicycles are stored. Its walls and roof are cedar-shingled, its doors and windows concealed by bamboo blinds.

Trees and shrubs are the bones of a garden and the most daunting to purchase. Garden centres, VanDusen and UBC botanical gardens, and *Sunset New Western Garden Book* are all user-friendly sources of information on which trees need sunshine and what likes shade. "Read," says Thompson, "and borrow. Look at nature — or other people's gardens — and observe what plants grow under the same conditions as in your garden. That's how I experiment and learn."

A laboratory it may be, but his Japanese-inspired garden is notably free of chemical pesticides. Puny plants, easy prey for disease, are ruthlessly ripped up. Only the Arnold Schwarzeneggers of the plant world are permitted to stay. The few bugs in the garden provide buffet lunches for the sparrows, grosbeaks, bush tits and lemon-yellow Wilson's warblers that constantly stream in.

Steve Thompson's next project is to introduce frogs into his pool. His first batch of tadpoles mysteriously disappeared so this year he's devised ways of protecting them. "Planting gardens is like raising kids," he says. "They require constant observation and adjustment. It takes patience. To be a good gardener you have to think in tree time." Natural Space Design can be contacted at 731-7341.

Jennifer Jones' Favourite Plants

Here are Landscape Consultant Jennifer Jones' picks:

Trees:
Stewartia pseudocomellia JAPANESE STEWARTIA
Acer griseum PAPERBARK MAPLE
Acer japonicum "Aconitifolium' FERN-LEAF MAPLE
Cornus kousa chinensis KOREAN DOGWOOD
Magnolia sieboldii OYAMA MAGNOLIA
Styrax obassia FRAGRANT SNOWBELL
Cercis canadensis 'Forest Pansy' EASTERN REDBUD
Amelanchier canadensis SHADBLOW
Arbutus unedo STRAWBERRY TREE
Salix babylonica WEEPING WILLOW

Shrubs:
Ceonothus CALIFORNIA LILAC
Enkianthus campanulatus REDVEIN ENKIANTHUS
Spiraea x *bumalda* 'Anthony Waterer' ANTHONY
    WATERER SPIREA
Senecio cineraria 'Sunshine' SENECIO SUNSHINE
Cistusladanifer COMMON GUM CISTUS
Vaccinium corymbosum BLUEBERRY
Salix lanata WOOLLY WILLOW
Chaenomeles nivalis WHITE FLOWERING QUINCE
Exochorda grandiflora 'The Bride' PEARL BUSH
Cotinus coggygria 'Grace' SMOKE TREE

What flowers grow between your nose and your chin? Tulips.

Julie Lane-Gay of the Hort-Line at UBC Botanical Garden.
Photo: UBC Botanical Garden

Donna Rodman just added her Master's degree in Landscape Architecture from UBC to her diploma in nursing, BA in Urban Geography and certification as a Building Technician. It has all come together, as Rodman specializes in Universal Design of accessible and adaptable gardens. For more information, check out her website: www.designsource.bc.ca or contact Donna by e-mail at: DonnaMarie_Rodman@bc.sympatico.ca

Perennials:
Nepeta 'Six Hills Giant' CATMINT
Centranthus VALERIAN
Echinacea CONEFLOWER
Sedum 'Autumn Joy' STONECROP
Geraniums—all varieties PERENNIAL GERANIUMS
Trollius x *cultorum* 'Alabaster' GLOBEFLOWER
Hemerocallis 'Gentle Shepherd', 'Catherine Woodbury' DAYLILY
Iris sibirica 'Sky Wings' IRIS
Corydalis ochroleuca CORYDALIS
Aster x *frikartii* ASTER

Annuals:
Echium lycopsis ECHIUM
Cerinthe retorta HONEYWORT
Heliotropium x *hybridum* CHERRY PIE
Nicotiana sylvestris TOBACCO PLANT
Brachycomeiberidifolia SWAN RIVER DAISY
Convolvulus mauritanicus MORNING GLORY
Cobea scandens CUP AND SAUCER VINE
Alyssum maritimum SWEET ALYSSUM
Helichrysum petiolatum 'AUREUM' LICORICE PLANT
Lathyrus odorata SWEET PEA

Claire Kennedy's Favourite Plant Combinations

Here are Vancouver Garden Designer Claire Kennedy's favourite picks:

Sunny Bed with Good Drainage:
(a dusky purple grey foliage combo)
Lavandula stoechas FRENCH LAVENDER; *Salvia officianalis* 'Purpurea' PURPLE LEAFED SAGE; and *Sedum* x 'Vera Jameson'.

Sunny Bed/Hot Colour Combo:
(deep purple foliage, yellow/orange flowers and black flowering grass – flowers well into autumn)
Cotinus coggygria 'Royal Purple' PURPLE SMOKE BUSH; *Crocosmia* 'Emily McKenzie' MONTBRETIA; and *Pennisetum alopecuroides* 'Moudry' FOUNTAIN GRASS.

Sunny Bed/Long Flowering Combo:
(a single yellow rose with repeat blooms; the Aster is lavender with yellow centres)
Rosa 'Golden Wings' ROSE; *Aster* x *frikartii* 'Monch' ASTER; and *Alchemilla mollis* LADY'S MANTLE.

Semi Shady Bed/Green and Gold Foliage Combo:
(evergold shrub with interesting structure, blue green Hosta with gold edges, and green and gold striped grass)
Lonicera nitida 'Baggesen's Gold' GOLDEN BOXLEAF SHRUBBY HONEYSUCKLE; *Hosta* 'Frances Williams' HOSTA; and *Hakonechloa macra* 'Aureola'.

Semi Shady Bed/Evergreen Combo:
(burgundy foliage with chartreuse flowers, burgundy-stemmed Hellebore with green flowers and Gold Creeping Jenny)
Euphorbia amygdaloides 'Rubra' SPURGE; *Helleborus foetidus* 'Western Flisk' CHRISTMAS ROSE; and *Lysimachia nummularia* 'Aurea' GOLD CREEPING JENNY .

Two private/public plantings by Alex Kurnicki and Michael Wilkes worth visiting: Boulevard and front of Happy Planet Juice on Union and Vernon; and the back of La Casa Gelato on Union at Glen.

Alpine Plant Recommendations

from The Alpine Garden Club

Easy Plants:
Erinus alpinus; Thlaspi rotundifolium; Campanula pusilla; Dianthus simulans; Dianthus glacialis; Draba aizoidies; Ramonda myconi; Saxifraga cotyledon; Orostachys spinosum; Polygola calcaria; Primula marginata; Primula alpicola; Sedum ewersii; Potentilla vernanana; Edrianthus graminifolius; Gentiana sino-ornato

Medium Difficulty:
Draba bryoides; rigida Dryas octapetala (N); *Edrianthus pumilis; Gentiana acaulis; Lewisia columbiana rupicola* (N); *Lewisia cotyledon* (N); *Petrophytum caespitosum* (N); *Saxifraga longifolia*

Difficult:
Tecophilia cyanocrocus; Primula allionii; Primula parryi (N); *Erigeron aureus* (N); *Eriogonum ovalifolium* (N); *Gentiana verna; Saxifraga griesbachii; Geranium argenteum; Gypsophila aretioides; Lewisia tweedyi* (N)

Not-Quite-Impossible Plants:
Erythronium montanum WHITE MOUNTAIN GLACIER LILY; *Eritrichium nanum* ALPINE FORGET-ME-NOT; *Primula angustifolia* ALPINE PRIMROSE; *Aquilegia jonesii* JONES COLUMBINE; *Androsace chamaejasme* ROCK JASMINE; *Trifolium nanum* DWARF ALPINE CLOVER; *Saxifraga oppositifolia* PURPLE MOUN-TAIN SAXIFRAGE; *Phacelia sericea* SILKY PHACELIA; *Polemonium viscosum* SKY PILOT; *Xerophyllum tenax* BEAR GRASS

Note: There are very few common names for alpine plants (except for the native list), hence the Latin names for plants.

Easy Care Hardy Perennials for Beginning Gardeners

by Odessa Bromley, Southside Perennial Gardens

For Sun:
Achillea spp. YARROW
Alchemilla mollis LADYS' MANTLE
Armeria spp. THRIFT
Aster spp. MICHELMAS DAISY
Centranthus rubra RED VALERIAN
Coreopsis spp. TICKSEED
Echinacea purpurea CONEFLOWER
Hemerocallis DAYLILY
Monarda didyma BEEBALM
Phlox paniculata SUMMER PHLOX
Sedum spectabilis STONECROP

For Part Shade:
Aquilegia spp. COLUMBINE
Astrantia camiolica MASTERWORT
Campanula spp. BELLFLOWER
Geranium spp. CRANESBILL
Iris ensata or siberica JAPANESE OR SIBERIAN IRIS
Polemonium ceruleum JACOBS LADDER
Primula spp. PRIMROSE

For Shade:
Anemone japonica WINDFLOWER
Astilbe spp. FALSE SPIREA
Dicentra spp. BLEEDING HEART
Geranium macrorrhizum SCENTED CRANESBILL
Helleborus orientalis LENTEN ROSE
Hosta spp. HOSTA
Heuchera spp. CORALBELLS
Lobelia speciosa LOBELIA
Pulmonaria saccharata LUNGWORT

The botanical names listed above with *spp.* have numerous species in their plant families that will thrive without much fuss. Your choice of species will depend on your colour preference and the overall size of plant that will suit your garden best. For example,

The Gardener's Prayer
O Lord, grant that it in some way may rain everyday, say from about midnight until three o'clock in the morning — but make it gentle and warm so that it can soak in; grant that at the same time it would not rain on Campion, Alyssum, Helianthemum, Lavender and the others which You in Your infinite wisdom know are drought-loving plants (I will write their names on a bit of paper if you like). And grant that the sun may shine the whole day long, but not everywhere (not, for instance, on Spirea, or on Gentian, Plantain-lily or Rhododendron) and not too much; that there be plenty of dew and little wind, enough worms, no plant lice and snails, and no mildew; and that once a week thin liquid manure and guano may fall from Heaven.
— Karel Capek (1920s)

for part shade, *Campanula siberica* is a small, mounding front-of-the-border plant with starry blue flowers, whereas *Campanula persicifolia* stands three feet tall with spikes of blue or white bell-like flowers and looks best near the back of the flower bed.

From the list above, chose a grouping that suits your site and follow the planting and care requirements recommended by the grower or nursery. Happy gardening!

What does a farmer give his wife on Valentine's Day? Hogs and kisses.

Master Gardeners

by Marg Meikle, Master Gardener, Class of 1993

When I'm on my knees in my garden hauling at the cursed Creeping Buttercup that is invading my flower beds, the last thing I feel like is a Master Gardener. But, in fact, I earned that title by spending a winter attending horticulture lectures, doing lengthy assignments, writing an intense (but open-book) exam and continuing to put in many, many volunteer hours talking to the public.

Despite the hopelessly pretentious handle, we Master Gardeners (or MGs, as we call ourselves) are a very grounded lot. Mention leaf miners, carrot rust fly or late blight of tomatoes and our eyes light up. Master Gardeners are trained to dispense horticultural information to the public and no question is too simple or too tough. We don't balk at botrytis or get riled by root weevils. Not one of the 1200 or more Master Gardeners in Canada would ever claim to know everything, but we sure know how to find answers.

The Master Gardener program began in 1972 in Washington State when an overworked agricultural extension agent who needed clones of himself decided to train others to answer gardening questions and provide information through community clinics and on the phone. Now the program operates in 44 states and four provinces: BC, Alberta, Saskatchewan and Ontario. The programs all have basically the same curriculum: landscaping, soil, irrigation, plant propagation, botany, physiology, Latin names, lawns, trees and shrubs, pruning, grafting, houseplants, vegetables, annuals and perennials, insects and pests, diseases, pesticide safety and organic alternatives to pesticides and herbicides.

Carol Boan, Dorothy Lee and Bunny Meikle, volunteers at VanDusen Garden's Master Gardener's Clinic.
Photo: VanDusen Botanical Garden

That's the curriculum, but the execution is different everywhere. Most programs screen applicants with an eligibility test. In BC, lectures are offered one day a week for a stretch. Once the formal training has been completed, the real learning begins – out in the community answering questions. The questions are generally the same across the country, but the answers depend on climactic zone. Set up on weekends at garden centres and garden events, armed with dozens of reference books and notes galore, we field question after question, most of which fall into one of two categories: "What can I grow where?" and "Why didn't this grow (or why did it die)"? The former lets us be creative and introduce people to great plant material. The latter demands detective work: where is the plant located?; how is it watered?; what about fertilizer, herbicides, soil conditions, weather, insect damage?; and on and on. As gardeners become more experienced, the questions get better, ranging from the common, "How do you keep geraniums over the winter?" to the more technical, such as botanical names of cultivars. We emphasize non-chemical alternatives, and we work hard at teaching people to do their own diagnosing – for example, explaining how something looks if it might be over or under-watered.

Master Gardeners have become a knowledgeable force. By focusing on the home garden — and spotting trends and problems like diseases and pests — we know exactly what is happening out there. As a group, we can anticipate what will be asked. If there is an early freeze before plants are totally dormant, we know the next summer will bring questions about dead plants. Nurseries and customers now expect to see MGs at many Lower Mainland garden centres in the spring.

Master Gardeners don't do hands-on gardening for others and we can't use the title for profit, but as well as advice clinics, we do advocacy and education. MGs constantly speak to groups about gardening, do TV or radio spots, write newspaper columns (for example, the question and answer section in Saturday's New Homes section in the *Vancouver Sun*) and answer hotlines (see page 51). Other volunteer work includes school gardening programs, displays, workshops, composting clinics, heritage garden projects and rooftop and patio demonstration gardens.

It is ironic that at the very time when interest in gardening has increased enormously and the demand for advice from Master Gardeners has too, problems in finding funding for this shoestring operation plagues programs across the country. In 1984, BC removed funding. Fortunately, VanDusen Botanical Garden received a small donation that covered the establishment of their MG program two years later and, since then, 50 students a year have taken the program. This valuable service is worth working for. Not only an excellent education, it's also a lot of fun for its volunteer participants.

For more information, contact:
Jennifer Sherlock • 257-8672
VanDusen Botanical Garden, 5251 Oak St.

Master Gardener Clinic Questions

from a 1995 tally

Major Topics:
How to Eliminate Pests: 18%
Plants for Particular Locations: 17%
How to Eliminate Diseases: 16%
Growing Conditions: 7%
How and When to Plant or Move Plants: 6%
Fertilizer and Soil: 6%
How and When to Prune: 5%
Varieties of a Specific Plant: 5%
Lawn Questions: 3%
Problems with Fruit: 3%
How to Propagate: 2%
How to Eliminate Weeds: 2%
Garden Books, Courses, Nurseries: 2%
Physiological Problems: 2%
Problems with Blooming: 2%
Hardiness of Plants: 2%
Overwintering of Plants: 1%
Miscellaneous: 1%

The Garden Party
A wealthy woman gives a garden party, and several well-to-do guests attend. While the party is going on, two gardeners are out on the back lawn working. One of the guests is watching the gardeners do their thing and sees that while one gardener is busy weeding the other jumps up and makes graceful swirling dance movements. Struck by the dancer's grace, the guest remarks to the host, "That man is such a talented dancer, I'd pay him a hundred pounds to demonstrate his dancing before my aerobics class!" When the host asks the first gardener about such an arrangement, the gardener yells out, "Hey Fred! Do you think for a hundred pounds you could step on that rake again?"

Toki Miyashita of Sogetsu Ryu says that Ikebana is extremely relaxing. She calls it "the Japanese lady's tranquilizer" and says that it is lovely to "retreat into the Ikebana world." Miyashita is in her sixties and many of her friends are in their eighties. They credit their youthful looks to the relaxation of Ikebana. "Psychiatrists will even advise that people take up Ikebana to get rid of their stress," she says.

GARDEN CLUBS AND HORTICULTURAL SOCIETIES

Name almost any plant in your garden: undoubtedly there is a club in the Lower Mainland devoted to its wonders. Like-minded devotees gather to sing its praises, to share the latest developments in its cultivation and to hear speakers on everything to do with that species or genera. Then there are community garden clubs, flower arranging and bonsai clubs. For the especially keen we worked it out — every weeknight of the month, save two, you could attend a garden club meeting; on five nights of the month you would have six or more to choose from.

Why do hundreds and hundreds of like-minded souls join clubs? Obviously to learn more about gardening, a subject that is infinite. Most of the clubs in the Lower Mainland have meetings that involve some business, an educational presentation (slide shows, guest speakers, classes, discussions) and a social time with coffee and goodies — a chance to chat with like-minded souls. Often clubs hold annual fundraising and educational functions such as plant sales, private garden tours for members only, and raffles. Before each meeting, many of these clubs have seed exchanges, pot shows, sales of cuttings or plants or books bought in bulk. Some clubs have deals with nurseries earning them a percentage discount. Others hold judging schools. Annual memberships are usually under $20 — a true Canadian bargain.

Because club officers change so frequently, meeting times and places have been included but names and telephone numbers haven't. Call the meeting venue or just show up — you will be welcome, for gardeners are a friendly lot. There's no doubt you will learn something, and you just might come home with a plant or two and a new friend.

Specialty Clubs

African Violets:

VANCOUVER:

Vancouver African Violet Club
VanDusen Botanical Garden, 5251 Oak St.
1 to 4 p.m., third Sunday of the month (Mar., May,
June, Oct., Nov.)

Alpine Plants:

VANCOUVER:

Alpine Garden Club of BC
VanDusen Botanical Garden, 5251 Oak St.
website: http://www.hedgerows.com/Canada/
clubbrochures/alpinegardenclub.htm
7:30 p.m., second Wednesday of the month (except
July and August).

Bonsai Clubs:

RICHMOND:

Wakayama Kenji Kai Bonsai Club
Steveston Japanese Cultural Centre
4111 Moncton Rd.
Meets 7:30 p.m. on the second and fourth Tuesdays
of the month.

SURREY:

BC Bonsai Society
Japan Bonsai, 2337 140th St.
Meets 7:30 p.m., third Tuesday of the month.

VANCOUVER:

BC Bonsai Federation
Japanese Gardeners Association, 4289 Slocan St.
Umbrella group for most of the bonsai societies in
BC. Meets six times a year.

Japanese Gardeners Association Bonsai Club
Japanese Gardeners Association, 4289 Slocan St.
Meets 7:30 p.m., fourth Friday of the month.

There isn't currently an active
local chapter of the Pacific
Northwest Bamboo Society,
but if you are interested in
bamboo, contact Graeme Bain,
bamboo aficionado, at 523-
0255 and he'll tell all.

There isn't a continuous display of bonsai in the Vancouver area. I recommend visiting the Weyerhauser Collection in Federal Way, Washington and Dan Robinson's Elandan Gardens in Bremerton, Washington (on Hwy. 16).
— Tim McDonnell, BC Bonsai Federation

Penjing Society of Canada (Chinese Bonsai)
Contact: Chinese Cultural Centre
50 East Pender St. • 687-0729
Chinese speaking.

Sun Yat-Sen Penjing Club (Chinese Bonsai)
Dr. Sun Yat-Sen Classical Chinese Garden
578 Carrall St. • 662-3207
Meets second Tuesday of the month at 7 p.m. at Dr. Sun Yat Sen Gardens. In the winter, club members meet at each other's homes.

Taguchi Bonsai Club
VanDusen Botanical Garden, 5251 Oak St.
Meets 7:30 p.m., third Monday of the month (except Dec., Jan., July and Aug.).

Taiwanese Canadian Bonsai Club
Taiwanese Canadian Cultural Society
101-1200 West 3rd Ave.
Meets 7:30 p.m., second Saturday of the month.

Vancouver Bonsai Association
VanDusen Botanical Garden, 5251 Oak St.
Call VanDusen for confirmation. Meets February to October, one Saturday morning a month.

Vancouver Sumi Bonsai Club
VanDusen Botanical Garden, 5251 Oak St.
Meets at 7:30 p.m. on the second Wednesday of the month.

West Coast Bonsai Society
VanDusen Botanical Garden, 5251 Oak St.
Meets at 7:30 p.m. on the first Friday of the month except during January and July.

Cactus:
BURNABY:
Burnaby Cactus & Succulent Club
Bonsor Community Centre, 6550 Bonsor Ave.
Meets at 12:30 p.m. every fourth Wednesday of the month, September through May.

Chrysanthemums:

VANCOUVER:
Point Grey Chrysanthemum Club
VanDusen Botanical Garden, 5251 Oak St.
website: http://www.hedgerows.com/Canada/
clubbrochures/PointGreyChrysanClub.htm
Meets at 8 p.m. on the second Thursday of each
month (except July and August).

WHITE ROCK:
White Rock & District Chrysanthemum Club
St. John's Presbyterian Church, George St.
website: http://www.hedgerows.com/Canada/
clubbrochures/WR&DChrysanSoc.htm
Meets at 7:30 p.m. on the first Tuesday of the month
from January through October.

Dahlias:

VANCOUVER:
Vancouver Dahlia Society
VanDusen Botanical Garden, 5251 Oak St.
website: http://www.hedgerows.com/Canada/
clubbrochures/VancDahliaSoc.htm
Meets at 8 p.m. on the third Wednesday of the month
(except November and December).

Daylilies:

ALDERGROVE:
Aldergrove Daylily Society
Contact: Pam Erikson • 856-5758
website: http://www.icangarden.com/clubs/adls.htm
Meets at 7:30 p.m. on the third Thursday of the month
from February to September. Meetings take place at
a member's home. Call for more information.

Desert Plants (see also: Cactus and Palms):

VANCOUVER:
Desert Plant Society of Vancouver
Italian Cultural Centre, 3075 Slocan at 12th Ave.
Meets at 7:30 p.m on the first Thursday of the month.

The Aldergrove Daylily Society
is the first Canadian daylily
club recognized by the
American Hemerocallis
Society, the governing body
for daylilies worldwide.

Ikebana is the Japanese art of flower arrangements.

Flower Arranging Clubs:

BURNABY:

BC Floral Art Society
Elks Hall, 6884 Jubilee Ave.
Meets at 10 a.m. on the second Monday of the month.

NORTH VANCOUVER:

Capilano Flower Arranging Club
Delbrook Rec Centre, Queens and Windsor St.
Meets at 7:30 p.m. on the second Wednesday of the month.

VANCOUVER:

BC Guild of Flower Arrangers
VanDusen Botanical Garden, 5251 Oak St.
Meets at 10 a.m. on the fourth Monday of the month (except August and December).

Vancouver Ikebana Association (the following five clubs belong to this association)
Vancouver Japanese United Church, 4010 Victoria Dr.
Contact: Joan Fairs • 524-3523
Meets four times a year. Call for dates and locations.
Member clubs:
• **Adachi Ryu**
Contact: Joan Fairs • 524-3523
• **Ikenobo Ikebana Society of Vancouver**
Contact: Joan Fairs • 524-3523
Classes are given in teacher's homes.
• **Ohara Ryu**
Contact: Joan Fairs • 524-3523
• **Sangetsu Ryu (Richmond)**
Johrei Centre, 10380 Odlin Rd.
Classes every other Sunday afternoon.
• **Sogetsu Ryu (Burnaby)**
Nikkei Place, 6677 South Oak
Meets at 10 a.m. on the third Monday of every other month, starting in January.

The BC Fuchsia and Begonia Society will be hosting an International Fuchsia Convention in September 2002.

Fuchsias and Begonias:

BURNABY:

BC Fuchsia and Begonia Society
St. Helen's Catholic Church Gymnasium
3971 Pandora St.

website: http://www.hedgerows.com/Canada/
clubbrochures/FuchsiaBegonia.htm
Meets at 8 p.m. on the first Monday of the month.

LANGLEY:
Valley Fuchsia & Geranium Club
St.Andrew's Anglican Church, 20955 Old Yale Rd.
website: http://www.hedgerows.com/Canada/
clubbrochures/ValleyFuchsiaGeranium.htm
Meets at 7:30 p.m. on the fourth Tuesday of the
month (except during December).

Geraniums:
BURNABY:
Canadian Geranium & Pelargonium Society
St. Helen's Catholic Parish, 3871 Pandora St.
Meets at 8 p.m. on the first Wednesday of the month,
except during January.

LANGLEY:
Valley Fuchsia & Geranium Club
St.Andrew's Anglican Church, 20955 Old Yale Rd.
website: http://www.hedgerows.com/Canada/
clubbrochures/ValleyFuchsiaGeranium.htm
Meets at 7:30 p.m. on the fourth Tuesday of the
month (except during December).

Gladiolus:
VANCOUVER:
Fraser Valley Gladiolus Society
Contact: Grant Wilson • 536-8200
Call for meeting times and places.

Herbs:
LANGLEY:
Fraser Valley Herb Society
H.D. Stafford High School, 20441 Grade Cres.
website: http://www.hedgerows.com/Canada/
clubbrochures/FraserValleyHerbs.htm
Meets at 7:30 p.m. on the fourth Tuesday of each
month.

There is an Ikebana show
every spring at Oakridge
Auditorium. There you can see
all the different styles and
schools so you can choose the
style you might be most
interested in learning. There
are also demonstrations.

North Vancouver:

Wild Thymes Herbal Guild
Rose Room, Park & Tilford Gardens
333 Brooksbank Ave.
website: http://www.hedgerows.com/Canada/
clubbrochures/WildThymes.htm
Meets at 7:30 p.m. on the second Wednesday of
month, except December, July and August.

Vancouver:

Canadian Herb Society
VanDusen Botanical Garden, 5251 Oak St.
website: http://www.hedgerows.com/Canada/
clubbrochures/CanHerbSoc.htm
Meets at 7 p.m. on the second Monday of the month
(except July and August).

Lilies:

Vancouver:

BC Lily Society
Contact: John Taylor • 589-0623
website: http://www.hedgerows.com/Canada/
clubbrochures/BCLilySoc.htm
No regularly scheduled meetings. Call for times.

Mushrooms:

Vancouver:

Vancouver Mycological (Mushroom) Society
VanDusen Botanical Garden, 5251 Oak St.
hotline: 878-9878
Meets at 7:30 p.m. on the first Tuesday of the month
except December, January, July and August.

Native Plants:

Vancouver:

Native Plant Society of BC (NPSBC)
Contact: Ross Waddell • 255-5719
e-mail: Npsbc@hotmail.com
No monthly meetings. Members receive newsletter.
Lots of local events: big sale at UBC, nursery tours,
field trips, lectures.

Orchids:

LANGLEY:

Fraser Valley Orchid Society
Langley Civic Centre, 42nd Ave. and 207th St.
website: http://www.ccn.cs.dal.ca/Recreation/
OrchidSNS/fvos.html
Meets at 8 p.m. on the first Wednesday of the month
(except July and August).

VANCOUVER:

Vancouver Orchid Society
VanDusen Botanical Garden, 5251 Oak St.
website: http://www.hedgerows.com/Canada/
clubbrochures/VancOrchidSoc.htm
Meets at 7 p.m. on the fourth Wednesday of the
month (except July and August).

Palms:

VANCOUVER:

Pacific NW Palm & Exotic Plant Society
VanDusen Botanical Garden, 5251 Oak St.
website: http://www.icangarden.com/clubs/
pnwpeps.htm
Meets at 7:30 p.m. on the last Monday in March,
May, July, September and November.

Perennials:

VANCOUVER:

Vancouver Hardy Plant Group
Contact: Beverley Merryfield • 921-6266
Perennial interest group. Spring and fall tours; events.
Bi-monthly newsletter. Call for details.

Primulas:

VANCOUVER:

BC Primula Group
VanDusen Botanical Garden, 5251 Oak St.
website: http://www.hedgerows.com/Canada/
clubbrochures/BCPrimulaGroup.htm
Meets at 7:30 p.m. on the third Wednesday of January, March, May, September and November.

The Pacific NW Palm and Exotic Plant Society would like to see Vancouver and Victoria promoted with the following slogans:
"Vancouver: Canada's Palm City" and "Victoria: Canada's Palm Capital"

We have a mild climate in Vancouver, perfect for the keen growers in the Pacific Northwest Palm and Exotic Plant Society. They work hard at spreading the word that *Trachycarpus fortunei* (the Windmill Palm) is relatively easy to grow here and ideal for beginners. Folks have been cultivating this fantastic tree for over 30 years. Contact the club for growing tips.

The Fraser Valley Rhododendron Society is creating an ornamental rhododendron garden at the Whonock Lake Community Centre. Most of the work is being done by members. Materials and plants have been donated by local members and businesses. Landscape design was donated by Ruth Olde of Blasig Landscape Design & Construction.

The Lynn Valley Garden Club is one of the Lower Mainland's oldest clubs. It started in the 1920s and is still very active with 100 members, some of whom help at the Lynn Valley Library with planting and maintenance. The club also sponsors a horticulture student at Capilano College.

Rhododendron:

LANGLEY:

Fraser South Rhododendron Society
St. Andrews Anglican Church Hall
20955 Old Yale Rd.
website: http://www.hedgerows.com/Canada/
clubbrochures/FrasSouthRhodoSoc.htm
Meets at 8 p.m. on the third Wednesday of month, except in December, July and August.

MAPLE RIDGE:

Fraser Valley Rhododendron Society
St. Andrew Presbyterian Church
22279 116th Ave.
website: http://www.hedgerows.com/Canada/
clubbrochures/fraservalleyrhodo.htm
Meets at 7:30 p.m. on the fourth Monday of the month.

VANCOUVER:

Vancouver Rhododendron Society
VanDusen Botanical Garden, 5251 Oak St.
website: http://www.hedgerows.com/Canada/
clubbrochures/VancRhodoSoc.htm
Meets at 7:30 p.m. on the third Thursday of the month (except July and August).

WHITE ROCK:

Peace Arch Rhododendron Society
St. John's Presbyterian Church, 1480 George St.
website: http://www.hedgerows.com/Canada/
clubbrochures/PeaceArchRhodoSoc.htm
Meets at 7:30 p.m. on the third Monday of every month from September to June.

Roses:

COQUITLAM:

Fraser Pacific Rose Society
Dogwood Pavilion, 624 Poirier St.
website: http://www.hedgerows.com/Canada/
clubbrochures/FrasPacRoseSoc.htm
Meets at 7:30 p.m. on the last Tuesday of the month (except August and December).

VANCOUVER:
Vancouver Rose Society
VanDusen Botanical Garden, 5251 Oak St.
website: http://www.hedgerows.com/Canada/
clubbrochures/VancRoseSoc.htm
Meets at 8 p.m. on the third Tuesday of the
month (except August and December).

Water and Koi:
DELTA:
Water Garden Club of BC
East Delta Hall, 104th St. and No. 10 Hwy.
website: http://www.hedgerows.com/
Canada/clubbrochures/watergardenclub.htm
Meets at 7:30 p.m. on the last Wednesday of the
month (February to May, September to November).

FRASER VALLEY:
Fraser Valley Koi & Water Garden Club
Contact: Merv Zakus • 462-9925
website: http://www.hedgerows.com/Canada/
clubbrochures/FrasVallKoi.htm
Call for meeting times. Meetings rotate around the
Fraser Valley at member's homes.

VANCOUVER:
Canada Koi Club of BC
Contact: Richard Adema • 596-0211
Meets on the second Sunday of the month at member's homes – call for information.

General Gardening Clubs

BOWEN ISLAND:
Bowen Island Garden Club
The Old General Store, [location??]
Meets from 1 to 3 p.m. on the second Monday of
the month.

BURNABY:
South Burnaby Garden Club
Bonsor Community Centre, 6050 Bonsor Ave.
Meets at 7:30 p.m. on the first Tuesday of the month
(except January, September and December).

Volunteers from the Fraser
Pacific Rose Society lovingly
maintain the Centennial Rose
Garden adjacent to the
Dogwood Pavilion in
Coquitlam. Members plant,
fertilize, deadhead and
generally tend the 800-plus
roses in the garden. They feel
strongly that it is the finest
rose garden in the Lower
Mainland. The fact that
volunteers provide the elbow
grease makes it unique.

Sharon Bélec, President of the Maple Ridge Garden Club, recommends visiting the heritage gardens at Haney House on the Fraser River at 224th Street in Maple Ridge.

The Maple Ridge Garden Club recommends this Nursery Hop in their area: start out at Cardinal Gardens and Ferncliff Gardens in Mission; stop at Cistos Pub at Hatzic Bench in Mission for lunch; go on to Hansi's Nursery on 112 Avenue (across from Whonnock Lake Rec. Area); then finish up at the Rainforest Gardens.

The Capilano Garden Club has members who range in age from 9 to 91.

COQUITLAM:
Dogwood Garden Club
Dogwood Pavilion, 624 Poirier St.
Meets at 8 p.m. on the third Wednesday of the month (except December).

DELTA:
Delta Diggers Garden Club
Royal Heights United Church, 9316 116th St.
website: http://www.hedgerows.com/Canada/ clubbrochures/DeltaDiggers.htm
Meets at 7:30 p.m. on the third Thursday of the month (except December and January).

LANGLEY:
Langley Garden Club
Sharon United Church Hall, 21562 Old Yale Rd.
website: http://www.icangarden.com/clubs/lgc.htm
Meets at 7 p.m. on the first Friday of the month.

MAPLE RIDGE:
Maple Ridge Garden Club
Centennial Centre, 11940 224th St.
website: http://www.hedgerows.com/Canada/ clubbrochures/MapleRidge.htm
Meets at 6:45 on the third Wednesday of the month, except December.

NEW WESTMINSTER:
New Westminster Horticultural Society
Centennial Lodge, Queens Park
website: http://www.hedgerows.com/Canada/ clubbrochures/NewWestHortSoc.htm
Meets at 7:45 p.m. on the second Tuesday of the month (except January).

NORTH VANCOUVER:
Capilano Garden Club
Canyon Heights Christian Assembly, Capilano Rd. and Mount Royal Blvd.
Meets at 7:30 p.m. on the second Monday of the month except July and August.

Deep Cove Garden Club
Seycove Community School, 1204 Caledonia Ave.
Meets at 7:30 p.m. on the fourth Thursday of the
month from January to June, September to November.

Delbrook Garden Club
Contact: Dorothy Mash • 985-6107
Meets at 7:30 p.m. on the fourth Monday of the
month in various members' homes.

Lynn Valley Garden Club
Lynn Valley United Church, 3201 Mountain Hwy.
website: http://www.hedgerows.com/Canada/
clubbrochures/LynnValley.htm
Meets at 7:30 p.m. on the third Thursday of the month
(except July and August).

Upper Lonsdale Garden Club
St Martin's Church, 195 E. Windsor St.
Meets at 7:30 p.m. on the second Thursday of the
month (except December).

PORT COQUITLAM:
PoCo Garden Club
Trinity United Church Hall, Prairie Ave. and
Shaughnessy St.
website: http://www.hedgerows.com/Canada/
clubbrochures/PocoGardenClub.htm
Meets at 7:30 p.m. on the third Tuesday of every
month (except July, August and September).

RICHMOND:
Richmond Garden Club
Minoru Sports Pavilion, 7191 Granville Ave.
website: http://www.hedgerows.com/Canada/
clubbrochures/RichmondGardenClub.htm
Meets at 7:30 p.m. on the fourth Wednesday of the
month (except August and December).

SURREY:
North Surrey Horticultural Society
Southside Community Centre, 12642 100th Ave.
Meets at 8 p.m. on the second Tuesday of the month
(March through November).

It wasn't on purpose, but the Upper Lonsdale Garden Club is all female! There are 50 members, and a waiting list to join.

The Delbrook Community Centre on Queens Avenue in North Vancouver has a Perennial Garden that was planted and is maintained by the Delbrook Garden Club. Plants are labelled with botanical names.

The Upper Lonsdale Garden Club helps maintain a garden at the Palliative Care Unit at Lion's Gate Hospital.

At the foot of 19th and Bellevue in West Vancouver there is a small garden and walkway that takes you to the sea wall. Members of the West Vancouver Garden Club maintain this primarily native garden.

South Surrey Garden Club
St. Mark's Anglican Church, 12953 20th Ave.
website: http://www.hedgerows.com/Canada/
clubbrochures/SsurreyGardenClub.htm
Meets at 7:30 p.m. on the fourth Wednesday of the month (except August and December)

TSAWWASSEN:
Evergreen Garden Club
Phoenix Hall, 6062 16th Ave.
Meets at 7:30 p.m. on the third Wednesday of the month.

VANCOUVER:
Dunbar Garden Club
Dunbar Community Centre, 4747 Dunbar St.
website: http://www.hedgerows.com/Canada/
clubbrochures/dunbargardenclub.htm
Meets at 7:30 p.m. on the fourth Tuesday of the month.

WEST VANCOUVER:
West Vancouver Garden Club
St. David's Church, 1525 Taylor Way
Meets at 7:30 p.m. on the first Tuesday of the month (except July and August).

WHITE ROCK:
White Rock and District Garden Club
Seaview Pentacostal Fellowship Hall, 14633 16th Ave.
website: http://www.hedgerows.com/Canada/
clubbrochures/WR&DGardenClub.htm
Meets at 2 p.m. on the second Tuesday of the month (except July and August).

Related Clubs and Organizations

COQUITLAM:
Riverview Horticultural Centre Society
290-9910 for recorded information on guided tours, or 942-7378
The purpose of the Riverview Horticultural Society is to preserve the Riverview lands (see arboretum list

page 194). Ask about their publication "The Riverview Lands: Western Canada's First Botanical Garden."

DELTA:
Burns Bog Conservation Society
202-11961 88th Ave. • 572-0373; fax: 572-0374
website: http://www.burnsbog.paconline.net/
Burns Bog is the largest undeveloped urban land mass in Canada – and it's in Delta, just by the mouth of the lower Fraser River. The society aims to "conserve and preserve Burns Bog for all life in perpetuity."

LANGLEY:
Butterfly Garden Resource Group
Campbell Valley Regional Park Visitors Centre
8th Ave. and 204th St. • 530-4983
Meeting and work party first Tuesday of the month except December and January. A hummingbird garden too!

Fraser Valley Heritage Tree Society
Kwantlen University College, Langley Campus
website: http://www.freeyellow.com/members/fvhtreesociety/
Meets at 8 p.m. on the second Thursday of the month, September through May.

VANCOUVER:
Garden Club of Vancouver
261-3126
The Garden Club of Vancouver has been meeting monthly since 1962. This group raises funds for the "beautification of Vancouver." They have supported the gardens at Canuck Place, VanDusen Botanical Garden, UBC Botanical Garden, St. Vincent's Langara, Roedde House, Queen Elizabeth Park and more. Membership is currently at capacity. Call the number above for information.

Hon. David Lam Garden Society
VanDusen Botanical Garden, 5251 Oak St.
Meets first Tuesday of the month at 7 p.m. This society's goal is to help new immigrants to learn about local gardening ways. The club was formed to help

The Butterfly Garden Resource Group designed and maintains the demonstration garden in Campbell Valley Regional Park in South Langley. They showcase butterfly-attracting and larvae-attracting plants. Members take an education program into the schools and to adult groups.

teach members how to grow indoor and outdoor plants, how to landscape and how to use a greenhouse.

On Our Hands and Knees

Started in 1998, On Our Hands and Knees is a time for gays and lesbians to get together and talk gardening, go on tours, hear speakers, hold sales etc. Meetings are held at members' homes every three weeks, and sometimes more often.

Vancouver Natural History Society

P.O. Box 3021, V6B 3X5 • 737-3074

There are four interest groups under the society's umbrella: birders, conservation, botany and general, as well as a wilderness camp. Call the number above for information on meetings and events.

GENERAL:

BC Council of Garden Clubs

Contact: Lorraine Martin • 820-2299

The BC Council of Garden Clubs is an umbrella organization for 115 garden clubs in the province. The council has two annual meetings and a bi-monthly newsletter. Their goal is to promote horticulture. The council has a resource slide library, and they provide grants, scholarships and bursaries to eight institutions (clubs donate to this fund). They train and certify judges in horticulture and floral arts for parlour shows and country fairs. They have a 175-page book on judging standards for non-specialized shows. Individual members can also subscribe to the newsletter for $7 per year. Information on upcoming meetings is published in newsletter. Call for a copy and times.

The Joy of Belonging to a Garden Club

by Dana Cromie

I had been to garden lectures before; they felt like tea parties at private school with well-published speakers (usually from England), everyone quite dressed up and me like the groundskeeper who had stumbled through the wrong door. Most uncomfortable.

My relationship with the Alpine Garden Club of BC is different. It began during a walk through VanDusen Gardens over 10 years ago. One of the gardeners there noticed my more-than-casual interest in many of the plants and he invited me to come to a club meeting. When I arrived, there were people carrying flats of beautifully potted plants, people with bits of plants in bags or bottles consulting or trading with one another, people putting out coffee and cookies at the back, people pulling seeds out of pockets and purses, people looking through books on alpines and rare plants. Everyone looked like a gardener, happiest with their dirty hands placing a precious new plant or pulling out weeds.

The evening started with a short discussion of club business. This was followed by a show-and-tell of the most amazing plants currently in bloom. Then the plants, which had been brought in for display, were judged — this is the "Pot Show." Plants were ranked on rarity, form, perfection and number of blooms, difficulty of cultivation and cleanliness of pot! All of this was done with humour — and bias. After a coffee break there was a slide presentation on the use of vines in the garden (very enlightening, especially to me, as I have a somewhat vertical garden).

Over the years, there have been travel lectures about every corner of the globe, lectures focused on a single genus, lectures and workshops on propagation and cultivation, and lectures on single gardens. There are two great plant sales a year — mostly plants not available elsewhere, many from member's gardens. There have been hikes to various local alpine areas. There is an annual walk about the Alpine Garden at UBC. There are open gardens of club members on spring weekends. And there is the famous seed ex-

The Maple Ridge Garden Club runs a plant reclamation line which can be reached by calling 465-1223. They reclaim plants from development sites to use in city beautification.

A Man of Words and Not of Deeds

A man of words and not of
   deeds
Is like a garden full of weeds;
And when the weeds begin to
   grow,
It's like a garden full of snow;
And when the snow begins to
   fall,
It's like a bird upon the wall;
And when the bird away does
   fly,
It's like an eagle in the sky;
And when the sky begins to
   roar,
It's like a lion at the door;
And when the door begins to
   rack,
It's like a stick across your
   back;
And when your back begins to
   smart,
It's like a penknife in your
   heart;
And when your heart begins
   to bleed,
You're dead, and dead, and
   dead indeed.

— *Mother Goose's Nursery
Rhymes* (Longmeadow Press,
1996)

change, where members send in seed from rare plants around the world — about 1500 varieties —which are listed, ordered, packaged and sent out, all without charge.

But what really makes the club work for me is knowing all these people and sharing plants and stories. If I looked at my garden now and took out everything I have gained — the plants, the knowledge and the advice — from club members, my garden would be a very different place. The Alpine Garden Club is not just about alpines — in fact, I don't actually have any in my garden. The club is about the love of plants and cultivation, and it is about sharing.

PUBLIC AND COMMUNITY GARDENS

For gardeners, a true joy is wandering streets and lanes peering, chatting, noting and inhaling. For this reason, public and community gardens are constant sources of inspiration and education. If you really want to learn something, join a botanical garden — the plants come with labels. Consider joining a botanical garden (both UBC and VanDusen are a deal) because then you won't think twice about dropping in. You don't have to tromp for two hours to "get your money's worth" — you can stop by for a short visit to see blossoms or look at a fully grown example of some plant or tree you have considered buying. Use the botanical gardens — they are like living research libraries. Need a little more colour in July or January? Before you visit a garden centre, a trip to the botanical garden will let you see lots of options in full bloom. But don't forget your notebook!

PUBLIC GARDENS

BURNABY:

Burnaby Centennial Rose Garden
100 Centennial Way
Admission Fee: No
Wheelchair Access: Yes (but hilly)
An oasis on the top of Burnaby Mountain.

Century Gardens
6344 Deer Lake Ave., Deer Lake Park
Admission Fee: No
Wheelchair Access: Yes
Located on the grounds of the Burnaby Art Gallery, this three-plus acre garden was created in 1967 for Canada's centennial. Overlooking a lake containing varied water fowl, the garden features rhododendrons, roses and azaleas.

COQUITLAM:

Centennial Rose Garden
624 Poirier St.
Admission Fee: No
Wheelchair Access: Yes.
This garden is the work of the Fraser Pacific Rose Society.

NEW WESTMINSTER:

Japanese Friendship Garden
4th St. and Queens Ave. (behind City Hall)
527-4567
Designed by Mr. Gordon Sales, the late Parks Director, the gardens were built in 1963 as a tribute to New West's sister city of Moriguchi, Japan. It is a blend of the basic Japanese garden and North American informal garden. In 1962, Hurricane "Freda" blew down most of the trees in this section of Tiperary Park and so the gardens came into being. In 1980, a 70-foot red cedar Cosmic Maypole was erected in the Friendship Garden. The carving, done by Georganna Malloff, is to be viewed in the round — it depicts a spiral of human social evolution. It incorporates carving techniques of the Northwest Coast Indians and of the traditional European Maypole.

Dozens of charming circular gardens are springing up all over Vancouver in the concrete borders of traffic circles. They seem to favour water-wise plants and grasses, but all kinds of plants are being used (lower-maintenance and low heights are preferable). If you are interested in adopting a traffic circle in your neighbourhood to plant and maintain, call City Hall (Greenways and Local Improvement Branch): 873-7155.

NORTH VANCOUVER:

Park & Tilford Gardens

440-333 Brooksbank Ave. • 984-8200

Admission Fee: No

Wheelchair Access: 80 percent accessible

Other Services: Giftshop: There are 38 stores and restaurants surrounding the gardens in the Park & Tilford Shopping Centre.

Park & Tilford Gardens consists of separate theme gardens or outdoor rooms, including: Roses, Herbs, Rhododendron, White Garden (perennials), Asian Garden, Townhouse Garden, West Coast Native plants, Yellow Garden, annual display gardens, hanging baskets (75), Victorian Greenhouse, florentine pergola covered in vines and more.

The purpose of the gardens is to display commercially available, quality plants suitable for our West Coast climate and grown with organic methods using Integrated Pest Management (IPM). The gardens also contain some of the finest and largest selections of unique trees in Western Canada.

Chiba Gardens

Waterfront Park, The Esplanade, south side

Admission Fee: No

Wheelchair Access: Yes

This garden is designed to be a traditional Japanese garden with stone lanterns donated by the city of Chiba (North Vancouver's sister city), some restful sitting areas and two streams that converge into one, representing the spirit of the two cities.

RICHMOND:

Fantasy Garden World

10800 No. 5 Rd. • 277-7777

Admission Fee: Yes

Wheelchair Access: Yes

Other Services: Shops

The 10-acre garden is located next to a European-style collection of shops. Also included in the area is a miniature railway, garden shop and restaurant. The best time to visit is in the spring when there are more than 200 varieties of tulips and

"My favourite part of VanDusen is the American Native section in the springtime. The tallest stuff is deciduous and the woodland floor is thick with rare stuff like *erythroniums* and *trilliums* and SOLOMON SEAL. It's a thick blanket and breathtaking in the spring."
— Thomas Hobbs, Southlands Nursery

masses of rhododendrons in bloom. In the spring and early summer, the rose garden is very popular. During the Christmas season a light display is worth visiting. Seasonal displays of annuals, perennials and roses can be seen throughout smaller gardens. Also included are a conservatory for tropical plants and an oriental garden.

Kuno Garden
Chatham and 7th Ave.
Admission Fee: Yes
Wheelchair Access: Yes
Located at the entrance to Garry Point Park, this small but lovely Japanese garden was created to commemorate the 100th anniversary of the arrival of Japanese immigrants to Canada.

Kwan Yin Buddhist Garden
9160 Steveston Hwy. • 274-2822
Admission Fee: Yes
Wheelchair Access: Yes
This garden contains a Buddhist temple which is open to the public. Call about special events such as bonsai demos, flower arranging and tea ceremonies.

London Heritage Farm
6511 Dyke Rd. • 271-5220
Admission Fee: No
Wheelchair Access: Garden – yes; house – limited
Site includes public park and gardens as well as a restored farmhouse (circa 1900). Tours can be arranged of gardens and house (now a museum)

SURREY:
Bear Creek Gardens
In Bear Creek Park on 88th Ave., east of King George Hwy. • 501-5085
Admission Fee: No
Wheelchair Access: Yes
Other Services: Some within park
This garden contains a variety of plant material including heathers, heaths, azaleas, rhododendrons, shade plants, ornamental grasses, a woodland bed and a cottage garden. During the spring and summer

months there is a colourful display of a large variety of annuals and bulbs. Also found in the garden is an impressive second growth forest of alders, western red cedars and cottonwoods as well as a "Native Walk" featuring plants indigenous to the Pacific Northwest. Also of interest is the massive western red cedar gateway to the gardens constructed in the fashion of a Native longhouse. The gardens have become very popular for weddings and a podium is provided for those wishing to marry within the garden.

Peace Arch Gardens
138 Peace Arch Park • 531-3068
Admission Fee: No
Wheelchair Access: Yes
These are actually two seaside gardens created between the Douglas International Border Crossing at Surrey and Blaine.

Pamela Cameron Forever Garden
South Surrey Athletic Park • 535-9936.
Admission Fee: No
Wheelchair Access: No
Dedicated to the memory of youth who were taken before their time. In a fledgling state, it is being developed by a group of volunteers who are always looking for more help (call Diane Pargee at the number above if you'd like to volunteer)

VANCOUVER:
Dr. Sun Yat-Sen Classical Chinese Gardens
578 Carrall St. (Chinatown) • 662-3207
Admission Fee: Yes
Wheelchair Access: Yes
Other Services: Giftshop
The Dr. Sun Yat-Sen Classical Chinese Garden is the first authentic, full-scale garden built outside China. Its tranquil ponds, natural rock sculptures, courtyards and plants create an environment which is harmonious and peaceful. The garden reflects the Taoist philosophy of yin and yang. Every stone, pine and magnolia flower in the garden has been placed purposefully and carries a

symbolic meaning. The Garden offers guided tours, which provide interesting perspectives on Chinese culture, life during the Ming dynasty, architecture and plants. A popular program offered at the gardens is the Enchanted Evening series. Every Friday night from July through September, visitors sip a cup of complimentary tea, enjoy a one-hour Chinese music program and then stroll through the garden.

Stanley Park
Entrances at West Georgia St., Nelson St. or Beach Ave. • 257-8400
For information on vegetation and nature walks, call: 257-8544
Admission Fee: No
Wheelchair Access: Yes
Other Services: See above
1,000 acres of heavily wooded park surrounded on three sides by water is home to many attractions which include a lake, a lagoon, swimming beaches, a variety of gardens, the Vancouver Aquarium, tennis courts, a miniature railway, a pitch-and-putt course as well as several restaurants. Of special interest in June and July is the Rose Garden, which features hundreds of roses divided in beds by colour. Also noteworthy, particularly in April and May, is the Ted and Mary Grieg Rhodendron Garden containing camellias, magnolias, maples, rhododendrons and azaleas. The park boasts a continuous seawall walk as well as many trails throughout the forested area.

Queen Elizabeth Park & Bloedel Conservatory
West 33rd Ave. and Cambie St. • 872- 5513
Admission Fee: Park, no; Bloedel Conservatory, yes
Wheelchair Access: Yes
Other Services: Coffee shop and store

The Bloedel Conservatory at Queen Elizabeth Park.
Photo: Dannie McArthur

High above sea level on Little Mountain, Queen Elizabeth Park is known for its beautiful view of the city and north shore mountains. It is a popular spot for wedding pictures, especially in June when the rose garden is in full bloom. Also within the park are ornamental gardens and colourful seasonal bedding plants, tennis courts, a pitch-and-putt course and a restaurant. Of note is the Quarry Garden at the peak of the mountain. Created in the 1960s, this garden emulates those of the Butchart near Victoria. The Henry Moore sculpture "Knife Edge-Two Piece" can be found close to the Bloedel Conservatory. This 70-degree triodetic dome is temperature controlled and contains a large variety of tropical, desert and exotic plants and over 100 tropical birds. A magnificent variety of trees create a jungle of palms, banana trees and orchids.

"Knife Edge—Two Piece" by sculptor Henry Moore at Queen Elizabeth Park.
Photo: Dannie McArthur

UBC Botanical Garden
6804 S.W. Marine Dr. • 822-9666
Admission Fee: Yes. Memberships available
Wheelchair Access: Majority of garden
Other Services: Shop-in-the-Garden and guided tours (Wed. & Sat.)
This 70-acre theme garden is used for teaching and research in addition to being open to the public. Located on the UBC campus, it includes: the E.H. Lohbrunner Alpine Garden; BC Native garden; the Physick Garden (herb garden); an arbor and a food garden. Of special interest is the classical Japanese Nitobe Memorial Garden. Within this 2 1/2-acre garden are many smaller ones, including the Tea Garden, the Nightingale Fence, the Tenth Bridge, several water crossings and a stroll garden. The garden reflects an idealized conception of nature and its harmony among natural forms. Also of note is the David C. Lam Asian Garden, which comprises 30 acres and contains a large variety of woody Asian plants, maples, clematis, roses, rhododendrons, azaleas, magnolias and rare Oriental plants. The support and volunteer organization is called Friends of the Garden Society (FOGS). In addition to many other activities, FOGS offer a horticulture information service line for the public. Call 822-5858.

Mary Allen and Rachel Mackenzie from FOGS at UBC Botanical Garden (see article on FOGS, page 233).
Photo: Dannie McArthur

VanDusen Botanical Garden
5251 Oak St.
• 266-7194
Admission Fee: Yes.
Memberships available
Wheelchair Access: Yes and special guided tours for those with limited mobility
Other Services: Gift shop, restaurant, courses, lectures and library
The VanDusen contains 55 acres of plants and trees for all seasons. At any time of the year you will see plants, trees and shrubs in bloom and most of them are well marked. The garden contains many theme gardens including Asian, heather, rose perennial, maze and fragrance gardens, a rhododendron walk, a Canadian Heritage garden and a holly garden. The garden is also host to many special events throughout the year. These include the very popular Festival of Lights at Christmas, the VanDusen Plant sale in April, the VanDusen Flower and Garden Show in June and various other clubs shows and sales throughout the spring and summer. The VanDusen is also home to the Master Gardeners Program (see education section) who provide horticulture information to the public. Call: 257-8662.

OUTSIDE GVRD:
We know that Minter Gardens is out of our GVRD focus area, but this is a garden worth seeing, and we appreciate all that Brian Minter has done to advance gardening in this area.
Minter Gardens
2892 Bunker Rd., Rosedale (Bridal Falls) • 794-7191
website: www.minter.org
Admission Fee: Yes
Wheelchair Access: Yes
Other Services: Restaurants and gift shop
Minter Gardens is 27 acres of floral artistry. The 11 theme gardens are designed to dazzle the senses with massive displays of colour and fragrance. Gently winding pathways progressively link each unique garden

such as the Victorian topiary, a living maze, an English cottage and beautiful waterfalls and ponds. Also featured is the Chinese Garden which includes a rare collection of Penjing rock bonsai. Over 1,000 rhododendrons are planted throughout the gardens. Thousands of brilliant annuals are carefully colour co-ordinated over 27 acres. Massive floral beds depict the Canadian flag and other uniquely designed features. Each summer the Rose Garden is full of colour and fragrance. And in the perennial gardens hundreds of well-known and rare perennials are blended together to create the cottage garden effect. After a garden stroll, visitors can visit either Bloomer's Garden Café or the Trillium Restaurant. And the 18-acre Minter Country Garden Centre (at 10015 Young St. North, in Chilliwack) is well worth the trip — it's a massive retail and greenhouse operation and very keen on being first with new introductions.

Private Gardens

VANCOUVER:

The Arthur Erickson Garden
4195 West 14th Ave. • 444-6894
Admission Fee: Yes
Wheelchair Access: Yes
Arthur Erickson, the renowned architect, bought the West Point Grey corner lot in 1957. The house, two original garages and a lean-to, occupies very little space. The rest belongs to this contemplative, poetic garden, incorporating many of Erikson's principles of design. The visitor enters a magic realm of trees, bushes and wild grasses surrounding a small pond. Beyond, there is the appearance of a small mountain. A marble slab (the moon-viewing platform) projects into this pond planted with lilies, rushes and wild irises. Above the wild grasses, several species of bamboo and rhododendron provide an evergreen privacy barrier under taller native dogwoods, pine trees and poplars. These visual layers of foreground water and tall trees give an illusion of far greater space. Guided tours are arranged through the Arthur Erickson House and Garden Foundation, founded in 1996 to rescue and preserve the property.

"My favourite public space in Vancouver is one I designed as part of the Robson Square Design (along with Arthur Erickson Architects) — it's the quiet area at the Provincial Courthouse Complex at Robson Square. If you ascend the mound at Robson Street and go up two more levels (up the "stramps" — stairs/ramps) to the level of the court house, you can wander through a grove of lodgepole pines under-planted with white-flowering azaleas and ferns. You are enveloped by nature and you forget about the noises of the city."
— Cornelia Hahn Oberlander, Landscape Architect

Why does a lawnmower think
it has a hard life?
Because it is always getting
pushed around.

SURREY:

"The Glades"

561-172nd St. • 538-0928
Admission Fee: By donation
Wheelchair Access: No
Open: Mother's Day annually to general public; by
appointment to garden clubs and other interested
groups; open (at a fee) for weddings and photos.

The five-acre garden called "The Glades" contains a
magnificent selection of over 1600 mature rhododendrons, azaleas and companion plants. The garden has
a superb selection of trees, many of which are now
designated as heritage trees. Native and exotics are
intermixed in a beautiful woodland setting. "The
Glades" is also a sanctuary for wild animals and birds
such as mallards and wood ducks. Owners Jim and
Elfriede DeWolf open their garden for the special
annual "Mother's Day" tour and tea, which is a
fundraiser for the Peace Arch Hospital. This is the
only day of the year the garden is open to the public.

Darts Hill Garden

1660-168 St. • 501-5085 (City of Surrey)
Admission Fee: Donations
Wheelchair Access: In future plans, when opened to
the public (date not determined)
Open: Not open to the public; limited tours are available for bona fide horticultural groups. For more
information, call: "The Friends of Darts Hill Garden"
at 501-5665

Darts Hill Garden is a botanical garden located on
7.5 acres in South Surrey. This relaxing garden comes
complete with a view of the ocean in the distance.
This is a planter's garden, containing a variety of rare
and precious plants and flowers, including witch hazel (hamamelis), wild azalea and coloneasier, along
with hundreds of rare and unusual perennials. Over
two dozen varieties of magnolias are grown in the
colourful flowerbeds, along with at least six varieties
of Mrs. Francisca Dart's favourite plant, thalietrum.
Visitors to the garden can also enjoy Spanish chestnut, mulberry salix and numerous maples.

Botanical Gardens

by Lolita Aaron

My introduction to the VanDusen Botanical Garden came about five years after I immigrated to Canada from South Africa. I was invited to join a French-speaking group of guides. I took a guide training course and found myself absolutely fascinated by the wonders the gardens had to offer. The fact that I came from South Africa — the place from which most of our flora emanates, with the richest floral kingdom in the world — did not mean that I had a clue about plants. In fact, I did not know the difference between parsley and a pansy. That is why it is thrilling for me to say words such as *"Cedrus atlantica* 'Glauca Pendula'"* when I feel like showing off — which I do quite often now, spouting my knowledge of botanical names.

That first day, a guide took me under her wing, walking me around and introducing me to the gardens. It was February, a time of the year in which one would not imagine there to be anything that looked like a "flower." In truth, I was utterly charmed and bewitched by what I saw and this motivated me to learn as much as possible. This was very easy because the gardens offer excellent courses on horticulture, garden design and floral design. I also attended every lecture I could on taxonomy and botany. I was privileged to have excellent teachers such as Gerald Straley, Roy Forester and the guides themselves, who have a wealth of knowledge to share.

Eventually, I joined the Floral Committee, took children on tours of the garden (conducted in French and English) and took adults on tours. I relished the gardens and what they had to offer from January to December. We are fortunate to have gardens which sustain their wonders throughout the year. The opportunity for learning and enhancing one's knowledge and appreciation is ongoing: there are Master Gardener programs, a lecture series and tours to Britain and Europe where knowledgeable tour leaders botanize, explore and encourage participants to discover more about plants in other parts of the world

"It is best to visit botanical gardens on the bleakest days, because if something catches your eye then, you definitely should have one"
— Michael Luco, Earthrise Garden Store

"Up around the back side of VanDusen — the Alma VanDusen Meadow Garden — that's my favourite. It is removed from everywhere else. In autumn, the gorgeous KATSURA TREE (*Cercidiphyllum japonica*) has the smell of burnt sugar."
— Terri Clark, Vancouver Park Board

with other climates and habitats. Closer to home, VanDusen conducts annual plant sales, a leaf compost sale, a manure sale, the Spring Garden Forum, a Christmas Lights celebration ... the list of events is endless, as are the opportunities for participating and volunteering.

The Perennial Group I joined pots and gathers plants from VanDusen as well as members' gardens in order to sell them at the plant sale. This is a wonderful way of learning about splitting, dividing and nursing young perennials. I have found that the people who do this work are fun, enthusiastic and full of energy. For me, it has been a place to meet good friends who share one's passion for plants and knowledge and pleasure. At the end of January, if we have had a mild winter, we go traipsing through the rain or snow to prostrate ourselves and look at a clump of emerging cyclamens. We seek out snowdrops and then Hellebores, and so it goes — more and more thrills! When things in our lives are difficult, VanDusen offers a place in which to become lost in the pleasure of growing things and to be comforted by what the gardens offer. It is a place to which I am terminally devoted.

It has been said that a city is only a city of note if it has an Opera House and a Cathedral. I would add a botanical garden — or two, in Vancouver's case, for we are blessed by having the UBC Botanical Garden which offers its members and volunteers equally wonderful opportunities for learning and expanding one's horticultural education. These two botanical gardens make it possible for us to have a charmed environment in which to grow.

Favourite Urban Landscapes

by Moura Quayle, Dean of the Faculty of Agricultural Sciences at UBC

Urban landscapes are the "outside" that exists inside the city. They are the places that some of us take for granted and others haunt because of their beauty, their ability to evoke Vancouver history, culture and geography, or their unique sense of space. Here are some urban landscapes that I think are wonderful:

- The False Creek Flats as the Grandview Cut explodes into the openness of the flats. This is where "rough" meets "refined."
- The railway tracks where their smoothness meets the tangled ecology of the derelict landscape. This intersection of tracks and landscape tells stories about what we did to make goods and people travel by train — and what happens when new transportation alternatives evolve. It is also one of the last "unbuilt" landscapes of our city. How we plan its use will say much about how we steward the city of the future. Let's hope that we don't sanitize it; let's hope that we ensure greenways and public ways give it structure and character; let's hope that the public makes its mark here. Let's make sure that there are places for artists to evolve some ephemeral art; and let's make sure that we don't lose the special character of this rough and ready landscape.
- The Leaf Tunnel streets of Vancouver at different times of the year. Streets like 10th between Arbutus and Macdonald are golden in the fall. In the spring, streets like the ones along the Ridge (Puget, Quesnel) form flower tunnels with their Flowering Crabs. These trees give spatial struc-

Moura Quayle, Dean of the Faculty of Agricultural Sciences at UBC.
Photo: UBC

Interesting Public Plantings in
West Vancouver include:
• The foot of 19th St. Seawalk
  garden, developed with
  donated funds on the old
  Wells' property. It has a
  wishing well, a wisteria-
  covered trellis, hanging
  baskets in the summertime
  and has lots of benches for a
  rest. MacDonald Creek runs
  through it.
• The foot of 18th St.: a native
  meadow with drought-
  tolerant native plant
  materials.
• Lighthouse Park has a native
  plant material garden
  outside the nature hut,
  planted by local Girl Guides.

ture to our city landscape. They give our streets identity and beauty. Streets in the future must perform better; we have to be aware that they are more than places for cars and the carriers of infrastructure. They must perform better ecologically (containing more trees and permeable ground) and perform better as community-building places (for meeting neighbours and sharing ideas). They should be enormous contributors to our daily restoration — the streets of the city should be replacing our need for a three-week stint in Hawaii. They should give us a nature "fix" every time we go outside.

• Greenways and public ways: The Ridgeway, our pilot-project greenway along 37th Avenue from Knight to Granville, is exciting because it represents some simple steps to make pedestrians and cyclists queens and kings above the car. You can get across Granville, Oak and Cambie streets without risking your life! And the greenway has idiosyncratic neighbourhood landscapes along the way. Check out Windsor Castle at Windsor and 37th Avenue. Garden Drive is another pilot project where citizens took to their street and their community to save it from wall-to-wall paving and from the insidious drug culture. It may not be everyone's cup of tea (it's a giant-rock traffic island) but it has the power of a community of people stamped on it and for this reason it is beautiful.

• The Vancouver Port is one urban landscape that should be more open to us as citizens of Canada. After all, we own it. There are places to explore in the port but access is tough. Try exploring BC Sugar, CRAB park (its official name is Portside) and all the way along to Wall Street (soon to be a greenway) and New Brighton. We should all write to our Port Corporation and our MPs to ensure that the port is planning for more public access, especially for children. We all need to see the Port as our window on the world — globalization that is happening in front of our eyes, not just in cyberspace.

• The Vancouver Food Lands are exciting places — check out all the community gardens from

Strathcona to Mount Pleasant to Maple and 6th to West Boulevard. Every place where people and landscapes interact are hot spots to me. If food, safety and security are taken seriously, we will be placing a much higher value on these lands.

• When the Park Board goes on strike, the 16th Avenue boulevard offers a glimpse of what would happen if we let more of our public realm "naturalize." When the mowers stop mowing, we start to see a different landscape evolve on the boulevards. This is not the landscape of the neat and tidy — the landscape with a "pedigree." No, this is the rougher landscape that cares for itself. This rough landscape is for people to whom weeds are beautiful and an important part of our diversity. For those who prefer a middle ground, we could sow some wildflowers into the mix and let them evolve. These are also the kinds of landscapes that could help us shape our future as a city. If we are serious about putting our energies into the "determinants" of health (like clean air, clean water and safe food) rather than on the results of ignoring these determinants (costly medicare), then many more of these landscapes will become critical to wellness and well-being.

"I like the row of chestnut trees you follow when you go down Yew Street on the way into Kits Park. They are especially beautiful in the spring with the flowering cherries in the foreground and the fresh green of the new leaves of the chestnut behind."
— Alan Duncan, Greenways Planner, City of Vancouver

Naturescape BC:
Caring for Wildlife Habitat at Home

by Edward Van Veenendaal, Naturescape consultant

The Greater Vancouver region is a favourite place to be – a fact that is true for people but also for plants and animals. Our natural surroundings offer wildlife a great diversity of habitats: a major fresh water river emptying out into an ocean; a topography that combines extremes, from valley floors to mountain tops; and all this within a mild climatic zone. The diversity of flora and fauna in this small corner of southwestern British Columbia has few parallels in the world.

As our human numbers grow and our expanding cities convert more and more natural areas into subdivisions, industrial areas and shopping malls, natural habitats are altered, if not destroyed. The evidence is all around us. The provincial government has been setting large areas aside for nature protection in the form of parks, yet most of BC's fertile valley bottoms are privately owned – by you and me. Here is where the Naturescape-BC program enters the landscape: since 1995, this grassroots movement has given homeowners the tools to be better stewards of their plot of land.

People who create wildlife habitats at home realize that animals need water, food and a safe place to hide and to raise their young. These needs are met differently by birds than by butterflies or amphibians in a pond. In the naturescaped garden, plants are chosen for function, not just ornamental value. For example, to attract birds, you will want to plant shrubs that produce edible berries and have a variety of trees that will provide different canopy levels in the garden. A cluster of shrubs will form a thicket for shelter. Colourful flowers all summer long will be a continuing source of nectar.

The naturescaped garden lets plants blend into each other, giving it a fuller, less manicured look than the average yard. It is not symmetric nor static. It caters to more than a few species of plants, and may try to complement nearby natural areas. The naturescaped yard requires more thought in the planning stage, but less maintenance in the long term. Reducing the lawn area and using native plants, for example, translates into reduced water and chemical usage.

Attracting nature into your yard will add a whole new dimension to the garden experience, one that goes well beyond gardening for the human eye or tastebud! Anyone who is interested in learning more about truly giving nature a hand can purchase the three "Naturescape BC" booklets, which are full of information on the Georgia Basin (our region), from the office in Victoria. The booklets walk you through an analysis of your property, explain the principles of naturescaping and what is needed to create or enhance habitat, and offer lists of native plants, birds and animals. There are tips on bird feeding, nest boxes, pond liners, composting, water-wise gardens and wildlife trees, to name just a few. A resource list of nature organizations, suppliers and consultants is also included.

Naturescape-British Columbia relies on ordinary citizens to do their part in restoring the natural environment at home, whether home is an acreage in the country, a city backyard or a balcony. Find out how you can do your part!

Naturescape British Columbia
PO Box 9354, Station Provincial Government
Victoria, BC
V8W 9M1
toll-free phone: 1-800-387-9853

Tuscan Farm Gardens

For a gardening retreat, take a drive to Langley. Tuscan Farm is an 80 acre family-run business with many facets. There are a number of gardens, fields of *echinacea* and lavender and a series of walking trails for recreational, informational or contemplative purposes. It's also a bed and breakfast, and there is a shop which carries local products. In the summer after your visit, stop for tea and some lavender biscotti.
24453-60th Ave., Langley •
530-1997; 532-0350 fax
e-mail:
heather@tuscanfarmgardens.com
website: http://
www.tuscanfarmgardens.com/

A Universal Garden For Vancouver

by the Universal Garden Society Steering Committee

The Universal Garden Society began as the vision of one inspired, community-focused individual. The idea was to have a Vancouver garden-park that incorporates "universal" design, or a design that would make the park welcoming to diverse groups of people. This vision has grown into a project supported by an ever-increasing number of enthusiastic volunteers. Today, the society is developing partnerships with the Vancouver General Hospital and the Vancouver Park Board to explore ways in which the community can contribute innovative and practical ideas to the planning of the Vancouver hospital grounds.

A park that is based on universal design is one that welcomes all people and accommodates their different backgrounds, abilities and experiences. In a hospital setting, this means that the local residents, hospital patients and hospital staff would all see the park as something that is there for them. For example, some patients may want an area that is accessible to wheelchairs where they can enjoy the healing properties of nature. Some staff may want a place to eat lunch where they can get away from the stresses of the hospital and come back to work rejuvenated. Some patients may want a sheltered area to meet with friends and family, outside the hospital walls. Residents in the area may want a place to go for a stroll — somewhere they can feel that they have escaped from the city. A universal garden that met these different requirements could have lots of paths, plots for horticultural therapy and plants that attract birds and butterflies. It could have peaceful corners with benches, surrounded by flowers and running water. It could have easy-to-reach visiting areas from which cars are not visible. These are only a few of the ideas for such a universal garden. The important thing is that future users of the park have the opportunity to come up with ideas, and that all kinds of people are able to use the park in many imaginative ways.

The Universal Garden Society is already going into the community for ideas. We have held art events where people created word-and-picture collages of their vision for the park; we are also working with the hospital on mini-projects that will build towards the universal garden and give the community an idea of what is possible. Some of our members are already working on a patio garden and horticultural therapy program at the Banfield Extended Care pavilion.

The role of the Universal Garden Society is to stimulate the process that will lead to a universally designed garden. We want to excite people's imaginations and provide a channel for the expression of ideas. We seek to gather up resources from the community — from individuals, other community groups, arts groups — and work in partnership with the hospital to inspire a truly innovative park design.

The Universal Garden Society is a non-profit organization, run entirely by volunteers. The Universal Garden Society Steering Committee is a collective of Vancouver residents with a total of 64 years of living near Vancouver General Hospital. Amongst them, they have 209 years of gardening activity and a wide range of educational, volunteer and occupational experiences. They are happily single/married/divorced/widowed with 15 great/grand/children.

The Universal Garden Society is interested in hearing from you, whether you want to become actively involved with the work of the society, transmit an idea or simply get more information. You can reach us at:

The Universal Garden Society
789 West 18th Ave.
Vancouver, V5Z 1W1
phone/fax: 874-6740

"My favourite garden is between Laurel and Willow Streets, and 7th and 8th Ave. It's all bamboo, and evocative of another world."
— Ann Bailey, garden activist, Douglas Park area and Universal Garden Society member

COMMUNITY GARDENS

The contacts for these gardens change fairly often, so if you are interested in getting involved we recommend going to the garden and asking someone there about who to call. Many community gardens have notice boards with this information. You can also call City Planning Departments for current contacts. Some have big waiting lists, but others are eager to accept new gardeners.

BURNABY:

Burnaby and Region Allotment Gardens Association
5500 block of Meadow Ave.
583-4240 (City of Burnaby)
15 acres.

Stoney Creek Community Garden
2898 Neptune Cres.
100 beds.

Heights Neighbourhood Garden
3897 Pender St.
43 plots.

SFU Community Garden
Burnaby Mountain next to Naheeno Park
99 plots.

COQUITLAM:

Burquitlam Organic Garden (BOG)
515 Ebert Ave. • 506-4766
contact: Don Violet
Size of three city lots. Starting spring 1999. Contact Burquitlam Community Association at number above.

Colony Farm GVRD
Colony Farm Regional Park, off Lougheed Hwy.
• 520-6442 (GVRD)
7-acre site; composting on site; shed with lots of tools and special-needs plot that's built up for those who are in wheelchairs or can't bend over.

DELTA:

Delta Recycling Society Community Garden
7046 Brown St. • 946-9828
25 plots.

LANGLEY:

Langley Family Services
5339-207th St. • 534-7921
Easy-access wheelchair plots available.

Sunrise Rotary Community Garden
Walnut Grove Community Park, 212 block off 88th
Ave. • 888-3376
contact: Rotary Club of Langley, Jane D'Silva
31 plots; two wheelchair-accessible plots; waiting list.

NORTH VANCOUVER:

Moodyville Garden Association, City of North Vancouver Planning Dept.
1st St. between Lonsdale and St. George St.
Six-year wait; zoned for development and planners are looking to relocate.

PITT MEADOWS:

Pitt Meadows Community Garden
465-2667
contact: Lynn and Ian Dick
28 plots; city-owned land

RICHMOND:

City of Richmond River Road Community Garden
6080 River Rd. (foot of No. 2 Rd. Bridge)
244-1208
A collaboration of the Richmond
Environmental Youth Corps and the
community. Three-year pilot project
beginning in 1999. Phone City of
Richmond Parks Department at number
above.

Richmond Allotment Gardens Association
10711 Palmberg Rd., north of Steveston Hwy.
130 plots (20-foot x 50-foot plots).

Why do gardeners hate weeds?
Because if you give them an inch, they'll take a yard.

North Vancouver recreation centres have great perennial borders. Roger Griffiths is the recreation-commission gardener with influence.

SURREY:

Dunsmuir Gardens
Crescent Beach (Surrey Parks and Recreation)
100 plots (25 feet x 25 feet)

VANCOUVER:

Acadia Park Community Garden
UBC Acadia Housing Complex

Arbutus Victory Garden
6600 block on East Blvd. beside railway tracks near 50th Ave.
Eight plots registered with city; each plot has a 50 foot frontage; plots rent for $11.50 per year. Operated by Vancouver Parks and Recreation Department.

Cottonwood Community Garden
103-700 E. Pender St. at south end of Strathcona Park
Operated by Strathcona Community Garden Society and Vancouver Parks and Recreation.

Cypress Community Garden (also known as Maple Community Garden)
Next to Arbutus rail line on 6th Ave. off Cypress St. 36-square-foot lots available. Plots cost $10 per year. Operated by Vancouver Parks and Recreation.

Elizabeth Rogers Community Garden
7th Ave. and Manitoba (northeast corner of park)
Operated by Urban Diggers Society.

Fraser Street Neighbourhood Garden
8th and Fraser St.
Plot rentals are $10 per year. Operated by Urban Diggers Society.

Gardeners by the Bay
1050 Beach Ave.
In the West End beside the Aquatic Centre.

Kitsilano Community Garden
6th and Maple St.
Sign up on garden shed; leave note. Operated by Kitsilano Community Garden Association.

McSpadden Park
South of 4th Ave. and west of Victoria Dr.
18 plots. Operated by Vancouver Parks and Recreation.

Mole Hill/Nelson Park
City block between Pendrell, Comox, Bute and Thurlow St.
Operated by Mole Hill Living Heritage Society.

Robson Park Community Garden
St. George and West 14th St., northwest corner
40 plots $10 per year. Operated by Urban Diggers Society and Vancouver Parks and Recreation.

Strathcona Community Garden
South of Prior St., west of Hawks Ave.
Plots are approximately 150 square feet and cost $15. Operated by Strathcona Community Garden Association and Vancouver Parks and Recreation.

WEST VANCOUVER:
Argyle Avenue Community Gardens, Argyle 1
1460 Argyle Ave.
28 plots at $75 per plot. Administered by West Vancouver Parks and Recreation.

Argyle Avenue Community Gardens, Argyle 2
1534 Argyle Ave.
28 plots $75 per plot. Administered by West Vancouver Parks and Recreation.

Navvy Jack Gardens
2000 Block Bellevue Ave.
26 plots. Administered by West Vancouver Parks and Recreation.

Want to start your own community garden? The City of Vancouver rents vacant lands like unopened lane allowances, street rights-of-way and empty lots that can't support buildings due to sewer easements. They are rented to neighbouring residents for $11.50. There are strict requirements as to who qualifies as a "neighbour."

Old Mother Old,
She lives in the cold,
And every year she brings
    forth young,
And every one without a
    tongue.
Who is it?
An apple tree

Strathcona Community Garden

by Marg Meikle

To the delight of residents and others who stumble upon it, a glorious three-acre garden blooms in the heart of Vancouver. Hidden from the city behind a berm of pine trees and broom, the Strathcona Community Garden elevates the downtown Vancouver neighbourhood known as Strathcona. Part of the poorest postal code in Canada, the neighbourhood has a high percentage of government-subsidized dwellings mixed in with gentrified row houses and trendy new developments. The neighbourhood is home to many third-generation Chinese-Canadian families and a large population of new immigrants — and also to prostitutes, drug users and street people. And while the garden is a surprising oasis in this hectic neighbourhood, it is part of a growing trend.

Community gardens are springing up across North America like weeds. For apartment dwellers who want to run their hands through earth, community gardens fit the bill. They date back at least a century to the allotment gardens of Britain, which were the model for the Victory Gardens of the Second World War; they work best when density is high and people don't own their own land. "They need a community base to survive," says Muggs Sigurgeirson, a founder of the Strathcona Community Gardener's Society, the non-profit association that manages Strathcona and the nearby Cottonwood Gardens. But they also foster the solidarity and growth of that same community.

The Strathcona Community Garden is the result of 14 years of backbreaking labour by hundreds of volunteers. But as with many successful joint ventures, it took one person to get the whole thing moving. Leslie Scrimshaw was volunteering for City Farmer, the urban agriculture resource office in Vancouver. She was a fan of community gardens and called meetings to gauge response and to talk about organic and allotment gardening. Residents' associations, various cultural associations and the neighbourhood itself showed immediate interest. And she got a major commitment from several very dedicated people.

The next obvious step was to find a piece of land. Scrimshaw took 15 supportive community groups to the Vancouver Board of Parks and Recreation meeting on April Fool's Day 1985. They were granted a one-year lease on a three-acre lot. The area had been covered with water until 1919, when it was turned into a landfill site. During the Second World War the military used the land to train women to drive heavy equipment. It was a wild space, taken over by broom and garbage. One section was still a swampy marsh.

With their work obviously cut out for them, the committed volunteers got down to it. Fortunately, Finning Ltd., a heavy-equipment dealer, and its union lent them a bulldozer and driver for a day to help get them started. Smithrite (now Waste Management of Greater Vancouver) donated a huge garbage dumpster, and an old veteran of logging camps helped make a "come along" device for pulling heavy objects. The volunteers dug up and dragged slabs of cement, bullied 1.5-metre-high boulders and battled blackberry brambles.

But clearing away the rubble was only a start. Additional soil was required because the existing clay was unworkable. Lacking the money to truck in manure or topsoil, the volunteers used their knowledge of composting to produce rich soil. People from Strathcona and the nearby Carnegie Community Centre began bringing kitchen scraps to the giant compost bins. Residents continue to compost, a landscaper brings grass clippings, and the city brings in truckloads of leaves every autumn. "The turning point for the garden," says Sigurgeirson, "was when the [nearby] Ray-Cam Co-operative Centre gave us $2,000 of its bingo take to put in a water line so people wouldn't have to carry water by bucket." With input from the group, Ellie Epp, a film-maker and garden society member who lives in the neighbourhood, designed the garden. It includes 200 two- by four-and-a-half-metre plots, an area that attracts wildlife and a shared public space.

The shared part of the garden includes an orchard with more than 100 varieties of espaliered apple trees, a huge herb garden, a social area, a section for raised beds that is wheelchair accessible and a children's wa-

As I was going through
    sloppery gap,
I met a little thing with a red
    cap,
A stone in its stomach, a stick
    in its side,
So answer me this, and I'll give
    you a ride.
What is it?
A cherry

Cicely sage sits in her cage,
And all her children die of age,
Yet she is alive and lusty.
What is she?
A tree and its leaves

ter-play area. Rather than fencing the perimeter of the garden, the volunteers planted shelter belts of broom, berries, herbs and flowering shrubs. These living borders, along with the "go organic" rule, have encouraged the return of 110 species of birds, including a large number of songbirds as well as ducks, pheasants and, most recently, red-tailed hawks. Now the swamp hums with frogs, snakes and salamanders.

The diversity of the plots gardened by the 100 members is overwhelming, and the range of colour and texture amazing. There are artichokes, tomatoes, beets, cucumbers, kale, beans, lettuce, potatoes, horseradish and every flower imaginable. Brian Tugwood, who works several plots, has exotic flowers, including the metre-high screaming red MONTBRETIA (*Crocosmia* 'Lucifer') and the voracious CALIFORNIAN POPPY (*Romneya coulteri*), surrounding 800 basil plants. "I love my pesto," he grins. Louie Ettling, originally from South Africa, has planted her plot full of different grasses to remind herself of home.

With the recent addition of a bee shed (funded by VanCity Savings Credit Union), the gardens are pollinated and blooming better than ever. The 227 kilograms of honey produced each year is sold to raise money. Members pay $10 a year and $5 per plot and raise funds for the rest of their financial needs, including insurance and water bills.

About three years ago the waiting list for plots was getting long. Inspired by the success of the Strathcona garden, a partner group established the Cottonwood Community Gardens on three acres of adjacent park board and city lands. Much of the work has been done by the Environmental Youth Alliance, a group dedicated to creating a healthy environment and sense of community.

Over the years, the garden society has proved itself a viable and important part of the community. The group now has a 10-year lease from the park board, and this summer building is under way on a permanent solar-powered garden house/ecopavilion for classes, meetings and seed storing. There will be a library and a kitchen which they hope to eventually use for mass community canning. It's the first public building to get a permit from Vancouver for a composting toilet and a grey water recycling system (which uses water that goes down sink, tub and shower drains to flush toilets).

There are no quiet routes into the garden. You have to cross main transportation arteries that cut up the neighbourhood. But then you slip in through the gate, and suddenly it is peaceful, visually soothing and fragrant. There are enough private spaces that you can feel alone here. It is an island of tranquility, a feast for the soul, amid the clatter of the city.

VANCOUVER ROSE SOCIETY'S RECOMMENDED ROSES FOR THE LOWER MAINLAND

Hybrid Tea Roses
Alexander (orange)
Berolina (Selfridges) (deep yellow)
Electron (deep pink)
Elina (Peaudouce) (light yellow)
Fragrant Cloud (orange)
Ingrid Bergman (red)
Liebeszauber (red)
Loving Memory (Bergund 1981)
 (red)
Marijke Koopman (pink)
Rosemary Harkness (orange pink)
Royal William (deep red)

Floribunda Roses
Anisley Dickson (Dicky) (orange)
City of London (light pink)
Fellowship (orange blend)
Friesia (Sunsprite) (yellow)
Glad Tidings (deep red)
Lavaglut (deep red)
Margaret Merril (white)
Pensioner's Voice (apricot)
Queen Elizabeth (pink)
Sexy Roxy (pink)
Tabris (pink blend)
Trumpeter (orange)

Shrubs & English Roses
Abraham Darby (orange pink)
Blanc Double de Coubert (white)
Bonica (pink)
Fair Bianca (white)
Fred Loads (orange)
Golden Wings (yellow)
Hansa (medium pink)
Heritage (light pink)
L.D. Braithwaite (red)
Leander (apricot)

Mary Rose (pink)
Penelope (light pink)
Sally Holmes (white)
Sweet Juliet (apricot)
Winchester Cathedral (white)

Miniature Roses
Beauty Secret (red)
Cinderella (white)
Cupcake (pink)
Gourmet Popcorn (white)
Green Ice (white)
Ko's Yellow (yellow blend)
Little Artist (red blend)
Loving Touch (apricot)
Pink Petticoat (pink blend)
Rainbow's End (yellow blend)
Snow Bride (white)
Sweet Chariot (cerise)

Climbing Mini Roses
Jeanne Lajoie (pink)
Laura Ford (yellow)
Warm Welcome (orange)

Old Garden Roses (OGRs)
Capitaine John Ingram (red/
 mauve)
*Duchesse de Montebello (pink)
*Fantin Latour (pink)
*Ispahan (pink)
Jacques Cartier (pink)
*Mme. Plantier (white)
Reine des Violettes (red/mauve)
*Rosa Glauca (pink)
*Rosa macrantha (light pink)
*Rosa Mundi (pink/white striped)
*Tuscany Superb (red/mauve)

Climbers and Ramblers
Altissimo (red)
*City of York (white)
Constance Spry (light pink)
Dortmund (red)
Dublin Bay (red)
Iceberg (white)
Lichtkonigin Lucia (yellow)
Mme. Alfred Carrière (white)
New Dawn (light pink)
Westerland (apricot)

*Albertine (orange pink)
*American Pillar (pink)
*Bobbie James (white)
*Félicité Perpétue (white)
*Veilchenblau (mauve)

*once blooming

TREE CITY

Trees are incredibly important to Vancouver. Not only are they the basis for our economy, they define the look of the city, are a home for birds, a source of calm and a great provider of shade in our summers. Consider the number of street names: Maple, Cedar, Larch, Elm, Fir, Oak, Alder, Hemlock, Willow and Birch, to name a few. Want controversy? Talk of removing trees raises the collective ire of Vancouverites more than just about any topic. To generalize, the west side of the city is notable for its large shade trees and the east side has spectacular shows of spring colour. We're lucky — we have more flowering trees for the area than any other city in Canada.

To achieve this splendour, the City of Vancouver has a full service tree department. It's a big job, with more than 110,000 trees on the streets and over 50,000 trees in the parks to maintain. And that doesn't count the trees in our urban forests such as Stanley Park or Jericho. The department has massive databases of information on all the trees in the city to help with managing planting, maintenance and complaints.

VANCOUVER'S FAVOURITE TREES

The city plants an average of 4000 trees a year, and 1300 of that number are usually replacements. How do they know which kind of tree goes where? There are lots of factors, such as soil condition, the width of the boulevard, where the power or trolley lines are, where the sun hits. Of course, in your own garden you can plant a much larger variety of trees, but the following lists of trees have proven to be healthy and safe for Vancouver's streets.

City of Vancouver Preferred Street Tree Species List

by the City of Vancouver Park Board

This list is a general guide. Other species/cultivars may do well on streets. Trees listed as unsuitable may be fine for park or garden settings. Remember to always plant the right tree for the right place.

LARGE TREES:

Trees over 50 feet in height and 25 feet in width. Suitable for boulevards with no overhead obstructions and eight feet of width. Listed by botanical name and common name respectively.

Acer platanoides NORWAY MAPLE
Acer pseudoplatanus SYCAMORE MAPLE
Aesculus x *carnea* 'Briottii' RED
 HORSECHESTNUT
Cercidiphyllum japonicum KATSURA TREE
Fagus sylvatica EUROPEAN BEECH
Fraxinus americana 'Autumn Applause'
 AMERICAN ASH
Fraxinus pennsylvanica 'Patmore Summit' GREEN
 ASH
Ginkgo biloba MAIDENHAIR TREE
Liquidambar styraciflua 'Worplesdon'
 WORPLESDON SWEETGUM
Liriodendron tulipifera 'Arnold' TULIP TREE
Metasequoia glyptostroboides DAWN REDWOOD
Platanus acerifolia 'Bloodgood' LONDON PLANE
 TREE

The Fraser Valley Heritage Tree Society is in the business of preserving trees of significant age, size, species and form in areas south of the Fraser River (Surrey, Delta, Langley, Abbotsford, Chilliwack).

Quercus acutissima SAWTOOTH OAK
Quercus palustris PIN OAK
Quercus phellos WILLOW LEAF OAK
Robinia pseudoacacia BLACK LOCUST
Tilia tomentosa SILVER LINDEN
Tilia cordata LITTLE LEAF LINDEN

MEDIUM TREES:

Trees maturing between 25 and 50 feet. Generally suitable for situating on a blockside tree lawn three feet or greater between curb and sidewalk. Listed by botanical name and common name respectively.

Acer campestre CAMPESTRE MAPLE
Acer cappadocicum CAPPADOCICUM MAPLE
Acer pennsylvanicum MOOSEWOOD
Acer rubrum 'October Glory'
'Autumn Blaze' RED MAPLE
Acer truncatum PURPLEBLOW MAPLE
Carpinus betulus EUROPEAN HORNBEAM
Fraxinus excelsior EXCELSIOR ASH
Fraxinus ornus FLOWERING ASH
Gleditsia triacanthos HONEY LOCUST
Magnolia kobus (Root Stock) NORTHERN
   JAPANESE MAGNOLIA
Parrotia persica PERSIAN PERSICA
Sorbus aria 'Lutescens' 'Majestica' WHITE BEAM
   MOUNTAIN ASH
Sorbus alnifolia KOREAN MOUNTAIN ASH
Tilia x *euchlora* CRIMEAN LINDEN
Zelcova serrata 'Green Vase'
'Village Green' JAPANESE ZELCOVA

SMALL TREES:

Trees maturing at 25 feet. Suitable for locating at or below overhead electrical conductors. Listed by botanical and common name respectively.

Acer palmatum (tree form varieties) JAPANESE
   MAPLE
Acer platanoides 'Globosum' GLOBE MAPLE
Cornus nuttallii 'Eddies White Wonder' DOGWOOD
Cornus kousa JAPANESE DOGWOOD
Crataegus crus-galli 'Inermis' THORNLESS
   COCKSPUR HAWTHORN

Vancouver Street Tree
Information Line: 257-8600

Crataegus phaenopyrum 'Treeform' WASHING-
TON HAWTHORN
Crataegus monogyna SINGLESEED HAWTHORN
Crataegus x *lavallei* LAVALLE HAWTHORN
Malus x *zumi* 'Calocarpa' REDBUD CRABAPPLE
(Other Disease Resistant Cultivar Recommenda-
tions Available)
Magnolia stellata STAR MAGNOLIA
Prunus cerasifera CHERRY PLUM
Prunus pissardii PISSARD PLUM
Styrax japonica JAPANESE SNOWBELL

COLUMNAR TREES:

Trees exhibiting a distinct upright branch arrangement.
Suitable for confined situations or on tree lawns off-
set from overhead electrical conductors. Listed by
botanical name and common name respectively.
Acer nigra 'Green Column' GREEN COLUMN
BLACK MAPLE
Acer platanoides 'Columnar',
'Olmstead', 'Crimson Sentry' COLUMNAR
NORWAY MAPLE
Acer rubrum 'Karpick','Bowhall', 'Scanlon'
UPRIGHT RED MAPLE
Acer freemanii 'Scarlet Sentinel','Armstrong'
FREEMAN'S MAPLES (Red And Silver Maple
Cross)
Carpinus betulus 'Fastigiata' EUROPEAN
HORNBEAM
Fagus sylvatica 'Dawyckiip' DAWYCKI BEECH
Gingko biloba 'Sentry' 'Lakeview' GINGKO TREE
(MAIDENHAIR)
Liriodendron tulipae 'Arnold' ARNOLD TULIP
TREE

UNSUITABLE TREES:

Trees considered inappropriate as streetside plantings
in Vancouver due to unsuitability to climate or unfa-
vourable characteristics. Listed by botanical name,
common name and reason for unsuitability.
Acer negundo MANITOBA MAPLE; weak wood,
suckers
Acer saccharinum SUGAR MAPLE; weak wood,
high pruning needs, invasive roots

VanDusen's Adopt-a-Tree Program

Mad for medlars? Batty about birches? VanDusen Botanical Garden offers an innovative way to support the garden and its plant collections. Adopt-a-Tree provides an opportunity for donors to "grow" a personal relationship with a "special" tree in the garden. For a minimum donation of $1,000 the donor may "adopt" a tree growing in the garden. The adopted tree is hung with a small gold plaque inscribed with the tree's botanical name and the donor's dedication. For more information, please contact Louise Dyer at 922-9798 or VanDusen Development Office at 257-8190.

Betula pendula EUROPEAN WHITE BIRCH; very
poor heat and drought tolerance, bronze birch
borer
Chamaecyparis lawsoniana LAWSON'S FALSE
CYPRESS; susceptibility to root rot
Cornus nuttallii PACIFIC DOGWOOD; susceptibility to anthracnose
Crataegus oxyacantha ENGLISH HAWTHORN;
leaf blight
Fraxinus velutina ARIZONA ASH; leaf blight
Laburnum x *watereri* 'Vossii' GOLDENCHAIN
TREE; profusion of poisonous fruit
Malus spp (unless specified FLOWERING
CRABAPPLE); scab resistent
Salix spp WILLOW; weak wood, invasive roots
Tsuga heterophylla WESTERN HEMLOCK;
tendency to blowdown, adelgids and mistletoe

How can you tell a dogwood
tree from a pine tree?
By its bark.

EXPERIMENTAL TREES:

Trees currently not in extensive use as street trees in
Vancouver but being monitored for possible inclusion
in the "recommended" list. Listed by botanical name
and common name respectively.
Acer davidii DAVID MAPLE
Acer ginnala AMUR MAPLE
Acer griseum PAPER-BARK MAPLE
Acer x *truncatum* 'Pacific Sunset' 'Norwegian
Sunset' SHANTUNG MAPLE
Betula jacquemontii Whitebarked HIMALAYAN
BIRCH
Cladastris lutea YELLOWOOD
Cornus mas 'Cornelian' CHERRY DOGWOOD
Davidia involucrata DOVE TREE (Medium)
Halesia carolina MOUNTAIN SILVERBALL(Small)
Koeleuteria paniculata GOLDEN RAIN TREE
(Medium)
Magnolia grandiflora SOUTHERN MAGNOLIA
(Medium)
Nothofagus antarctica CHILEAN BEECH (Large)
Nyssa sylvatica BLACK TUPELO (Medium)
Parrotia persica PERSIAN PARROTIA (Medium)
Pterocarya fraxinifolia CAUCASIAN WINGNUT
Robinia pseudoacacia 'Globe' GLOBE BLACK
LOCUST (Medium)

Sorbus tianshanica 'Dwarfcrown' TIANSHANICA MOUTAIN ASH (Small)
Sophora japonica JAPANESE PAGODA TREE (Large)
Stewartia pseudocamellia STEWARTIA TREE (Medium)
Ostrya virginiana EASTERN HORNBEAM

Arbor Week is the third week of October.

Good Performers for Vancouver Gardens

by Ann Kent, Master Gardener and Horticulturist

These trees and shrubs perform well in Vancouver gardens. Consult a good reference text for photographs and site requirements. Criteria for selection include seasonal interest, suitability for small gardens, attractive form and relative disease resistance when compared to other cultivars or species.

TEN GOOD TREES:

Acer palmatum 'Bloodgood' JAPANESE MAPLE
Cercis canadensis 'Forest Pansy' EASTERN
  REDBUD
Chamaecyparis obtusa 'Nana Gracilis' HINOKI
  CYPRESS
Cornus florida rubra FLOWERING DOGWOOD
Magnolia x loebneri 'Leonard Messel' STAR
  MAGNOLIA
Prunus yedoensis 'Akebono' JAPANESE
  FLOWERING CHERRY (disease resistant)
Pyrus salicifolia pendula 'Silver Cascade' WILLOW-
  LEAVED PEAR
Sorbus hupehensis 'Pink Pagoda' MOUNTAIN ASH
Stewartia pseudocamelia JAPANESE STEWARTIA
  (CAMELIA TREE)
Tsuga mertensiana MOUNTAIN HEMLOCK

TEN GOOD SHRUBS:

Aucuba japonica 'Picturata' JAPANESE SPOTTED
  LAUREL
Euonymus alatus BURNING BUSH
Forscythia x intermedia 'Lynwood Gold' FOR-
  SYTHIA
Hammamaelis mollis CHINESE WITCH HAZEL
Pieris japonica 'Forest Flame' LILY-OF-THE-VALLEY
  BUSH
Rhododendron 'Jean Marie de Montague'
Rosa 'Bonica' SHRUB ROSE
Sarcoccoca ruscifolia SWEET BOX
Skimmia japonica 'Bronze Knight' JAPANESE
  SKIMMIA
Weigela florida variegata WEIGELA

A good resource for tree fanciers is *West Vancouver Tree Book*. It includes a descriptive list of 140 trees and large shrubs that will not exceed an ultimate height of 35 feet. The book can be purchased at the Municipal Hall, 750-17th St. Price: $9. Municipal Hall also has a range of pamphlets available on trees. They are put out by the ISA (International Society of Arboriculture) and by BC Hydro. They are all free.

FIVE GOOD TREES AND SHRUBS THAT ALSO MAKE GOOD FORMAL AND INFORMAL EDGES:

Buxus sempervirens 'Faulkner' COMMON
  BOXWOOD
Lonicera nitida 'Baggesen's Gold' SHRUB
  HONEYSUCKLE
Rhododendron 'Snow Lady'
Taxus x *media* 'Hicksii' YEW
Thuya occidentalis 'Smaragd' HEDGING CEDAR

"The tree which moves some to tears of joy is in the eyes of others only a green thing which stands in the way ..."
  —William Blake

Favourite Trees of Some Vancouverites

PAUL MONTPELLIER'S FAVOURITE TREES

Paul Montpellier is the City of Vancouver's Arborist. When asked to list his favourite trees in the city, he chose mature (or in some cases, huge) specimens. "I think that given the stress of the urban situation on trees, never mind on us, that they should get extra points for hanging in with such splendour, for so many years." Paul Montpellier's favourites, in no particular order:

The RED OAK (*Quercus rubra*) in Alexander Park
  at the corner of Bidwell St.
The AMERICAN LINDEN tree (*Tilia americana*)
  in the centre of Brocton Point picnic ground.
The WESTERN RED CEDAR (*Thuya plicata*) at
  the top of Third Beach trail in Stanley Park.
The SIERRA REDWOOD or BIGTREE
  (*Sequoiadendron giganteum*) on the Cambie
  median at King Edward.
The common HORSE CHESTNUT (*Aesculus
  hippocastanum*) at the east end of the crescent in
  Shaughnessy.
The TREE-OF-HEAVEN (*Ailanthus altissima*) in the
  traffic island on Kingsway at Fraser.
The WEEPING WILLOW (*Salix babylonica*) on
  West 16th at Trafalgar St.
The NORWAY MAPLE (*Acer platanoides*) on
  Garden Dr. at East 2nd Ave.
The KATSURA (*Cercidiphyllum japonicum*) on
  Beechwood Cres. near Fraserview Golf Course.
The LONDON PLANE TREES (*Platanus
  acerifolia*) on Broadway west of Alma.

GERALD STRALEY'S TREES

Dr. Gerald Straley was Research Scientist and Curator of Collections at the UBC Botanical Garden. He is the author of the extremely useful book *Trees of Vancouver* (UBC Press, 1992). Dr. Straley died in 1998 and is truly missed. A couple of years earlier he had put together this list of his favourite trees. He said: "Most of my favourite trees are relatively uncommon or underused and they are attractive for several seasons or all year long, rather than having a short season of interest. They are also small trees."

Acer griseum PAPERBACK MAPLE
Grown for its wonderful peeling, coppery bark and soft pink-red fall colour. Asian and Alpine Gardens, UBC Botanical Garden; Sino-Himalayan Garden, VanDusen Botanical Garden; east of tennis courts, Stanley Park.

Betula utilis var. jacquemontii HIMALAYAN WHITE BIRCH
Nice dark green leaves and the whitest of white-barked trees. Asian Garden, UBC Botanical Garden; Sino-Himalayan Garden, VanDusen Botanical Garden; around Pitch & Putt Golf Course, Stanley Park; street planting along 7th Ave. at Oak St.

Cornus kousa KOUSA DOGWOOD
The latest flowering of dogwoods. Four white bracts surround the tiny flowers in June. Attractive and edible cherry-like fruits in fall. Becoming more popular. Asian Garden, UBC Botanical Garden; street plantings along Cambie St. from 49th to 54th Ave. and along Charles St. from Nanaimo to Renfrew St.

Cercidiphyllum japonicum KATSURA TREE
Delicate pale copper to green in spring, dark green in summer, early fall colour in soft pastel shades. Asian Garden, UBC Botanical Garden; around parking lot at VanDusen Botanical Garden; row in front of Vancouver School of Theology on the UBC campus; street planting along Selkirk St., between 40th and 41st Ave.

For information about getting permits to remove trees from your property in the City of Vancouver, call: 871-6378

Parrotia persica PERSIAN IRONWOOD
A graceful, usually multi-trunked, tree with attractive bark, excellent fall colour and small red flowers in late winter to early spring, which have to be cut and brought indoors to enjoy. It is related to the witch hazels. There is a street planting along 37th Ave. outside VanDusen Botanical Garden; in containers on the north side of Bloedel Conservatory in Queen Elizabeth Park and in the Asian Garden, UBC Botanical Garden.

Robinia pseudoacacia 'Frisia' GOLDEN LOCUST
Fairly narrow habit, with the best golden colour all summer and fall. Around the parking lot, VanDusen Botanical Garden; at the corner of 41st Ave. and S.W. Marine Dr.; street planting along 8th Ave. from Scotia to Prince Edward St.

Koelreuteria paniculata GOLDEN-RAIN TREE
A very ornamental, but little-known, small tree with a rounded crown, large compound leaves, yellow flowers in great clusters and attractive seed pods in autumn. Three trees in entrance courtyard to UBC Botanical Garden and several west of the pine woods at VanDusen Botanical Garden.

Sorbus hupenhensis HIMALAYAN MOUNTAIN ASH
Probably the most attractive of mountain ashes. A small tree with sea-green leaves, turning multi-coloured in fall, with white flowers and pink fruits in large clusters, Asian Garden, UBC Botanical Garden and Sino-Himalayan Garden; and in Sorbus Collection, VanDusen Botanical Garden.

Stewartia pseudocamellia JAPANESE STEWARTIA
After these small trees reach maturity, they develop very nice bark that peels in irregular plates. White camellia-like flowers in mid-summer, often good fall colour and attractive coppery seed pods over winter. Several in the Asian Garden, UBC Botanical Garden; around the Pitch & Putt Golf Course in Stanley Park; and along the Rhododendron Walk, VanDusen Botanical Garden.

Styrax japonica JAPANESE SNOWBELL
A desirable small tree that is gaining popularity. It
has a profusion of hanging white bells in June. There
are two fine old specimens in The Crescent; several
in the Asian Garden, UBC Botanical Garden; a planting along Hudson St. from 40th Ave. to 41st Ave.

ELISABETH WHITELAW'S FAVOURITE TREES
Landscape Architect Elisabeth Whitelaw compiled
Vancouver's Heritage Tree Inventory in 1983. Copies
of the inventory are in the UBC Fine Arts Library
and the Science Division of the main branch of the
Vancouver Public Library. These are some of her favourite trees in the city.

The CAPPADOCICUM MAPLES (*Acer cap-*
padocicum) on Barclay St. These were likely planted
in the early 1890s, the same time as the houses on
the street were built. The CAPPADOCIAN MAPLES,
which originate in the Cappadocian area of central
Turkey, turn a bright butter-yellow colour in the fall.

The NORTHERN RED OAK (*Quercus rubra*) at the
southwest corner of Alexandra Park. The park was
named in honour of Queen Alexandra, who reigned
with King Edward VII from 1901-1910, when the park
was acquired. Likely the tree was planted at that time.
It is the broadest tree in the city with its horizontal
branches spanning over 30 metres.

At the southern end of English Bay there are six ENG-
LISH ELMS (*Ulmus procera*) that the Park Board
lights each Christmas. They once sheltered the cottage of Joe Fortes, who taught hundreds of Vancouver
children to swim in the early part of this century.

There is a WHITE MULBERRY (*Morus alba*) in the
Shakespeare Garden in Stanley Park (across Pipeline
Rd. from the Rose Garden). It was transplanted from
the Kerrisdale back garden of Mr. John Wesley
Morgan, an active member of Vancouver's Shakespeare
Society, in 1936. The Mulberry started as a cutting
from a tree in Anne Hathaway's garden in England
in 1925.

"I think that I shall never see
A billboard lovely as a tree.
Indeed, unless the billboards
     fall
I"ll never see a tree at all."
—Ogden Nash, from "Song
of the Open Road"

189

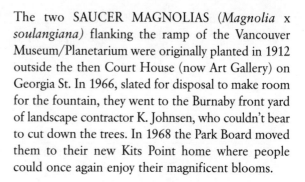

The two SAUCER MAGNOLIAS (*Magnolia* x *soulangiana)* flanking the ramp of the Vancouver Museum/Planetarium were originally planted in 1912 outside the then Court House (now Art Gallery) on Georgia St. In 1966, slated for disposal to make room for the fountain, they went to the Burnaby front yard of landscape contractor K. Johnsen, who couldn't bear to cut down the trees. In 1968 the Park Board moved them to their new Kits Point home where people could once again enjoy their magnificent blooms.

"Trees: Concerns and Solutions" is a pamphlet put out by the District of North Vancouver (987-7131) and District of West Vancouver (925-7000). It is free.

The HANDKERCHIEF TREE (*Davidia involucrata*) in a private garden at the southeast corner of SW Marine Dr. and West 49th Ave. is a spectacular landmark, especially in the early summer when its large, white bracts decorate the tree like handkerchiefs.

The ENGLISH OAK (*Quercus robur*) at Cambie and 12th Avenue (Vancouver City Hall). This was planted in 1937 to celebrate the coronation of King George VI and Queen Elizabeth (the Queen Mother). A tiny seedling from the Royal Forest at Windsor was wrapped in cotton and sent to the Vancouver Horticultural Society to be planted in commemoration of this special occasion.

Eddie's White Wonder

by Marg Meikle

Since 1956, British Columbia has claimed the dogwood as its provincial flower — even though other North Americans have made similar claims. The dogwood is Missouri's state tree, and North Carolina's and Virginia's state flower. Officially, Atlanta bears the honour of being nicknamed the Dogwood City.

Ask anyone to describe the tree's flower and they will probably say it has four or six creamy white or pink petals that look like leather, and a button centre. Wrong. What we assume to be the petals are, in fact, bracts like those on a poinsettia. The actual flower is the round centre, which turns from green to bright yellow when in bloom.

The Nanticoke Indians of the eastern United States have a legend that explains the dogwood's distinctive shape. There was once a chief so greedy that he insisted the braves who would win the hands of his four daughters would be those who brought him the most riches. The gods were so angry with this calculating chief, who had a lodge piled with furs and other valuables, that they turned him into the gnarled dogwood tree. His daughters are the four white bracts and the flowers in the centre are all the gifts.

But it is the story of Henry M. Eddie and "Eddie's White Wonder" that provides British Columbians with a bit of folklore of our own to stake a claim to the dogwood. At the corner where the University Endowment Lands (now Pacific Spirit Park), Musqueam Park, and the city of Vancouver meet, there was a dogwood so magnificent that when it bloomed each May it would cause a pileup of drivers, bicyclists and joggers. This specimen was on the property of J. Henry Eddie, across the street from where his father, Henry M. Eddie, provided mail order plants to gardeners across the continent — and by the carload around BC — until his death in 1953. It was Henry Eddie Sr. who developed Eddie's White Wonder, a celebrated dogwood hybrid now grown all over the world.

After training in Scotland, Eddie Sr. had immigrated to Canada in 1910 and eventually became the owner

"Give me a land of boughs in leaf,
A land of trees that stand;
Where trees are fallen, there is no grief;
I love no leafless land ..."
—A.E. Housman

of Eddie's Nurseries in Vancouver, with a branch in Everson, Washington. He experimented with growing better roses, azaleas, rhododendrons, fruit trees – and dogwoods. Eddie particularly liked the scarlet fall leaf colour of the dogwood from the eastern United States, *Cornus florida* ("cornus" is Latin for horn, referring to the toughness of the wood). So he tried to combine that quality with the large flower size of the native British Columbian *Cornus nuttallii* (named by John James Audubon after Thomas Nuttall, who collected specimens from the Columbia River Valley while marching to the Pacific Ocean). He cross-pollinated the two, searching for a resilient new dogwood without sacrificing any of its beauty.

In 1948, disaster struck. The Fraser River flooded and submerged Eddie's nursery for three months. All the hybrids were destroyed – except one. A 1945 cross had been progressing so quickly that Eddie had planted some at a site in Richmond, near what is now the airport. The miraculous Eddie's White Wonder was released for sale in 1955. The Royal Horticultural Society of England eventually honoured it for its hardiness, large creamy-white flowers, vivid fall foliage and resistance to blight (common in the Pacific Northwest).

In 1989, a group of BC nursery owners pledged $600,000 to form the Henry M. Eddie Plant Development Foundation at the UBC Botanical Garden. "My father was always keenly interested in research, but there was never any money," says J. Henry Eddie. "After he died, I thought it would be worthwhile to have some kind of a co-operation between the university and the nursery industry, with the objectives of developing new and better plants and encouraging young people to follow in his footsteps."

The foundation funds research, development and the introduction of new plants, and aims to increase its trust to $1 million over the next five years. Of the four million plants (and 13 varieties) that have been sold, 20 percent were sent to Europe. Henry M. Eddie should rest easy at the thought of the thousands of Eddie's White Wonder bursting into bloom all over the world. In the minds of horticulturists, Vancouver has finally supplanted Atlanta as the Dogwood City.

ARBORETUMS AND INTERESTING TREE WALKS

Arboretums

An arboretum is a collection of trees that are cata-
logued, labelled and planted by genus/family or by
geographical area. Vancouver's Lower Mainland boasts
a number of very interesting arboretums. Here is a
list to prompt exploration and further reading.

1. The Old Arboretum on the UBC Campus: What
remains of this arboretum is what was originally much
of the campus. Look just west of West Mall, from
the Fraser River Parkade south to University Boulevard, behind the Ponderosa Cafeteria. There are 88
trees. The native trees were planted in 1916; the
exotics were planted after WWII. See Gerald Straleys
book *Trees of Vancouver* (UBC, 1992) for a complete map and listing.

2. Stanley Park is a rain forest in the city. There is
even a 17-inch-diameter cedar tree (near the Hollow
Tree on Meadow Trail). The tree collection is especially fine and diverse around the Park Board Office
and the Pitch & Putt. See Richard Steele's book *The
Stanley Park Explorer* for a map and tree listings.

3. The north end of **Queen Elizabeth Park** was
planted as an arboretum in the 1950s and is now
maintained as a tree walk. City arborists have identified holes in the 1950s collection and work with the
donations program to fill out the collection. Call the
Communications Manager at the Park Board for more
information. There is a booklet available for a tree
walk in Queen Elizabeth Park and in the Quarry Garden (published by the Park Board).

4. UBC Botanical Garden: Here you'll find a large
collection of trees, especially in the David C. Lam
Asian Garden. You can find pretty much every tree
native to BC somewhere in the Native Garden.

For information on tree walks
in Stanley Park call the Nature
House: 257-8544

Derry Walsh and Linda Wright labelling trees and shrubs at the VanDusen Plant Sale.
Photo: VanDusen Botanical Garden

5. **VanDusen Botanical Garden** (Oak St. and 37th Ave.): a large collection, labelled with botanical names.

6. In **Shaughnessy,** one of the oldest neighbourhoods in Vancouver, there is a round park in the middle of "The Crescent." It has a collection of unusual trees, some of which are over 100 years old. See Gerald Straley's *Trees of Vancouver* for a complete map and listing.

7. Along the wide medians of the city there are varied plantings. King Edward Ave. (25th Ave.), 22nd East between Renfrew and Nanaimo, West 16th Ave. and Cambie St. are the most interesting. Cambie Street boasts the Heritage Boulevard.

9. **Vancouver Park Board Tree Walk:** this is comprised of seven blocks around Alma and 11th to Trutch and 13th. Call for a booklet about the various trees (257-8600) or pick up the booklet at the Park Board Office.

10. **Riverview Lands Davidson Arboretum** (500 Lougheed Hwy., Coquitlam, 524-7120) The Davidson Arboretum is 244 acres located on the grounds of Riverview Hospital. It contains over 150 varieties of trees including oaks, tulip trees and silver maples. Each tree is labelled. There are guided tours available or you can just wander. There are a total of about 1,800 trees throughout the 244 acres. The arboretum was initially created by the first provincial botanist, Professor John Davidson, who established a botanical garden with a collection of Western Canadian native plants. It was one of the first arboreta in Canada. In 1916, Davidson orchestrated the move of over 25,000 of the plants and trees planted at Riverview to the newly created Point Grey Botanical Garden (now UBC

Botanical Garden). Currently, Riverview is waiting for direction from the Provincial Government about their expectations for the arboretum.

11. **Redwood Park**: Enter at 17,900 block of 20th Ave. in Surrey, just east of Pacific Hwy. This 74-acre park is home to a wild assortment of trees planted by a couple of avid and eccentric seed collectors, twins David and Peter Brown. They lived in a two-story tree house in South Surrey with a spectacular view of Semiahmoo Bay. Their goal was to create their own exotic forest, so they grew trees in forest stands, or large groupings of 36 non-native or exotic species. Look for the chestnut and walnut trees and the 100 amazing *Sequoiadendron giganteum* GIANT SIERRA REDWOOD or BIGTREES. Some of the trees are approximately 76 metres (250 feet) tall. This is one of 293 developed parks in Surrey.

12. **Darts Hill** has a large collection of labelled trees planted over the past 50 years. There is a particularly large collection of exotic magnolias. (See public gardens section, pages 152-159)

13. **Green Timbers** is near 140th St. and the Fraser Hwy. It is the 160-acre provincially owned site of the first silvaculturally planted forest in BC. When this area was planted in the 1920s and 1930s, an arboretum was established.

The Cambie Street Heritage Boulevard

In 1993, Vancouver's city council designated the Cambie Street Boulevard from King Edward Avenue to S.W. Marine Drive as a Heritage Landscape. This came as a result of lobbying by a group called the Cambie Boulevard Heritage Society who were concerned that the city preserve the trees on the "elongated park" from future development or from the possibility of it becoming a rapid transit route.

The boulevard has interesting origins. Harland Bartholomew and Associates, the St. Louis, Missouri Landscape Architecture firm who had been responsible for developing Vancouver's town plan in 1928,

The City of Vancouver tree by-laws are long and complicated. They're available at City Hall or at the city website: http://www.city.vancouver.bc.ca/COMMSVCS/PLANNING/TREEBYLAW/treebylw.htm

designed the Cambie Boulevard in 1940 when they updated the city plan. It was planted in stages over the next few decades. Bartholomew's idea was for the street to be a "pleasure drive." He considered Vancouver a "year round garden city" and wanted Cambie Street to be a marvellous gateway to the city. He suggested using a diversity of species to provide interesting textures and colours, niches and other design interventions to distinguish Cambie from other streets. The boulevard boasts 264 trees from the original plantings. The Giant Sierra Sequoias are 60 years old. Here is the list, block by block.

King Edward Ave.:
Sequoiadendron giganteum GIANT SIERRA REDWOOD or BIGTREE
Ulmas procera 'Van Houtei' GOLDEN ENGLISH ELM
Prunus serrulata var. 'Kwanzan' KWANZAN FLOWERING CHERRY
Sequoiadendron giganteum GIANT SIERRA REDWOOD or BIGTREE
Forsythia intermedia 'Lynwood Gold' LYNWOOD GOLD FORSYTHIA
Sequoiadendron giganteum GIANT SIERRA REDWOOD or BIGTREE
Ulmas procera 'Van Houtei' GOLDEN ENGLISH ELM
Picea pungens glauca COLORADO BLUE SPRUCE
Crategus oxycantha paulii PAUL'S SCARLET HAWTHORNE

27th Ave.:
Crataegus oxycantha paulii PAUL'S SCARLET HAWTHORNE
Sequoiadendron giganteum SIERRA REDWOOD or BIGTREE
Picea pungens glauca COLORADO BLUE SPRUCE
Forsythia Intermeda 'Lynwood Gold' LYNWOOD GOLD FORSYTHIA
Sequoiadendron giganteum GIANT SIERRA REDWOOD or BIGTREE
Ulma procera 'Van Houtei' GOLDEN ENGLISH ELM

28th Ave.:
Picea pungens glauca COLORADO BLUE SPRUCE
Forsythia intermedia LYNWOOD GOLD FOR-
SYTHIA
Sequoiadendron giganteum GIANT SIERRA
REDWOOD or BIGTREE
Ulmus procera 'Van Houtei' GOLDEN ENGLISH
ELM
Sequoiadendron giganteum GIANT SIERRA
REDWOOD or BIGTREE
Ulmus procera 'Van Houtei' GOLDEN ENGLISH
ELM
Picea pungens glauca COLORADO BLUE SPRUCE
Crataegus oxycantha paulii PAUL'S SCARLET
HAWTHORN or MAY TREE

29th Ave.:
Cedrus deodara DEODAR CEDAR
Sequoiadendron giganteum GIANT SIERRA
REDWOOD or BIGTREE
Larix x *eurolepsis* HYBRID LARCH
Sorbus aria 'Lutescens' EUROPEAN WHITEBEAM
Taxodium distichum BALD CYPRESS OR SWAMP
CYPRESS
Larix x *eurolepsis* LARCH

Entrance to Queen Elizabeth Park at 30th Ave.:
Sorbus aria 'Lutescens' EUROPEAN WHITEBEAM
Tilia x *euchlora* 'Redmond' REDMOND
CAUCASIAN LIME, REDMOND BASSWOOD

31st Ave.:
Cornus 'Eddies White Wonder' EDDIE'S WHITE
WONDER DOGWOOD
Sequoiadendron giganteum GIANT SIERRA
REDWOOD or BIGTREE
Pinus sylvestris SCOTCH PINE
Quercus x *turneri* TURNER'S EVERGREEN OAK

32nd Ave.:
Quercus x *turneri* TURNER'S EVERGREEN OAK
Pinus sylvestris SCOTCH PINE
Sequoiadendron giganteum GIANT SIERRA
REDWOOD or BIGTREE

If you want beauty for a year,
plant a garden;
If you want beauty for a
lifetime, plant a tree.

Acer saccharum SUGAR or ROCK MAPLE
Betula pendula EUROPEAN or WEEPING BIRCH
Thuya plicata WESTERN RED CEDAR or WEST-
    ERN ARBORVITAE
Rock (Basalt) Outcropping
Sorbus aucuparia MOUNTAIN ASH,
    ROWANTREE

33rd Ave.:
Chamaecyparis lawsoniana 'Stewarti' GOLDEN
    LAWSON'S (FALSE) CYPRESS
Acer circinatum VINE MAPLE (a native tree)

McGuigan St.:
Celtis occidentalis HACKBERRY, NETTLE
Cornus mas CORNELIAN CHERRY or SORBET
Celtis occidentalis HACKBERRY, NETTLE TREE
Pinus ponderosa WESTERN YELLOW PINE
Cornus nuttallii PACIFIC DOGWOOD (BC's
    official flower)
Sorbus aria 'Lutescens' EUROPEAN WHITEBEAM
Celtis occidentalis HACKBERRY, NETTLE TREE

35th Ave.:
Sorbus aria 'Lutescens' EUROPEAN WHITEBEAM
Cornus 'Eddies White Wonder' EDDIE'S WHITE
    WONDER DOGWOOD
Celtis occidentalis HACKBERRY, NETTLE TREE
Cornus nuttallii PACIFIC DOGWOOD
Cornus 'Eddie's White Wonder' EDDIE'S WHITE
    WONDER DOGWOOD

37th Ave.:
Fagus sylvatica fastigiata EUROPEAN PYRAMIDAL
    BEECH
Prunus serrulata var. 'Takasago' ORIENTAL
    FLOWERING CHERRY
Thuya plicata 'Aurei' GOLDEN FORM of our
    WESTERN RED CEDAR
Pinus nigra var.nigra AUSTRIAN PINE
Prunus serrulata var. 'Takasago' ORIENTAL
    FLOWERING CHERRY

38th Ave.:
Gleditsia triacanthus inermis SUNBURST LOCUST
Cornus 'Eddie's White Wonder' EDDIE'S WHITE
    WONDER DOGWOOD
Prunus serrrulata ORIENTAL FLOWERING
    CHERRY

39th Ave.:
Prunus serrrulata var. 'Shirofugen' ORIENTAL
    FLOWERING CHERRY
Cornus 'Eddie's White Wonder' EDDIE'S WHITE
    WONDER DOGWOOD
Chamaecyparis nootkatensis ALASKA CEDAR or
    NOOTKA FALSE CYPRESS
Prunus serrulata var. 'Shirofugen' ORIENTAL
    FLOWERING CHERRY

40th Ave.:
Sequoiadendron giganteum GIANT SIERRA
    REDWOOD or BIGTREE
Cornus 'Eddie's White Wonder' DOGWOOD
Chamaecyparis nootkatensis ALASKA CEDAR or
    NOOTKA FALSE CYPRESS
Pinus nigra austriaca var. *nigra* AUSTRIAN PINE

41st Ave.:
Prunus serrulata var. 'Shirofugen' ORIENTAL
    FLOWERING CHERRY
Chamaecyparis nootkatensis ALASKA CEDAR or
    NOOTKA FALSE CYPRESS
Sorbus aria 'Lutescens' EUROPEAN WHITEBEAM

42nd Ave.:
Prunus serrulata 'Kwanzan' KWANZAN
    FLOWERING CHERRY
Prunus serrulata 'Kwanzan' KWANZAN
    FLOWERING CHERRY
Sorbus aria 'Lutescens' EUROPEAN WHITEBEAM

43rd Ave.:
Prunus serrulata 'Kwanzan' KWANZAN
    FLOWERING CHERRY
Chamaecyparis nootkatensis ALASKA CEDAR or
    NOOTKA FALSE CYPRESS

On 41st Ave. at Yew (in front of the Shopper's Drug Mart) there is a *Gingko Biloba* tree planted "In Honour of Dr. Gerald Straley."

Crataegus oxycantha fastigiata UPRIGHT
   HAWTHORN
Prunus serrulata 'Kwanzan' KWANZAN
   FLOWERING CHERRY

45th Ave.:
Prunus serrulata var. 'Shirofugen' ORIENTAL
   FLOWERING CHERRY
Chamaecyparis lawsoniana 'glauca' BLUE
   LAWSON'S CYPRESS
Sequoiadendron giganteum SIERRA REDWOOD
   or BIGTREE
Prunus serrulata var. 'Shirofugen' ORIENTAL
   FLOWERING CHERRY
Chamaecyparis lawsoniana 'Stewartii' GOLDEN
   LAWSON'S CYPRESS
Prunus serrulata var. 'Shirofugen' ORIENTAL
   FLOWERING CHERRY

48th Ave.:
Prunus serrulata var. 'Shirofugen' ORIENTAL
   FLOWERING CHERRY
Chamaecyparis lawsoniana 'glauca' BLUE
   LAWSON'S CYPRESS

49th Ave.:
Chamaecyparis nootkatensis ALASKA CEDAR or
   NOOTKA FALSE CYPRESS

50th Ave.:
Chamaecyparis nootkatensis ALASKA CEDAR or
   NOOTKA FALSE CYPRESS
Prunus serrulata var. 'Pink Perfection' ORIENTAL
   FLOWERING CHERRY
Taxodium distichum BALD CYPRESS or SWAMP
   CYPRESS
Chamaecyparis nootkatensis ALASKA CEDAR or
   NOOTKA CYPRESS
Prunus serrulata var. 'Pink Perfection' ORIENTAL
   FLOWERING CHERRY
Taxodium distichum BALD CYPRESS or SWAMP
   CYPRESS
Chamecyprus nootkatensis ALASKA CEDAR or
   NOOTKA CYPRESS

Prunus serrulata var. 'Pink Perfection' ORIENTAL
  FLOWERING CHERRY
Quercus macrocarpa BUR OAK
Thuya plicata 'Aurea' GOLDEN WESTERN
  ARBORVITAE
Quercus macrocarpa BUR OAK (A Manitoba
  native)
Chamaecyparis nootkatensis ALASKA CEDAR or
  NOOTKA FALSE CYPRESS
Prunus serrulata var. 'Pink Perfection' ORIENTAL
  FLOWERING CHERRY

54th Ave.:
Prunus serrulata var. 'Shirofugen' ORIENTAL
  FLOWERING CHERRY
Chamaecyparis nootkatensis ALASKA CEDAR or
  NOOTKA FALSE CYPRESS
Quercus macrocarpa BUR OAK
Chamaecyparis obtusa aurea GOLDEN HINOKI
  FALSE CYPRESS
Chamaecyparis nootkatensis ALASKA CEDAR or
  NOOTKA FALSE
CYPRESS
Prunus serrulata var. 'Shirofugen' ORIENTAL
  FLOWERING CHERRY
Chamaecyparis nootkatensis ALASKA CEDAR or
  NOOTKA FALSE CYPRESS
Thuya plicata 'Aurea' GOLDEN WESTER
  ARBORVITAE

57th Ave.:
Chamaecyparis nootkatensis ALASKA CEDAR or
  NOOTKA FALSE CYPRESS
Prunus serrulata var. 'Pink Perfection' ORIENTAL
  FLOWERING CHERRY

58th Ave.:
Quercus macrocarpa BUR OAK
Thuya plicata 'Aurea' GOLDEN WESTERN
  ARBORVITAE
Quercus macrocarpa BUR OAK

The Great Tree Hunt is a descriptive book with colour photographs of "trees of significance" as nominated by the citizens of Burnaby and compiled by the Burnaby Beautification Committee. Available at Burnaby City Hall for $6.

59th Ave.:

Prunus serrulata var. 'Pink Perfection' ORIENTAL FLOWERING CHERRY

Thuya plicata 'Aurea' GOLDEN WESTERN ARBORVITAE

Chamaecyparis nootkatensis ALASKA CEDAR or NOOTKA FALSE CYPRESS

60th Ave.:

Prunus serrulata 'Kwanzan' KWANZAN FLOWERING CHERRY

Chamaecyparis nootkatensis ALASKA CEDAR or NOOTKA FALSE CYPRESS

Prunus serrulata var. 'Pink Perfection' ORIENTAL FLOWERING CHERRY

61st Ave.:

Prunus serrulata var. 'Pink Perfection' ORIENTAL FLOWERING CHERRY

Chamaecyparis nootkatensis ALASKA CEDAR or NOOTKA FALSE CYPRESS

Prunus serrulata var. 'Pink Perfection' ORIENTAL FLOWERING CHERRY

62nd Ave.:

Prunus serrulata var. 'Pink Perfection' ORIENTAL FLOWERING CHERRY

Castanea sativa SWEET CHESTNUT

Chamaecyparis nootkatensis ALASKA CEDAR or NOOTKA FALSE CYPRESS

63rd Ave.:

Prunus serrulata var. 'Pink Perfection' ORIENTAL FLOWERING CHERRY

Chamaecyparis nootkatensis ALASKA CEDAR or NOOTKA FALSE CYPRESS

Thuya plicata 'Aurea' GOLDEN WESTERN ARBORVITAE

Sequoiadendron giganteum SIERRA REDWOOD or BIGTREE

64th Ave.:

Prunus serrulata var. 'Pink Perfection' ORIENTAL FLOWERING CHERRY

Chamaecyparis nootkatensis ALASKA CEDAR or
NOOTKA FALSE CYPRESS
Quercus macracarpa BUR OAK

65th Ave.:
Chamaecyparis nootkatensis ALASKA CEDAR or
NOOTKA FALSE CYPRESS
Prunus serrulata var. 'Pink Perfection' ORIENTAL
FLOWERING CHERRY

66th Ave.:
Prunus serrulata var. 'Pink Perfection' ORIENTAL
FLOWERING CHERRY
Chamaecyparis nootkatensis ALASKA CEDAR or
NOOTKA FALSE CYPRESS
Sophora Japonica PAGODA TREE (native to
China)

The Fraser Valley Heritage Tree Society and the City of Surrey have a poster of the heritage trees of the area ($5). Contact Surrey Parks and Recreation at: 501-5050.

Marine Dr.:
After the heritage designation, the Cambie Boulevard Heritage Society encouraged city council to plant more trees to carry on Bartholomew's vision. There are six zones identified along the median, and the plantings are done to stagger colour and shape along the seasons and to suit the context of these zones.

25th to 29th, residential, single family; both sides:
Juniperus communis COMMON JUNIPER
Thuya plicata 'Aurea' GOLDEN WESTERN
ARBORVITAE
Cornus nuttallii PACIFIC DOGWOOD

29th to 33rd, west side:
Acer campestre 'Queen Elizabeth' CAMPESTRE
MAPLE
Pyrus calleryana 'Chanticleer' CHANTICLEER
PEAR

33rd to 40th, both sides:
Platanus acerifolia 'Bloodgood' LONDON PLANE
TREE
Acer campestre 'Queen Elizabeth' CAMPESTRE
MAPLE
Cornus kousa 'Chinensis' KOUSA DOGWOOD

41st to 49th, west side:
Prunus serrulata 'Kwanzan' KWANZAN
   FLOWERING CHERRY
Fagus sylvatica 'Dawykii' DAWYCKI BEECH

41st to 49th, east side:
Prunus cerasifera 'Pissardii Nigra' PISSARDII
   NIGRA FLOWERING CHERRY PLUM
Fagus sylvatica 'Dawykii' DAWYCKI BEECH

49th to 57th, west side:
Carpinus betulas 'Fastigiata' HORNBEAM
Cornus kousa 'Chinensis' KOUSA DOGWOOD

57th to Marine Dr., both sides:
Acer rubrum 'Karpick' UPRIGHT RED MAPLE
Acer freemanii 'Scarlet Sentinell' FREEMAN'S
   MAPLE
Cornus kousa 'Chinensis' KOUSA DOGWOOD

GROWING FRUIT TREES IN GREATER VANCOUVER

by Derry Walsh

All sorts of fruit trees can be grown in south coastal BC — apples, pears, peaches, plums, cherries — but some are simply not worth the effort.

Cross-pollination is necessary for most fruits. This means you or your neighbour or someone in the same block must have a fruit tree of the same kind (plums for plums, apples for apples) which blooms at the same time and which has fertile pollen. Then you must have sunny, dry, warm weather when the blossoms are open, and the temperature must be warm (above 10°C for plums and above 14°C for apples)

Insects — especially bees — are essential for carrying the pollen from one tree to another during bloom time. Honeybee populations have declined drastically in the 1990s. Alternate pollinators include the Blue Orchard bee (BOB), a native solitary bee. Cardboard straws can be set out in the home garden to provide nesting sites for the BOB, ensuring she visits your fruit trees when collecting pollen. For more on BOB, check out this website: http://www.interchg.ubc.ca/wchase/HTML/

Some points to note about fruit trees in this area:

Cherries: There is no dwarfing rootstock available for cherry trees so all cherry trees are very big, take up most of a city lot and the birds get the fruit or the rain splits the fruit. Most cherry varieties require cross pollination. In many old neighbourhoods, there are huge old cherry trees, but the most they provide is shelter from the sun in summertime.

Peaches: These must be sheltered to prevent peach leaf curl and must be planted in the warmest, sunniest spot in your garden. Almost all are self-fertile, so cross-pollination is not necessary. One peach tree will do well in your yard so long as the weather is dry and sunny at bloom time and there are bees around.

Plums: There is a semi-dwarfing rootstock, St. Julien A, for plums. Most plum trees need cross-pollination. Only Japanese plums will cross-pollinate Japanese

"Microscopic purses, little beads,
Each holding in its patient dark a store
Of apples, flowering orchards, countless seeds.
—Vernon Scannell, from "Apple Poem"

plums, and only European plums will cross-pollinate European plums. Most Japanese varieties flower earlier than the European varieties and are more likely to be damaged by late frosts. Bees are needed to transport the pollen, but plum blossoms are low in nectar so bees will visit other garden flowers before visiting plum blossoms. Some plum varieties suffer from Black Knot, a disease where big lumps form on the branches, but if your yield is good, just cut out the lumps and burn them.

Pears: European pears are usually grafted on to pear seedling rootstock or quince, which has an interstem of Old Home or German Butter. Asian pears are grafted directly on to *Pyrus betulaefolia*. Cross-pollination is essential. European pears can be used to cross-pollinate Asian pears as long as they bloom at the same time and there are bees and insects present. Pears have a low sugar content in their nectar. Bees will often go elsewhere for nectar and this results in poor pollination.

Apples: Apple trees are the fruit trees of choice for south coastal BC. There is dwarfing rootstock (M9), really dwarfing rootstock (M27, P22) and semi-dwarfing rootstock (M26). The rootstock of choice for city property is M9; for the patio in a pot, the rootstock of choice is M27 or P22. Flavour, time of ripening and susceptibility to disease are the main things differentiating the apple varieties, so before selecting an apple tree you must taste lots of varieties and choose the best one for you. The best opportunity for tasting apples is at the UBC Apple Festival on the third weekend in October.

UBC Apple Festival, UBC Botanical Garden
6804 SW Marine Dr. • 822-9666
There are about 60 apple varieties for tasting, 40 apple varieties for buying and 40 varieties of dwarf apple trees for sale. Most of these are heritage varieties which grow well in south coastal BC. At the same event, the BC Fruit Testers Association (BCFTA) has more than 120 varieties of apples on display, including many crabapples and some other fruits (pears, quince, medlars). The BCFTA runs grafting and budding demonstrations, a bee display — including nests

of the Blue Orchard bee and bumblebees – a cider juicing demo and a discussion of juicing. Master Gardeners with a display of fruit diseases and insect damage will give advice on growing fruit trees and dealing with problems. There is no admission charge to the UBC Botanical Garden on the weekend of the Apple Festival.

While at the UBC Botanical Garden, visit the Food Garden, where there are many espaliered apple and pear trees including stepovers, single and multiple cordons, candelabra, goblets and Belgian fences. The UBC Botanical Garden often runs courses on "espaliering" in the spring and "summer pruning" in July.

Another place to view espaliered apple trees is the Strathcona Community Garden (no admission charge), between Prior and Malkin Streets, off Hawkes St., near Chinatown. There are oblique cordons and a Belgian fence with many varieties of apples including heritage varieties.

Maurice Lavoie at the UBC Botanical Garden Apple Fest.
Photo: UBC Botanical Garden

Local Orchards and Rootstock Suppliers

<u>ALDERGROVE:</u>

Annie's Orchard
4092-248 St. • 856-3041
owners: Jim & Mary Ann Rahe
e-mail: rahe@sfu.ca
40 varieties of apples, many scab-free. Open 9 a.m. to 6 p.m., Monday to Saturday, and Sunday from 2 p.m. to 6 p.m., early August to December.

Rootstock
contact: Derry Walsh • 856-9316
e-mail: wchase@interchange.ubc.ca
website: http://www.interchange.ubc.ca/wchase/
HTML

LANGLEY:

Dave's Orchard
5910-216 St. • 534-9979
e-mail: Dave_Ormrod@bc.sympatico.ca
40 varieties of apples, 6 varieties of pears. Open 9
a.m. to 9 p.m. daily from mid-July to mid-February.

Dwarf Fruit Trees (including custom grafting)
4549-220 St. • 530-8440
contact: Valle Lunzmann

Fruit Growers Association

BC Fruit Testers Association (BCFTA)
PO Box 48123, 3575 Douglas St.
Victoria, V8Z 7H5
e-mail: bcfta@islandnet.com
website: http://www.islandnet.com/~bcfta/
An association of amateur and professional fruit
growers. Lower Mainland Representative: Derry
Walsh, Aldergrove (call: 856-9316 or e-mail:
wchase@interchange.ubc.ca).

EDUCATION AND EVENTS

Confused about compost, stymied by soil or flummoxed by flowers? There are terrific educational resources for the home gardener in the Lower Mainland. Check the seasonal course catalogues from your local community centre, school board, community college and botanical garden, and ask at your local nursery. There is a huge range of non-certificate, fun and practical offerings where you can meet like-minded gardeners and learn a thing or two.

PROGRAMS IN HORTICULTURE

Certificate and Degree Programs

For those considering a career in the horticulture business, or for the serious hobbyists, here is information on the programs offered in the Lower Mainland. The programs are listed in alphabetical order.

BC HORTICULTURE CENTRE
Kwantlen University College
20901 Langley Bypass, Langley • 599-3254
The Centre offers several levels of training. Below is a basic description of the different programs.

Horticulture Citation Programs for Entry-Level Horticulture Workers
Program details: 15 credits; part-time classes only
Specializations:
1. Landscape Maintenance
2. Parks Arboriculture
3. Turfgrass
4. Greenhouse Production
5. Retail Horticulture
6. Landscape Design

Horticulture Certificate Program:
Program details: 30 credits; 10 months full study
Specializations:
1. Greenhouse Vegetable Production
2. Landscape Maintenance (introduced in fall 1999)

Horticulture Apprenticeship Program
Program details: four years of employment-based training; 24 weeks of technical training at Kwantlen University College
Specializations:
1. Landscape Horticulture
2. Production Horticulture

Horticulture Technology Program
Program details: 60 credits; 18 months of full-time study

Specializations:
1. Landscape Specialization
2. Garden Centre/Nursery Production
3. Greenhouse Production
4. Turf Management
5. General Horticulture Studies

Commercial Florist Program
Program details: 30 credits; eight months of full-time study
To train florists and flower-shop owners.

CAPILANO COLLEGE

2055 Purcell Way
North Vancouver • 984-4960; 984-4993 (fax)
Landscape Horticulture Program (one year)
Since 1978, the Landscape Horticulture Program at Capilano College has been training individuals in the prerequisite skills and knowledge required for a career in landscaping and landscape-related industries. Set in 34 acres of second-growth forest on the edge of the Seymour Watershed in North Vancouver, Capilano College offers a unique setting for the Landscape Horticulture Program. The program emphasizes classroom instruction while learning applications and practical skills. Students work in the greenhouse and nursery facility on campus as well as in ongoing work-experience co-operatives with the Park & Tilford Gardens in North Vancouver and West Vancouver Parks & Recreation.

Main study areas include: plant materials; growing media; plant nutrition; basic landscape design; landscape irrigation and drainage; turf management; greenhouse and nursery production; landscape installation and management; and pest control and management.

Classes run daily throughout the week from 8:30 a.m. to 4:30 p.m., September to April.

NORTH SHORE CONTINUING EDUCATION

Residential Landscape Design Certificate
Lucas Centre, 2132 Hamilton St., North Vancouver • 986-8888
This centre offers a professional certificate that com-

Why does Santa have a garden?
To hoe, hoe, hoe.

211

bines classroom and field instruction in the design of residential gardens in the Lower Mainland. Through lecture, practical assignments and field trips, the program exposes participants to the techniques and language used in the garden design industry. Developed for practitioners in the horticultural industry who are seeking professional development and for amateur gardeners who are considering a career in residential garden design.

Capilano College students do their practicums at Park and Tilford Gardens.

Successful completion, with demonstrated competency of all components in the program, with the exception of Business Fundamentals, is necessary to fulfill graduation requirements. Completion of the certificate can be accomplished at the participant's own pace.

Required courses for certificate program: Landscape Methods & Materials I; Landscape Methods & Materials II; Landscape Methods & Materials III; Residential Landscape I; Residential Landscape II; Residential Landscape III; Plant Identification & Design Workshops; Business Fundamentals.

General gardening courses are also offered through the North Shore Continuing Education Program.

THE UNIVERSITY OF BRITISH COLUMBIA CONTINUING STUDIES

Certificate in Garden Design

2075 Westbrook Mall, UBC Campus • 822-1450; fax: 822-1499

e-mail: gardendesign@cce.ubc.ca

The UBC Certificate in Garden Design offers comprehensive and innovative instruction in the design of residential gardens in the Pacific Northwest. Developed in co-operation with Vancouver garden designer Ron Rule to appeal to keen amateur gardeners and professionals alike, the program explores — in depth and in logical sequence — all of the stylistic forms and techniques of good garden design. Participants receive practical training in drafting, horticulture, construction and maintenance, along with an opportunity to apply this knowledge to the design of an actual case-study garden. The Certificate program is unique in that it is geared specifically to the making of smaller gardens; it is innovative because it is focused on exploring the design possibilities inherent in the Pacific Northwest region; it is unusual in that it has a diverse and dedicated faculty comprised of university instructors and distinguished regional experts practising in the field.

Who should apply? Horticultural practitioners and those in the nursery trades seeking professional development; landscapers who wish to provide more comprehensive and professional services to clients; keen amateur gardeners who want to make their own gardens more attractive and interesting, or are considering a career in landscape design.

Classes are held on the UBC campus, utilizing the space and facilities of the Landscape Architecture Program and the Botanical Garden. The Landscape Architecture Program building, situated on West Mall near the Botanical Garden, provides the main space for lectures and studio work.

The UBC Botanical Garden – renowned for its 70 acres planted with over 10,000 different trees, shrubs and flowers in a combination of natural and cultivated styles – is used as a laboratory to study plant combinations and the aesthetics of native planting.

Off-campus activities include visits to nurseries and suppliers, well-designed local residential gardens and the site of a designated case-study garden.

Program Requirements: The curriculum for the UBC Certificate in Garden Design encompasses a variety of courses related to garden design. These courses are referred to as certificate-credit courses to differentiate them from regular university credit and non-credit courses.

Certificate-credit courses are measured in hours of instruction. Participants must complete all six courses (up to 175 hours) to receive the certificate. Participants must complete all requirements for graduation within the prescribed six-month period. The courses are designed to be taken sequentially – each one utilizing and building upon the knowledge gained in earlier ones. All courses must be taken in the same year.

In New Westminster, Parks Horticulture Manager Claude LeDoux teaches an immensely popular hanging basket course in the spring. Not just for beginners or the more advanced, the course is open to all. Call Queens Park Arena at 524-9796. But hurry — classes fill up very quickly.

Want to learn more? Almost all of the gardening clubs have guest lecturers for most of their meetings. Here are some garden lectures about town:

The VanDusen Garden Show runs lectures continuously for the three days of the Garden Show which is always held during the first weekend in June.

The UBC Noon Lecture Series is held at UBC or in downtown Vancouver. Judy Newton and David Tarrant of the UBC Botanical Garden do a great number of garden talks on a variety of topics. Call the UBC Botanical Garden at 822-3928.

Ask at VanDusen Botanical Garden about the Cedar Series of Garden Lectures.

Enrollment in this program is limited to ensure appropriate class size for group learning and to achieve a balance between professional and hobby gardeners and landscapers. The fee is $4250 for the complete certificate program and may be paid in three installments.

VANCOUVER SCHOOL OF GARDEN DESIGN
Suite 200, 840 Howe St. • 687-1600
e-mail: info@vec.bc.ca
Classes are held at 609 West Hastings St., Vancouver. Call for information.

Certificate in Garden Design, Level One
Courses include:

Design 1, which includes 12 three-hour classroom sessions and three Saturday field trips. It offers an introduction to design theory including the history of garden design, principles and elements of design, the design process and the use of structures in garden design.

Drafting 1, which includes 12 three-hour classroom sessions and offers an introduction to Landscape Drafting including the use of instruments, materials, conventions and symbols, the lettering and labelling techniques, the preparation of the plan view and colour rendering.

Plant Material Studies 1, which includes 10 three-hour sessions and offers an introduction to hardy plants suitable for use in private garden schemes including botanical nomenclature and plant identification.

Successful completion of Level One is a prerequisite for entry into Level Two (professional level) of the program.

Certificate in Garden Design, Level Two
Courses include:

Design II: Practical application of design theory, including conceptual drawings, aesthetic expression, preparation of a detailed planting plan, study of theme gardens and specifications and standards.

Drafting II: Preparation of detail drawings, including cross-sections, elevations and axonometrics.

Plant Material Studies II: An in-depth study of various groups of hardy plants, with particular reference to their cultural requirements and design characteristics in evaluating them for use in private garden schemes.

Non-Certificate/Degree Programs

BURNABY:

Burnaby Adult & Continuing Education
Residential Landscape Technician Program
Burnaby Central School, 4939 Canada Way
• 664-8888
The Residential Landscape Technician Program provides participants with all the information required for employment as a residential landscaper, including business fundamentals. This part-time program is industry approved and developed in co-operation with the BC Landscape & Nursery Trades Association. It also prepares participants to write the Canadian Certified Landscape Technician and Provincial Trade Qualifications exam. This program will be of interest to: those considering a career in the landscape industry; those considering starting their own business in the landscape industry; and those currently in the industry who wish to update their knowledge and provide more comprehensive and professional services to clients.

Participants can complete this program on a part-time basis in two semesters (January-March/April-June). Coursework includes a combination of classroom and field experiences.

Mandeville Gardens
The Gardener's School
4746 SE Marine Dr. • 434-4111.
Various seasonal courses throughout the year.

VANCOUVER:

VanDusen Botanical Garden
5251 Oak St., VanDusen Education Department
Garden Course Co-ordinator: 257-8151
Master Gardener Program: 257-8672
Family/School Programs: 257-8669

In Abbotsford, check out the Lower Mainland Horticultural Improvement Association at 1767 Angus Campbell Rd. (556-3001).

Burnaby has an annual contest put on by the Burnaby Beautification Committee. The contest is advertised in local newspapers and applications are available at City Hall, the libraries, garden centres and community centres. Call Burnaby Parks and Recreation at 294-7450 for more information.

website: www.vandusen.org
The education department at VanDusen Botanical Garden is dedicated to increasing the awareness and appreciation of the Plant Kingdom through public education and training in botany, horticulture, ecology and related fields. Call for a current calendar of courses and special lectures or check their website.

OUTSIDE GVRD:

University College of the Fraser Valley
Ornamental Horticulture Production (OHP) Certificate
45635 Yale Rd., Chilliwack, V2P 6T4 • 792-0025
Graduates of the one-year OHP certificate program are qualified to seek work as assistants in greenhouse, nurseries, garden centres and landscaping companies or as grounds maintenance personnel. All fall courses are 15 weeks in length; winter semester courses are 12 weeks in length. Students then complete a required three-week practical lab course on campus. Applications are accepted throughout the year. Interested students must arrange an interview with the agriculture director (call: 795-2813) before admission to the program.

HORTICULTURAL THERAPY

Horticultural Therapy Around Here:

Sowing the Seeds of Health and Well-Being

by Shelagh Smith, horticultural therapist

Horticultural therapy is a process which assists people with special needs to access gardening and other plant-related activities. Professionally conducted programs are currently being run in several hospitals, correctional centres, schools and seniors' centres in the Lower Mainland. Horticultural Therapy is also offered in a number of centres for people with mental health issues, people with developmental and physical disabilities, and youth at risk. Program design varies according to the needs of the clientele and the site of the facility. Gardens can be designed to be accessible to everyone and tools can be adapted to bring gardening — a formerly impossible task for some people — within reach.

What is a gardener's motto?
A peony saved is a peony earned.

The quality of life in an institution can be greatly improved when horticulture is introduced. A large rooftop garden provides a haven of beauty and relaxation for the residents of Banfield Pavilion, the extended-care facility at the Vancouver General Hospital. Raised planter boxes allow the residents to access the plants from their wheelchairs. Weekly activities range from outdoor gardening to indoor crafts and flower arranging, starting seeds and bus tours to local gardens. The residents enjoy social interaction, mild physical exercise and, for many, the continuation of a lifelong interest. In addition, the garden and the horticultural therapy program make the hospital feel more like a home for the residents and their visitors.

Horticulture is a versatile pursuit that can be adapted to suit different levels of ability and a wide range of interests. Program goals are therapeutic, rehabilitative, social, vocational or a combination of these. Prison inmates are learning transferable floristry skills at the Burnaby Correctional Centre for Women. Marpole Place for Seniors has been revitalized with a garden created by and for community members of all

ages. In the downtown east side, the Environmental Youth Alliance teaches local young people how to grow food in the Cottonwood Community Gardens. The Coast Foundation drop-in centre offers adult mental-health clients the opportunity to contribute to their community by performing landscaping tasks. As this article is being written, therapeutic and rehabilitative gardens are being created at G.F. Strong Rehabilitation Centre and at St. Mary's Hospital in New Westminster. Research has shown that gardens in hospitals can shorten recovery time.

As a profession, horticultural therapy is relatively new in Canada, but is well established in the United States. Kansas State University runs a degree program in horticultural therapy and the American Horticultural Therapy Association provides an equivalency point program for anyone who wishes to become professionally registered.

Locally, the BC Chapter of the Canadian Horticultural Therapy Association started up in 1994 and offers a yearly conference and the opportunity to share information and resources. VanDusen Botanical Garden holds an introductory class and Langara College offers a series of three full-length courses.

Each of us has some sort of affinity for plants, whether through gardening, enjoying fresh cut flowers, cooking with herbs, walking in the forest or making crafts with plant materials. These activities can provide physical exercise, stimulate our senses and restore our spirits. Our problems can disappear for awhile as we become engrossed in the natural world. Horticultural therapy offers these opportunities to people who require a little assistance opening the garden gate.

Horticultural Therapy Projects:

BURNABY:
Burnaby Women's Correctional Centre (BWCC)
"Beginnings" Florist Shop
7900 Fraser Park Dr. • 436-6020, local 173; 660-9724 (fax)
contact: June Strandberg
Three times a year, this program trains residents to

be florists. After the initial training, residents work in the flower shop. For those who wish to go on in the profession, there is a high job placement rate after residents leave BWCC. In fact, the job placement program has to do very little footwork — florists most often call them. The program has been in business for eight years. Weddings are the program's mainstay and they operate by word of mouth. They have a very pretty flower shop in the heart of the prison. Clients have to make an appointment and come through eight locked doors to see the flowers, but the shop has built a solid list of regular customers and business customers.

What do gardeners like to read? *Weeder's Digest.*

NORTH VANCOUVER:

Kiwanis Lodge

Mount Seymour Pkwy. • 924-8300

Kiwanis Lodge is a long-term care facility where Barb Tocher and three other master gardeners work with residents. Tocher feels that the main purpose is to get the residents involved in the soil and to have them participate in other activities such as making cuttings and seed propagation. The residents also participate in crafts that are related to the gardens, such as dried-flower arranging, potpourri and paper making with dried flowers.

The residents work with the master gardeners all the way through the life of the garden, from planting the garden in spring through putting it to bed in the fall. Half barrels on the outside deck make it easier for those in wheelchairs to work and there's a greenhouse with a long table that the wheelchairs fit under. Those residents who are more active can plant bulbs in pots outside and water the plants. The residents get a great deal of pleasure when the tomato plants they've cared for ripen and they can go out, pick and eat them. Most of the residents involved in the garden previously had gardens of their own and they really enjoy getting back to it. Last year the City of North Vancouver donated dozens of hyacinths and bulbs to put in the garden and such donations make the garden even more beautiful and rewarding for the residents.

The Coast Foundation Society
Horticulture Therapy Program
293 East 111 Ave. • 488-0035

Wolf Schmitz uses hort therapy with mental health consumers at a downtown drop-in centre run by the Coast Foundation Society. The program was started three years ago and operates on two levels:

1) Through three of the society's downtown affordable-housing organizations, Schmitz runs classes on a volunteer basis. Residents started a community garden at one of the homes. There are weekly classes to discuss gardening techniques;

2) Schmitz runs a landscape work program where mental health consumers do landscape maintenance for community homes in the Coast organization. They do landscape maintenance, cut grass, weed and plant flowers. Some of the workers have advanced enough to go to the sites on their own. They get paid eight dollars an hour to do the work.

Marpole Intergenerational Garden Project
1305 West 70th Ave. • 266-5301
contact: Eduardo Ottoni

This project involves children from the David Lloyd George Elementary and seniors from Marpole Place. The groups got together to discuss how they could strengthen their sense of community and from these discussions came the plan to build an intergenerational garden on the grounds of Marpole Place. Through weekly workshops facilitated by two members of BC Environment's Eco-Education Program, seniors and children developed relationships and planned for the garden. With the help of two community work parties the construction got under way, and with the added help of the

Marpole-Oakridge Family Place and the Spare Time children's day camp, the garden grew to its potential.

This project began in the spring of 1997 and already hosts many community groups including pre-schoolers, elementary and high school students, the Developmental Disabilities Association and the Elizabeth Fry Society. Keys to the garden's success have been its ability to transcend age barriers and its accessible garden beds, pathways, sitting benches and tables. For those who envisioned the garden as a place to strengthen community ties, it has been a great success.

What is a gardener's favourite game?
Mow 'n Tell.

Yaletown House

Foundation Office, 1099 Cambie St.
contact: Lynn Parkin, foundation co-ordinator
• 689-0022, ext 308.

What's a farmer's favourite game?
Hoe 'n Tell.

Yaletown House is a residence for 130 people who need intermediate care. The house has two gardening programs. The second, third and fourth floor overlook a courtyard and greenhouse with a fountain. There are raised flower beds so those who can't bend over can garden with ease. There are also kneeling pads and other adaptive aids for clipping and pulling weeds. The garden has been in place since Yaletown opened in 1986 — it was something that the architect fought tooth and nail to have included in the house plans. Apparently many people felt that gardens would be wasted on those who were so near the end of their lives. The programs that have developed around the gardens have gone on to prove its naysayers wrong and have provided all those involved with Yaletown house with many years of pleasure. There are volunteer possibilities and donations are welcomed. Donations and inquiries can be made through the foundation co-ordinator at the number above.

Training and Education in Horticulture Therapy

VANCOUVER:

Canadian Horticulture Therapy Association
BC Chapter
101-1001 West Broadway
Fees: $15.00 per student; $20.00 per individual (non-student); $50.00 per organization.

Langara College
Program Planning for Horticultural Therapy
100 West 49th Ave. • 323-5322
The course takes place over eight Saturdays from 9 a.m. to 4 p.m. Learn how to access goals and objectives, client's needs, interests, current skills and the capacity of a facility to support horticultural activities.

VOLUNTEERING

Places to Volunteer

DELTA:
Delta Farmland & Wildlife Trust
203-4882 Delta St. • 940-3392
e-mail: dfwt@axionet.ca
The trust helps to promote farmland stewardship programs.

PORT MOODY:
Riverview Horticultural Centre Society
8-2929 St. John's St. • 290-9910
Formed to preserve and protect the lands and trees of the Riverview Hospital site as a community oriented, financially viable centre for horticultural, educational and therapeutic activities. Activities include: administrative duties; lobby to save lands; Fall Tree Fest; fundraising events; public presentations; hosting tours; production of graphics; work on committees; table/booth displays; horticultural education; research into plant history; plant information.

VANCOUVER:
The Arthur Erickson House & Garden Foundation
709-700 West Pender St. • 444-6894
Volunteer activities include helping with preservation of the garden as a public heritage site and becoming a tour guide.

City Farmer
Canada's Office of Urban Agriculture
2150 Maple St. • 736-2250
801-318 Homer St. • 685-5832
The first address is for the teaching garden; the second is the office address. Volunteer activities include: help with public education programs in composting, organic gardening and water conservation; the promotion of urban food gardening; setting up community and school gardens and rooftop gardens.
e-mail: cityfarm@unixg.ubc.ca
website: www.cityfarmer.org (this is the most popular website for urban agriculture in the world)

One: I make pressed flowers for a living.
The Other: Is it fun?
One: No. It's cut and dried.

Dr. Sun Yat-Sen Garden
578 Carrall St. • 662-3207
Activities include helping with a variety of tasks, from guiding, garden maintenance, office work, admissions, shop clerks, docents and/or special events.

Friends of the Garden (FOGS)
UBC Botanical Garden
6804 SW Marine Dr. • 822-3928
Interviews for volunteers are conducted in November and December. Write for application. Volunteers help run "Shop in the Garden," guide tours, collect seeds, grow plants for the Mothers Day plant sale, answer hot-line questions, work in the herbarium and present the "Apple Festival" each October.

Vancouver General Hospital Horticultural Therapy Program
Banfield Pavilion, 855 West 12th Ave. • 875-4189
Volunteers welcome on Wednesdays. Activities include assisting with therapy programs in hospital and garden maintenance.

VanDusen Botanical Garden
5251 Oak St. • 257-8674
Orientations are held bi-monthly throughout the year. Volunteer opportunities fall into three categories: education (e.g. school program leaders, garden guides or master gardeners) and plant information line (257-8662); special events and fundraising (e.g. annual plant sale, flower and garden show, Festival of Lights); general garden assistance (e.g. seed collecting, propagating, garden shop, library, etc.). The garden also sponsors a Horticultural Therapy Program.

OUTSIDE GVRD:
Naturescape British Columbia
P.O. Box 9354, Stn Prov. Govt.
Victoria, V8W 9M1 • 387-9853
toll-free: 1-800-387-9853
This organization welcomes volunteers to do slide programs and community outreach. Call or write for more information. Membership required for volunteers. Fee is $20 (includes three booklets).

Volunteering at Friends of the Garden Society

by Rachel Mackenzie and Mary Allen, FOGS

A small group of eight gathered round a crackling fire in a gracious room overlooking the Pacific Ocean. The date was February 24, 1976. The location: the UBC Botanical Garden office, which at that time was located in the Norman Mackenzie House (now the home of the UBC president). The group included Dr. Roy Taylor, Director of the Garden, David Tarrant, Educational Co-ordinator, and six people who had responded to a notice in the UBC *Alumni Bulletin* asking that "anyone interested in forming a support group of the Botanical Garden please come to a meeting." Thus the Friends of the Garden Society (FOGS) was born.

The aims of this new group were twofold: to act as a liaison between the Botanical Garden and the community, and to provide an educational experience for the members. The original aim of being ambassadors for the garden continues today. Public awareness of the garden has been carried out in ever expanding ways — through plant sales (indoor and perennial), public education (special lecture series and

Doreen Ingram, Beverly Merryfield and Liz Litherland, the book buyers with FOGS at the UBC Botanical Garden Shop.
Photo: Dannie McArthur

guiding) and art shows ("Two Hundred Years of Botanical Art" and "Cloud flowers"). Since the beginning, the weekly meetings have been an important element of the FOGS program. Each Wednesday from September to June, we meet for a lecture or discussion. As well as being educational, these meetings provide a forum for the exchange of ideas. No matter what one's particular area of interest, everyone keeps in touch so that FOGS can function as a whole. Originally, the structure of FOGS was quite relaxed. We

A prisoner in jail receives a letter from his wife:

"Dear Husband: I have decided to plant some lettuce in the back garden. When is the best time to plant them?"

The prisoner, knowing that the prison guards read all mail, replies in his letter:

"Dear Wife: Whatever you do, do not touch the back garden. That is where I hid all the money."

A week or so later, the prisoner receives another letter from his wife:

"Dear Husband: You wouldn't believe what happened! Some men came with shovels to the house, and dug up all the back garden."

The prisoner writes back:

"Dear Wife: Now is the best time to plant the lettuce!"

took turns being monthly co-ordinator, which meant chairing meetings, writing the "diary" and, with the staff, planning our Education workshops. The chair was always available when National and International meetings were hosted by the Botanical Garden. At the same time, we were busy students learning about all areas of the garden, writing garden guides and researching the plantings of the Physick Garden.

In 1986, we wrote bylaws and the group became more structured. The bylaws gave us a simple, workable and flexible set of rules with which to govern ourselves. They continue today. As our guidelines changed, so did our aims. During the recession in the 1980s, fundraising became a necessity. Greater emphasis was placed on the "bottom line" of the early projects such as the Special Lecture Series and Student Plant Sale. Our longed-for Shop in the Garden became a reality in 1986, just in time for Expo. Now open seven days a week, it provides excellent public relations for the garden. Recently, an enlarged Plant Centre was built adjacent to the shop and has proved to be a busy and popular place. 1991 saw the first annual Perennial Plant Sale. In 1992, due to a generous donation by David Lam and an anonymous donor in Victoria, the David Lam Centre was built in the Asian Garden at 16th Avenue and SW Marine Drive. For the first time in its history, the garden, the garden and office staff and FOGS were together in one place. Offices, a reception centre and the shop provide a delightful entrance to the Botanical Garden. The recession, with its inevitable staff cutbacks, provided more opportunities for FOGS. The "hortline" is answered by FOGS volunteers twelve months of the year and "Weeding Days" in the Garden are an annual part of the spring program. We've staged art shows, special lectures, plant sales and more recently our fall Apple Festival. In addition, volunteers from FOGS act as guides in the Nitobe and Main Gardens, collect and package seeds, photograph the garden, help with the Botanical Garden courses, mount herbarium specimens, make plant labels, work the "Back 40" area, harvest the produce from the Food Garden (which is then sent to a needy cause), catalogue the books in the Botanical Garden library, operate the Shop in the Garden and conduct research in the garden (i.e., the Magnolia Study). Those with computer skills produce posters and signs for the shop. The FOGS activities and plant lists for sales are also computerized.

The FOGS have enjoyed day trips to Dease Island Park and Honeymoon Bay on Vancouver Island, and longer trips to California to visit the Strybing Arboretum and the Los Angeles State and Country Arboretum. Members of FOGS also made a trip to the Eastern United States, visiting the Brooklyn Botanic Gardens, Longwood Gardens and Winterthur. At each garden, ideas were exchanged with other volunteers. These were great sharing sessions and FOGS returned realizing how privileged its members were to be part of the garden at UBC. We are able to create new projects as needed by the garden and enjoy a very co-operative relationship with the staff in the office and the garden, who are always available to answer questions and give excellent advice. Each FOG has a personal involvement with the garden and has the satisfaction of seeing it grow.

Today, both the garden and FOGS continue to evolve. There is a twelve-week training course each year for 20 new FOGS and this provides a continuous source of new talent and new ideas. Where will we be 20 years from now? Still, we hope, giving of ourselves as well as enjoying ourselves helping this wonderful garden grow!

The *Surrey Leader* newspaper sponsors a gardening competition called "Surrey's Greatest Gardens."

GARDEN TOURS

How To Arrange a Private Garden Tour

by Terri Clark

White Rock and Surrey Garden Tour is put on by the University Women's Club. Check local papers and garden centres for information.

About a dozen years ago I made a visit to Victoria where the Conservatory of Music sponsored a private garden tour in aid of their organization. Though the tour was wonderful, the garden attendants were less than informed on the delicacies of each garden – but then, as they were all music afficianados, this was to be expected. And Victoria's effort became the inspiration for an event I helped introduce to Vancouver the following year: the annual VanDusen Private Garden Tour.

It is now over a decade since we arranged the first Private Garden Tour and in that time we have also assisted well over a dozen other organizations to do the very same thing in cities and towns as diverse as Prince Rupert, Montreal, Vancouver's east side and Bowen Island – to name just a few. What better way to have a wonderful time while earning substantial funds for your local botanical garden or other charity?

A private garden tour is *not* hard to organize. Here's how to do it:

1. Seek out interesting gardens whose owners would be willing to share their knowledge and space over a one- or two-day period during specific hours.
2. Choose an interesting time of year. The end of May to the middle of June is best for flower gardens; late summer is good for vegetable gardens. Many people have tried to convince me to arrange an early spring or late fall tour but until more gardens are available with a substantial breadth of choice, I'll stick to the glory of that special month between mid-May and mid-June. The gardens can share a theme or be a good mixture of themes.
3. Mail out a notice of the tour or advertise at least two months in advance, and include the cost, times and details of the tour in your ad.

4. Ask participants to mail back a cheque with a self-addressed stamped envelope in which their tickets, and directions to the gardens, will be mailed back.

5. Drop off flower signs (on stakes) the week before the tour to open gardens. Owners can put out their signs each morning, thereby making it easier for tour-goers to find out where they should go.

6. Show appreciation for all the gardeners who have so graciously opened their private spaces. Invite them to a "Champagne and Dessert Party" later in the summer. This is an opportunity to officially thank the gardeners and give them a chance to meet all the other gardeners on that year's tour. (Remember not to scrimp financially on this part of the job. The party is fun and the gardeners deserve a wonderful time for having made your event a success. Give them free tickets to next year's tour as an added thank-you.)

West Coast Garden Friends arranges special interest garden tours and seminars for groups. Call Pat Kramer at 463-0890.

Arranging a successful private garden tour is easy if you remember this: If you love to garden, you probably love to share your discoveries and results with people who appreciate beautiful or inspirational landscapes. The size of the garden never matters; weather never matters. All that really counts is that those who open their gardens are fully appreciated and that those who visit are grateful, polite and inspired by what they see. Can a private garden tour really make money? The VanDusen Private Garden Tour has raised nearly $100,000 in its 12 years.

What about a very private Private Garden Tour, you ask? Just last spring, four dear friends and I picked a day in which we visited each of our gardens and it was really a lot of fun. We started at 8:30 a.m. at my house, for an English Breakfast and then a jaunt around the property. Next we went to our friend Lolita's, where we sat under her shady tree while sipping rich coffee and home-made biscotti. Then it was on to Deborah's, where we had a lovely luncheon salad and lemonade; and then to Dagmar's for a fresh fruit plate with goblets of chilled white wine. Plants

Another garden tour: Eastside Private Garden Tour of "eclectic and creative gardens." This is a fundraiser for Mosaic Creek Park and is usually held on Father's Day Sunday. Call 254-4212 for information.

were exchanged, horticultural secrets uncovered, advice given, notes taken – and there were smiles all around. It was so much fun we plan to do it next year and start at my friend Donna's garden which, though far afield, offers us the perfect environment in which to peruse her divine annuals, grown from seed.

In the end, any private garden tour is about giving and taking, appreciating' and saying out loud what we love about nature's exuberance in entrancing us from one season to another, over and over again.

To find. out about the VanDusen Private Garden Tour, check your spring "VanDusen Botanical Garden Bulletin" or call VanDusen Botanical Garden at 878- 9274.

Annual Private Garden Tours

BOWEN ISLAND:
Bowen Island People, Places and Plants
Snug Cove, Bowen Island
contact: *Undercurrent Newspaper* • 947-2442
Tour generally takes place biannually in the second weekend in July.

BURNABY:
Burnaby Private Gardens Tour
Burnaby Parks and Recreation • 294-7128
The tour is conducted by the Burnaby Beautification Committee. Call for information.

NORTH VANCOUVER:
North Shore Private Garden Tour
contact: *North Shore News* or call the parks departments of any of the municipalities:
City of North Vancouver: 985-7761
District of West Vancouver: 925-7000
District of North Vancouver: 987-7131
This tour is conducted by the North Shore Contest Society. Each year they tour gardens of the previous year's winners.

GARDEN SHOWS AND ANNUAL EVENTS

The Joy of a Good Plant Sale

by Steve McQueen, 1999 VanDusen Garden Plant Sale chair

For me, a black plastic gallon pot offering a stem or two, a few green leaves and maybe a bud beats chocolate-covered ginger, hands down! Multiply this scene by a hundredfold, add a large group of people, some sunshine and a mug of coffee — it must be heaven or a good plant sale.

Beginning in September, plans start at VanDusen for the Annual Plant Sale, always held the last Sunday in April (rain or shine). My first job was guarding the washrooms by the Floral Hall. It was pouring rain that year and volunteers were hanging the dollar bills (this was before the loonie) on clotheslines to dry. I wasn't to let any stray shoppers near the classroom door, either — inside, soggy cheques were being blotted to keep the signatures from running!

For the next four years I worked in "Services"— said to be another easy job — just ordering tables and chairs to go with the different plant categories. My work crew, lent to me each year by the courts, consisted of several interesting — though not necessarily interested — characters, most of whom probably only knew grass of another ilk! They would drift in and follow me about all day, lugging signs, tables, ladders, hammers, etc. I remember one particularly tough-looking character with his cigarettes rolled in his shirt sleeve, which covered a tattoo. He ended up buying a Fuschia basket for his mother at the end of the day — he was thrilled and so was I. My crew was known as "Steve's Bad Boys." By the end of the weekend most of my boys had endeared themselves to the other hard-working volunteers, digging in and helping where help was needed.

Steve McQueen getting ready for the annual plant sale at VanDusen Botanical Garden.
Photo: VanDusen Botanical Garden

For Garden Getaways throughout the Pacific Northwest, call Cindy Coombs at 206-285-1145. The trips include stays at bed and breakfasts, educational seminars and hands-on practice. Check out the website at:

www.gardeninggetaways.com

Setting up the actual plant sale site on the great lawn begins three days before the sale. The garden becomes a hubbub of trucks, tables, people and plants. Hundreds of registered volunteers appear, eager to participate and do their stuff in one of the 12 plant categories. Latin is the language of the day, and although it comes a little easier now, I still stare blank-eyed through many conversations, just nodding a lot. Of course the weather is the main topic of conversation — and we are all prepared to take what comes.

Sale day arrives and excitement mounts as the word "line-up" is murmured over the hill. Line-ups at a plant sale should, I think, be looked on as miniature gardening courses. No one is there to buy books or shoes. We're all there for one thing only — *plants* — and what a great time to exchange tips and information. I wonder how many people buy a plant they have only just heard about in the line-up?

It's finally time, and we watch as the flood of eager shoppers rushes down the path armed with wheelbarrows, boxes, shopping carts, babies in buggies, reluctant spouses, wagons and wishes. (My favourite customer was a man on his bicycle who left happily with several plants of various sizes stuffed in his knapsack.) And the crowd keeps coming — and coming — and coming! Devoted shoppers know exactly what they're after, and within minutes Plant Hold is busy checking plants like coats — shoppers choose and check, choose and check. Questions like "Where did you find that?" and "What is that?" and "Last year I found such-and-such. Do you have more this year?" are heard as folks rush to fulfill another green dream.

How, when, where and what are the key questions of the day, and smiles are the expression of choice. Laden with trees, shrubs, vines and plants of every description, gardeners stagger from the sale, happy, tired, maybe a bit damp, only to face the biggest challenge of all — how to fit everything into a garden already full. But there's always a way ... because there's always another plant sale!

A SEASONAL CALENDAR

On any given weekend from April through September you can find dozens of plant sales and gardening events in the Lower Mainland. To find out more, check Saturday's *Vancouver Sun*, Sunday's *Vancouver Province* or your local community paper. We have listed the annual gardening events that take place at the same time each year. Remember, most of the gardening clubs have annual sales throughout the year too. For more information on the clubs see Chapter 3 or log on to: http://www.hedgerows.com/Canada/Information/Calendar

Here is a list of events, arranged within each month in roughly chronological order.

JANUARY
Stay home, read mail order catalogues (see Chapter 2) and dream about spring.

FEBRUARY
Northwest Flower and Garden Show
Washington State Convention Centre
1515 NW 51st St. Seattle, WA • 206-789-5333

BC Home and Garden Show
Southex Exhibitions
BC Place Stadium • 433-5121
website: www.southex.com

VanDusen Seedy Saturday (seed sale)
5251 Oak St., Vancouver • 878-9274
Takes place during the last Saturday of February.

MARCH
Spring Garden Forum
VanDusen Botanical Garden
5251 Oak St. • 878-9274
Public education presented by the VanDusen Guides. Usually held the first Saturday of March.

Nomination forms for Coquitlam's community beautification awards program are available in April at local nurseries and most municipal buildings. Judging happens in the last week of July. Call 933-6224 for more information.

Fraser Valley Home & Garden Show
Southex Exhibitions
Tradex: Fraser Valley Trade and Convention Centre, Abbotsford • 412-2288
website: www.southex.com

VanDusen Garden Annual Manure Sale
5251 Oak St., Vancouver • 878- 9274

Celebration of Native Plants and Sale
UBC Botanical Garden
6804 Southwest Marine Dr., Vancouver • 822-9666
Generally takes place the last weekend in March.

APRIL

Bradner Spring Flower Show (Daffodil City)
Bradner Hall, 530 Bradner St. • 856-8441
Takes place in the second weekend of April.

Granville Island Market Farm Truck Sales
1669 Johnston St., Vancouver • 666-6477
Runs from middle of April to end of October. In-season bedding plants and perennials available. Inside the market there are seasonal plants too.

Bowen Island Garden Club Plant Sale
Snug Cove, Bowen Island
contact: *Undercurrent Newspaper* • 947-2442
Takes place during the last Saturday in April at the Old General Store.

VanDusen Plant Sale
5251 Oak St., Vancouver • 878-9274
Takes place during the last Sunday of April.

MAY

St. George's School Fair
4175 or 3851 West 29th (alternates between junior and senior schools), Vancouver • 224-1304
Takes place during the first Saturday in May. Includes a couple of booths selling plants.

East Vancouver Farmer's Market
Trout Lake parking lot at 15th St. and Victoria St.,

Vancouver • 879-FARM (3276)
Takes place Saturday mornings mid-May through Thanksgiving.

The Douglas Park Plant Sale
801 West 22nd St., Vancouver • 879-7954
Always held on the weekend between VanDusen's Plant sale and Mother's Day.

New Westminster Horticultural Society Plant Sale
Royal City Centre, McBride and 8th St., New Westminster
Held on the weekend before Mother's Day.

South Surrey Garden Club
St. Mark's Anglican Church
12953 20th Ave., Surrey
Held on the Saturday before Mother's Day.

Richmond Garden Club Plant Sale
Broadmoor Shopping Mall, No. 3 Rd. and Williams St.
Held on the Friday and Saturday of Mother's Day weekend.

Beach Grove Plant Sale
1547 Enderby Ave., Beach Grove, Tsawwassen
contact: Donna Guillemin
Unusual annuals and climbers including blue Morning Glories as well as many blue flowers such as *Heliophila longifolia*. Edible, fragrant and cutting flowers. Some hardy geraniums. Always held the Saturday of the Mother's Day Weekend, from 10 a.m. to 3 p.m.

UBC Botanical Garden Perennial Sale
6804 SW Marine Dr.
Vancouver • 822-9666
Held on Mother's Day.

A satisfied customer at the UBC Perennial Plant Sale.
Photo: UBC

The weekend of Mother's Day is one of the busiest for plant sales and displays throughout the Lower Mainland. Check the club listings for individual club sales, or log on to http://www.hedgerows.com/Canada/Information/Calendar, or watch local community papers for listings of events.

The Glades Tour and Tea (annual fundraiser for Peace Arch Hospital)
561-172nd St., Surrey • 538-0928
Held on Mother's Day. Open to the public one day a year.

South Burnaby Garden Club
Maverick Sports Bar parking lot, Kingsway at Sperling
Held on Mother's Day.

Vancouver Rhododendron Society Sale
VanDusen Botanical Garden
5251 Oak St., Vancouver • 878-9274
Held on Mother's Day.

Simon Fraser University Plant Sale
Between Strand Hall and East Parking Lot, SFU • 291-4636
website: www.sfu.ca
Held on the Wednesday of the week before the May long weekend. For information, check campus paper and events listing on the SFU website. Rainforest Gardens in Maple Ridge is very involved with this sale, and half of one of their September Sunday's revenues go to the SFU Student Bursary fund.

PoCo Garden Club
Poco Recreation Centre
2150 Wilson Ave., Port Coquitlam
Held the Saturday after the Victoria Day long weekend.

Mayfair Perennial Society Plant Sale and Fair
3776 West 28th Ave. (Immaculate Conception School)
Held the last Saturday in May. Proceeds fund grassroots projects in a village in India.

JUNE

Coquitlam Farmer's Market
Coquitlam Recreation Centre on Poirier St. • 461-5387
Held Sunday mornings June through Thanksgiving.

Dr. Sun Yat-Sen Gardens
578 Carrall St., Vancouver • 662-3207
Midsummer's Eve celebration.

VanDusen Flower and Garden Show
5251 Oak St., Vancouver • 878-9274
Held the first weekend in June.

Fraser Pacific Rose Society Annual Show
Dogwood Pavillion, 624 Poirier St., Coquitlam
Held the last weekend of June.

JULY
Dr. Sun Yat-Sen Gardens, Enchanted Evening Series
578 Carrall St., Vancouver • 662-3207
Held Friday nights through September. Chinese music program and garden stroll.

Brock House Plant Sale
3875 Point Grey Rd., Vancouver
Held the second Saturday in July.

AUGUST
Richmond Garden Club Annual Two Day Horticultural Show
Minoru Arena, 7551 Minoru Gate • 277-8663
Usually the first weekend of August.

SEPTEMBER
Vancouver Dahlia Society
VanDusen Botanical Garden
5251 Oak St., Vancouver • 878- 9274
Held Saturday and Sunday of
the Labour Day weekend.

**UBC Botanical Garden
Indoor Plant Sale**
6804 SW Marine Dr.
Usually held one week after
the UBC term starts. Watch
for signs and ads.

The volunteers who run the Perennial Sale at UBC Botanical Garden every Mother's Day look forward to the annual arrival of a limousine full of gardening gal pals from Nanaimo. The Nanaimo contingent are always in good cheer and ready to seek out a bargain.

Lia Indla at the UBC Botanical Garden Perennial Plant Sale.
Photo: UBC Botanical Garden

VanDusen Art Show & Sale
5251 Oak St., Vancouver • 878-9274

Tree-mendous Compost Sale
Parking lot, VanDusen Botanical Garden, 5251 Oak St., Vancouver • 878-9274
Held during the last Saturday of September.

VanDusen Tree Fest (to celebrate arbor month)
5251 Oak St., Vancouver • 878-9274

Riverview Horticulture Centre Society
500 Lougheed Hwy. (Riverview Hospital), Coquitlam • 524-7120
Fall tree tours during September and October.

OCTOBER

VanDusen Autumn Colour Day
5251 Oak St., Vancouver • 878-9274

UBC Botanical Garden Apple Fest
6804 SW Marine Dr., Vancouver • 822-9666
Held the weekend after Thanksgiving.

NOVEMBER

VanDusen Artisans Crafts Christmas Market
5251 Oak St., Vancouver • 739-9002

DECEMBER

UBC Botanical Garden Spectacular Wreath Sale
6804 SW Marine Dr., Vancouver • 822-9668
Held throughout December. Wreaths are made by volunteers with material from the gardens.

VanDusen Festival of Lights
5251 Oak St., Vancouver • 878-9274

Park & Tilford Gardens: Christmas Light Display
440-333 Brooksbank Ave., North Vancouver • 984-8200

Fantasy Garden World Christmas Light Display
10800 No. 5 Rd., Richmond • 277-7777

KIDS AND GARDENS

To wildly paraphrase an old saying: Give a child a vegetable and that child will eat for a day. Teach a child to grow vegetables and flowers and he or she will eat for life (and be delighted too). We started collecting information on children and gardening in Vancouver and realized that we had a whole chapter. We're delighted and we hope that with more gardening awareness and education, this section will grow in future editions of *Garden City: Vancouver*. Let us know if you have any tips.

A special issue of *Green Teacher* (April/May, 1994) focused on "The Promise of Gardening" in schools. It includes articles on "Children and Gardens in Japan" and "Multicultural Gardens." Contact *Green Teacher*, 95 Robert St., Toronto, ON, M5S 2K5. Phone: (416) 960-1244

GARDENING WITH KIDS

Ready, Set, Grow!

by Joette Heuft, Master Gardener

Every parent dreams of working side by side with their attentive happy children, sharing a mutually rewarding activity. Yet, as every occasionally harassed parent will admit, effective teaching and parenting techniques provide practical support to good intentions. Here are some parenting concepts and tools, adapted for the garden, which can help you enjoy gardening together, provide an educational, fun, healthy and lifelong activity for your child, and make an environmentally sustainable contribution to your neighbourhood.

Children, especially young ones, love nothing better than your time. Your enthusiasm for gardening, and your willingness to share your knowledge and to offer them a role in the garden, is a good starting point. Engage them by capitalizing on the special characteristics of the young — their abundant energy, curiosity, idealism and playfulness. Some of that energy can be burned off doing chores, especially if you call those chores by another name. While you may not want all that high energy tromping about in your spring perennial beds, children can dig manure or compost into the vegetable bed. They can also clean pots and assist in preparing potting mixes for growing seeds indoors or for containers.

Throughout the summer and fall, children can harvest food and flowers for the dinner table. A kitchen garden containing lettuce, parsley, chives, basil and cherry tomatoes, and located close to the house or in containers on an attached deck, makes it easy for the child to contribute regularly to meals shared by the family. The removal of mature flowers ("dead-heading") — a necessary task to prolong the blooming period and to defer seed-setting — is another task which can be assumed by children. The spent blossoms, although often not "perfect" enough for dried flower arrangements, are fine for making potpourri, which not only smell wonderful but are visually beautiful as well. Peonies, roses, *calendula*, cornflowers, *alchemilla mollis*, baby's breath, lemon balm, mints, lavender and many other flowers and leaves can be air-dried successfully simply by hanging them upside down (where there is good air circulation) and away from direct light. Books containing potpourri recipes are readily available in libraries and bookstores.

Finally, kids can be taught to do early morning or evening bug patrol (and many kids rise to the task). This can be an educational project for both of you — an opportunity to research the life cycles of bugs, to identify those bugs which are unwanted in the garden as opposed to those which either pollinate plants or prey upon or parasitize insects which are harmful in the garden. Together you can learn to recognize the eggs and larvae of the ones to leave alone and the ones to dispose of. In the battle against bugs, four hands (even little ones) are better than two!

Kids are people too; they differ individually but share common human attitudes and aesthetics. Therefore, some children will love getting dirty, others will hate it; some will be fascinated by the insect world, others horrified. However, just like us, most children will respond to working with their hands, to the feel and smell of sun-warmed soil and to the satisfaction of seeing and sharing the results of their efforts — not the least of which is popping something they've grown into their mouths! Children also experience pride of ownership and respond to the challenge of caring for their own garden area, plants and containers. I know of a family where a grandparent gave each child, at birth, a tree of their own — a life partner to grow up with.

Your attitudes and an ecological education will help children in overcoming fears and reservations. Children need to feel that it's okay to get dirty but, for their comfort and safety, they should also have gardening gloves, slush pants, shoes and a few tools. I believe kids should be encouraged to always wear gloves in the garden. Clean-up is less tedious and they will be protected from cuts, stings and allergic reactions. Gloves will only be worn, though,

Many simple picture books (some quite old) on growing various food plants can be found in the children's section of public libraries. There are also books and photos available on school garden programs from the turn of the century.

Sea Spray is a local company harvesting and producing organic kelp fertilizer. They believe in environmental education and have started something called the "Growing Awareness Program." Its motto is "Preserving our natural community environment one backyard at a time." Sea Spray has a speaker's bureau which includes members from more than 50 environmental organizations who will visit schools for 45-minute presentations. They also have an animated character called "Kelpman" who is used with kids under age 10 as a learning tool. A "Kelpman" mascot is being developed. For further information, fax: 925-1430.

if they fit. Three pairs are best: rubberized ones for spring mucking about in wet soil; a general work pair for planting and weeding; and a thin cotton pair for seed sowing. Another safety note: pesticide and fertilizer application is not a child's task, and kids should be educated as to when and where in the garden these substances have been applied. Tools, too, should fit — that is, they should be sturdy, but a little smaller and lighter than an adult's and have smaller handles. Quality garden stores today do carry some "real" tools for kids.

Be aware of those characteristics, particularly prominent in children, which make gardening tough — a lack of patience, a desire for immediate results, discouragement caused by failure. A first strategy in overcoming these difficulties is to plant to please and plant for success. Appeal to a kid's interests; plant plants which are dramatic in form, size or colour, or which are quick-growing and/or edible. Encourage giant pumpkin or zucchini competitions, or theme gardens like a pizza-toppings garden, butterfly gardens or Hallowe'en party garden. Some plants that meet some of these criteria are scarlet runner beans, peas, tomatoes, strawberries, sweet peas, snapdragons, marigolds, cornflowers, sunflowers, nasturtiums, Sea Holly, *Echinacea*, *Allium*, Globe Thistle, Chinese Lanterns, *Lunaria*, *Nigella*, blueberry bushes or crabapple or apple trees. A child's interest is more easily sustained if there is some garden activity all the time, so if you can, plant a mix of bulbs, perennials, annuals and seeds.

Seed size should be appropriate to a child's manual dexterity — the fat seeds of beans, peas, sunflowers, pumpkin, corn and cucumber are great for young children. Be generous with the seeds — one for the slugs, one for the aphids and wireworms, one for the birds to fatten them for the winter and one for me! Successive plantings (an initial planting followed by one or two other plantings a week or two later) also help to overcome losses due to weather or pests. Planting in a range of locations is another means of increasing the survival rate, and seeds planted in pots for planting out later are less likely to become lunch for some hungry larva.

Try to foster the attitude that from each season in the garden, some things are to be used, some are to be saved and some are to be given away. Plants that can be used include succulent strawberries, peas, tomatoes and rhubarb dipped in honey and eaten on the spot or brought in for dinner, and also those flowers and shrubs enjoyed for their beauty. As for saving, I allow some plants to go to seed and encourage the children to pretend that they are pioneers and collect the seed for next year's planting. Seeds can usually be shaken out of ripe pods into a paper bag and, when completely dry, stored in a labelled and dated airtight container. Geraniums, dahlia tubers and bulb offsets can be over-wintered in dry cool storage for the following year. There are so many ways for children to make gifts of their gardening. Those extra seeds sown can be given as seedlings, and divided perennials, rooted cuttings and saved seeds also make welcome gifts. Herbs can be dried for oils and vinegars and teas or made into pesto, and flowers can be dried for potpourri, soaps, dried wreaths and other floral gifts. Children can also make gifts of their gardening knowledge by giving demonstrations at school and at community centres.

If children can be shown that gardening is really just human participation in natural, recurrent cycles of growth, death and decay, they will develop a broader focus and more realistic expectations about the art and pleasure of gardening. Worm composting is a fascinating way of convincing them that the creepy crawlies of the natural world have an ecological role to play. Trapping an insect in a bug box with a magnified top will allow you and your child to later check references for a positive ID or to hold the insect to observe its life phases. Play guessing games with your child: Which garden pest leaves a slimy trail and chews irregular holes around leaf edges? What causes the new growth of roses to look wilted and the buds fail to open? Can you think of a shrub with

Students ripping newspapers for worm composting workshop at the Vancouver Compost Demonstration Garden (see Chapter One). Photo: City Farmer

The Rotary Heritage Forest Stewardship and Treekeepers Program is a continuing environmental project sponsored by the Rotary Club of Vancouver South and six other Vancouver and Burnaby Rotary Clubs. It is an awareness and education program for grades four and five in Vancouver and Burnaby elementary schools, centred around existing trees in their local community. Since 1992, some 3700 students from 35 Vancouver and Burnaby schools planted 7000 trees at the Rotary Heritage Forest site beside the TransCanada Highway. Out of these students, some 300 children from seven schools participate in a Treekeeper program at their school. Each student takes on the responsibility for learning and caring for a large tree in the Urban Forest, on their school grounds, on adjoining streets or in nearby parks. An integral part of the Treekeeper program is each class' stewardship of their section of the Rotary Heritage Forest. The Rotary Heritage Forest sites are along the TransCanada between Burnaby and the Second Narrows Bridge to North Vancouver. The Rotary Heritage Forest now consists of over 5000 healthy trees. For more information, call 327-1851 or fax 327-1851. The program offices are located at: 879 West 61st Ave.

edible berries that is a relative of the salal we saw on our walk? Find the seeds in a banana. In nature, how do plants come to be in different places? Judging from the growing conditions that sage likes, where do you think it originates from? Also, sometimes seeing larger examples or masses of a given plant will form in a child's mind an image of that plant that is transferred to the less dramatic version in his or her own garden. For example, a visit to the rhododendron walk in full bloom may cause one to see the potential of the three or four rhodos at home. Red poppies, by association, always transport me to sunlit fields in the Italian countryside.

Children whose minds and hands are exploring, year round, nature in their backyards, will come to see gardening as an aesthetic, healthy and ecologically relevant activity, and their garden as a microcosm of the larger environment of human, animal, insect and plant life.

HAVING FUN WITH SEEDS

by Roy Jonsson

Most gardeners look at seed catalogues when trying to decide what to grow, but there is another source of seeds that may be of interest to you and your children. Have you ever thought of growing some tropical houseplants from the fruit seeds or vegetables that come from the produce store?

Raising plants from exotic fruit seeds can be a great way to get children interested in growing things and learning a little elementary botany as well. Many of the seeds are very large and the parts of the newly germinated plant are easy to observe as they develop. Adults in the family might also be surprised to see what some of these plants look like.

Most people have eaten peanuts but would not recognize a peanut plant if they saw one. Coffee in particular makes an excellent potted plant. It has holly-sized leaves that are deep green and after several years will produce clusters of white flowers and green berries. After the berries ripen and turn dark red, the coffee beans can be extracted, roasted, ground and brewed. Possibilities for good houseplants include avocado, cherimoya, citrus, litchi nut, loquat, mango, persimmon and pomegranate. Passion fruit can also be grown but the plant will be a vine rather than an upright plant. Coconuts and dates are interesting to germinate but grow too large to keep in the house for long.

With few exceptions, seeds must be extracted from the ripe fruit and dried briefly before being germinated. If the fruit or produce has been cooked, roasted or pickled, the seed is dead and of no value. Use a semi-sterile medium such as "mica-peat" or "Reddi-earth" to plant the seeds in (regular potting soil contains too many microbes and fungal spores). Choose a container that is large enough to accom-

Seedy Saturday (sponsored by VanDusen Botanical Garden during the last Saturday in February) has art activities for children.

Joette Heuft and Aaron Michael, sharing the load.
Photo: Joette Heuft

What do female gardeners wear when they get married? Weeding dresses.

modate the type of seed. Avocado, coconut and mango can be quite large and the seeds need to be completely covered with 5 to 20 millimetres of medium to maintain the moisture. Dampen the medium before planting (like a wet sponge) and place some loose plastic wrap over the container.

Seeds from tropical plants generally need a higher temperature to germinate so choose a warm spot above a hot water tank or fridge or set up a 25-watt bulb below your seeds to provide that extra constant heat. If you have a small thermometer, check the temperature and try to keep it between 24 and 28 degrees Celsius.

The length of time it will take for germination varies greatly. Be patient! Some plants will come up within two to three weeks and others will take two to three months. If they are not in constant view, they must be checked on a regular basis as the seedling will not survive for long in the dark or without food and water. Lifting the new seedling out of the rooting medium can be interesting. On the large seeds the radical (root) and the cotyledon (sprout) are very evident and grow in opposite directions, one with and one against gravity. Most of the seed is stored food and the seed casing slowly withers and drops off as the food is consumed by the new seedling. Use any quality potting soil and a 5 to 10 centimetre container for the first potting. Too large a pot will kill your seedling.

Papaya seeds have to be treated differently. They will not germinate unless planted along with some of their own pulp, which contains a digestive enzyme called papain. The enzyme helps break down the seed casing, allowing germination. It is the same enzyme used as meat tenderizer.

Pineapples are grown from cuttings, not seeds. Tug on the green leaves coming out of the top of the pineapple and if they do not come free then the top section can be used. Cut the top section off with a 20 millimetre layer of fruit and let it sit in a warm dry place for several days until there is no sign of moisture on the cut surface. Plant it in a damp rooting medium so the fleshy section is buried and then place it in a warm bright area. In three or four weeks, lift the pineapple top gently and check for roots.

There are several vegetables that can also be grown from cuttings. Sweet potatoes and yams are both vines and can be grown the same as seed potatoes. These tubers, like most potatoes, are treated to prevent them from sprouting. It may help to soak them in water for a day before planting. They also need to be quite warm to break dormancy.

Peanuts or ground nuts will sprout as long as they have not been roasted. After the plant matures and flowers, the seed heads burrow under the ground and form the seeds or new peanuts.

The Trans Canada Trail is a nation-wide millennium project with plenty of gardening opportunities. The trail will be going through Templeton Secondary's schoolyard. They are building a greenway with two paths, one for walkers and one for cyclists. The greenway will include a couple of large domed mosaics (of provincial birds and a map of the route) and plantings from various regions of Canada. Gilmore Community School and neighbouring businesses in Vancouver Heights are also planning to enhance two kilometres of the trail in their area. For more information on the Trans Canada Trail call Leon Lebrun at Trails BC (942-6768) or go to the TCT Pavilion behind the False Creek Community Centre at Granville Island. You can also check out their website at: www.tctrail.ca

What did the spaceman grow in his garden?
Alien beans.

RESOURCES FOR KIDS

Here are some gardening projects and resources for children throughout the Lower Mainland.

ABBOTSFORD:

BC Agriculture in the Classroom Foundation
Abbotsford Agricultural Centre, 1767 Angus Campbell Rd. • 556-3088
contact: Lindsay Babineau
Develops resources to support the curriculum.

BURNABY:

Burnaby North Secondary School Meditation Garden
751 Hammarskjold • 664-8550
In 1996, under the direction of Landscape designer Heide Hermary and Career Preparation Advisor Dave Warnett, students and community volunteers turned an asphalt-covered courtyard into a lush meditation garden. It's a refuge from the bustle of the school, a place where poetry classes are taught peacefully, where students come to read or think quietly. Heide wanted to design a garden that would be a place to find happiness and peace and become rejuvenated. The garden is respected and loved by the students – their favourite spot is a pond that the students built.

Burnaby North Students, along with students from a Burnaby School Board Continuing Education course for landscape technicians, look after the garden. The amazing thing is that the plants grow at a phenomenal rate as it is a very protected area – a warm micro-climate. Plants were carefully selected to be low maintenance.

Burnaby South Secondary School
5455 Rumble St. • 664-8560
This gardening program was set up for special needs students. A greenhouse facility on school grounds is used to grow plants for hanging baskets and planters. Fuchsia and geranium cuttings are taken in autumn and seedlings are raised in the spring. These are used to plant 40 or more hanging baskets and planters in April which are then sold for Mother's Day. The pro-

gram is so successful that most years everything is pre-sold. Students now take orders before they start to plant the containers. Flower arranging is also taught, using the cut flowers that weren't sold at the United Flower Growers auction. Teacher Pat Ponti is helped by volunteers from VanDusen gardens. With additional help from some folks in the industry, the students created arrangements for the visit of H.R.H. Prince Charles and sons William and Harry in the spring of 1998.

Gardenworks
6250 Lougheed Hwy. • 299-0621
Gardenworks provides tours for preschoolers and kindergarten classes. It also has hands-on demonstrations of gardening techniques for young kids.

NORTH VANCOUVER:
Highland Community School
3150 Colwood Rd. • 985-7478
This school has created a butterfly garden on the school grounds. Students have planted flowers and plants known to attract butterflies.

RICHMOND:
Richmond Garden Club
Contact: Katrina Dnistransky • 435-5471
The club has a pilot program now in an early stage. Club members have provided bulbs and rhizomes to three schools in Richmond School District to help students gain hands-on experience in planting and maintaining a garden.

VANCOUVER:
City Farmer
801-318 Homer St. • 685-5832
Call City Farmer for booklet entitled "School Garden Guidelines." City Farmer was involved in the setup of the kids' garden at Lord Roberts Elementary School at 1100 Bidwell St. in the early 1980s. It was designed as a hands-on project for young students to learn about planting, composting and garden maintenance. The garden is still in existence and is now maintained solely by the students and teachers.

The majority of schools in North and West Vancouver have started clubs called "Earthshakers: Environmental Caretakers." The four pillars of the program are increased awareness of nutrition, organic gardening, recycling and composting. See also: information on Sea Spray, page 242.

What did the big flower say to the little flower?
Hi, Bud.

The Evergreen Foundation (West Coast Office)
106-163 West Hastings Ave. • 689-0766; 689-0768 (fax)
e-mail: sgn-bc@evergreen.ca
website: www.evergreen.ca
The Evergreen Foundation does "School Ground Naturalization," which aims to change bleak areas into more livable, balanced environments through the planting of indigenous species. Twenty schools are currently participating in the two-year re-greening program. Schools may apply to the foundation for a $500 grant to assist with the start-up. The Foundation provides resources such as workshops, resource personnel, facilitators and fundraising expertise. Students are involved in the preparation of "Habitat Creation Sites" and are encouraged to use native plants. Restored habitat areas become learning classrooms. Students, teachers, parents and community members are encouraged to participate. Call the foundation for more information. The office has lots of resource material. One of these garden projects has just begun as a co-operative venture between Lord Strathcona Elementary School and Strathcona Community Centre in Vancouver.

Farm Folk/City Folk
730-0450
Each year a children's tent is set up at the Farm Folk/City Folk festival. Kids are taught about composting and helpful bugs in gardens. Call for more information.

Pacific Spirit Park
16th Ave. and Sasamat • 224-5739
The park has programs run by the GVRD. Their nature walks include bird watching and tree identification.

Ray-Cam Co-operative Centre
920 East Hastings St.
Their daycare program has a garden. Kids plant beans, sweet peas, carrots etc. The kids also weed the garden and share the crops.

Southlands Elementary School
5351 Camosun St. • 713-5414
A "greening" project on the school grounds was started by a group of parents to encourage active participation of students. Students helped with the digging, fertilizing and planting in the native garden. They learned to loosen root balls, how to plant bulbs at varying depths, how to use bone meal as a bulb rooster and many other things. This will eventually become a teaching garden with all plants labelled and a reference book compiled.

VanDusen Botanical Garden
5251 Oak St.
contact: Grant Withers, Children's and Family Program Co-ordinator • 257-8669
In addition to school programs (call the above number for brochure), the garden runs children's programs with the goal of enhancing awareness and appreciation of the plant world and its interdependence with all living things.

More information about Laurel and Jan is available on their website:
http://www.laurelandjan.com/jukebox.htm

PESTICIDE BLUES

Children's entertainers Laurel and Jan of North Vancouver sing environmentally conscious songs. Their latest CD, *Flights of Imagination*, is all about gardening. A sample of the lyrics:

Well, I'm looking at our garden, can't believe what I
    see there
Leaves and flowers chewed and ragged; berry canes
    are bare!
I see slippery, slimy, silvery trails of snails and slugs
Well, I'm gonna get out skull and crossbones —
I'm gonna take care of those bugs!

Chorus:
We've got the DDT, the PCB, the Diocide,
    insecticide blues
We've got the modern-day technology
What happened to ecology blues ...
Think before you spray ...
And look to Mother Nature for the Natural Way.

We could wait until the night falls, when crawly
    things come out
Could blast them with our spray and spread the
    chemicals about,
But then we'd start to cough and sneeze, so let's
    find a better way
With 100 million years behind them, those bugs are
    here to stay.

(Chorus)

So we asked some questions, read some books and
    learned just what to do
Got some garlic and hot pepper, made a herbal
    brew
We sprayed them on the creepy crawlers munching
    in the night
The flowers bloomed, the leaves got greener
Now everything is all right!

(Chorus)

FURTHER RESOURCES

If you think this book is dense with information, we've got news. There's a lot more out there. We've stayed away from how-to's, but fortunately there are lots of talented writers and broadcasters who tackle how-to's and who's who and what's what on the gardening scene around here. Here's our list.

FURTHER RESOURCES

Umbrella Organizations

SURREY:

BC Horticultural Coalition
203A-15225 104th Ave. • 588-1958; 588-1010 (fax)
The Council is responsible for research, lobbying and monitoring of legislation associated with the horticultural industries.

OUTSIDE GVRD:

BC Agricultural Council
101-266 Lawrence Ave. • Kelowna
(250) 171-0360; (250) 717-0370 (fax)

LOCAL GARDENING RESOURCE PUBLICATIONS

There are so many great publications on gardening that we had to work hard at focusing on those about gardening locally. Some of these books are out of print, but the public libraries have copies. Also, check out used book stores and don't forget the excellent library at VanDusen Botanical Garden.

Gardening Books

Allen, Christine
Roses for the Pacific Northwest (Steller Press, 1999)
Past president of the Vancouver Rose Society and owner of Killara Farm Old Rose Nursery. Recommended varieties in every category and practical information on planting and maintenance.

Bradbury, Elspeth and Judy Maddocks
The Garden Letters (Polestar, 1995)
Two friends, one in West Vancouver, the other in New Brunswick , exchange musings about their gardening lives.

Bradbury, Elspeth and Judy Maddocks
The Real Garden Road Trip (Polestar, 1997)
The same two pals cross Canada seeking interesting gardens and gardeners.

Clearview Horticultural Products, Inc.
The Concise Guide to Clematis in North America (Clearview Horticultural Products, 1996)
A colour guide from the Wein family, who have been growing clematis in Aldergrove since 1970.

Cranshaw, Whitney
Pests of the West: Prevention and control for today's garden and small farm (Fulcrum, 1992)
Line drawings of bugs, diseases and weeds.

Croft, Philip
Nature Diary of a Quiet Pedestrian (Harbour, 1986)
The writings of a gentle walker, a gardener, painter and chronicler of life, mostly in West Van.

Grant, John and Carol
Trees and Shrubs for Coastal BC Gardens (Whitecap, 1990)
The original 50-year-old tome has been up-dated extensively by four horticulturists from the Seattle area.

Grescoe, Audrey
Giants: The Colossal Trees of Pacific North America (Raincoast, 1997)
This is a large book about the biggest trees, with good information and lyrical writing.

Heinen, Greta
In Your Greenhouse: A Beginner's Guide (Birch Publishing, 1994)
A beginner's guide to managing your home greenhouse with a year's calendar of chores geared for locals.

Hobbs, Thomas
Shocking Beauty (Raincoast, 1999)
The gift book of the decade by the entertaining and informative Thomas Hobbs of Southlands Nursery.

Johnson, Lorraine
Grow Wild: Native Plant Gardening in Canada (Random House of Canada, 1998)
Native plants are water-wise and ideally suited for your garden. This resource guide tells you why.

Keswick, Maggie, Judy Oberlander and Joe Wai
In a Chinese Garden: The Art & Architecture of the Dr. Sun Yat-Sen Classical Chinese Garden (Dr. Sun Yat-Sen Garden Society of Vancouver, 1990)
A photo essay about this remarkable garden.

Kramer, Pat
Gardens of British Columbia (Altitude Publishing, 1998)
Gorgeous colour photo essay guide to the entire province.

Kruckeberg, Arthur
Gardening with Native Plants of Pacific Northwest: An Illustrated Guide (U of Washington, 1982/1992)
The authority on this topic.

Lyons, C.P. and Bill Merilees
Trees, Shrubs and Flowers to Know in British Columbia (Lone Pine, 1995; revision of 1952 work)
Line drawings, lots of info. geared to amateur naturalists rather than botanists. Useful "quick check" info. for identifying trees.

Merilees, Bill
Attracting Backyard Wildlife (Whitecap, 1989; revised for 1999)
Want birds, bees and beasts? Read this.

Minter, Brian
Brian Minter's New Gardening Guide (Whitecap, 1998)
Minter's guide is incredibly practical and has very useful plant lists.

Newton, Judy
Gardening in Vancouver (Lone Pine, 1992)
A great primer with lots of useful info – especially on garden planning and soil improvement.

Noble, Phoebe
My Experience Growing Hardy Geraniums (Trio Investments Ltd, 1994)
Everything you need to know by the woman responsible for the cultivar "Phoebe Noble."

Parish, Roberta and Sandra Thomson
Tree Book: Learning to Recognize Trees of BC (BC Ministry of Forests, 1994)
Very useful guide to the entire province.

Pettinger, April
Native Plants in the Coastal Garden: A Guide for Gardeners in British Columbia and the Pacific Northwest (Whitecap Books, 1996)
Plants particularly for our local growing conditions.

Pojar, Jim and Andy MacKinnon
Plants of Coastal British Columbia including Washington, Oregon and Alaska (BC Ministry of Forestry and Lone Pine Publishing, 1994)
Detailed botanical information; excellent reference colour photos.

Reynolds, James I.
Sub-Tropical Gardening in a Temperate Climate (Hylea Publishing, Vancouver, 1997)
Very local. By a member of the Pacific Northwest Palm and Exotic Plant Society (and the editor of the journal).

Steele, Richard M.
The Stanley Park Explorer (out of print; Whitecap, 1985)
An invaluable guide. Out of print, but worth looking for.

Stevens, Elaine, Dagmar Hungerford, Doris Fancourt-Smith, Jane Mitchell and Ann Buffam
Twelve Month Gardener (Whitecap, 1997)
Excellent contemporary and local information on what to do in your garden each month, from five members of VanDusen's Volunteer Master Gardeners. Good plant lists too.

Stoltmann, Randy
A Hiking Guide to the Big Trees of Southwestern BC (Western Canada Wilderness Society, 1991)
Lots of detail on these amazing trees.

Straley, Gerald B.
Trees of Vancouver (UBC Press, 1992)
Interested in trees? This is the book—clear, complete and very useful.

Stubbs, Betty
From Golf Course to Garden: A History of VanDusen Botanical Display Gardens (VanDusen Botanical Garden Association, 1985/1994)
If you are interested—go to the VanDusen library to read this.

Sunset
Sunset Western Garden Book (Sunset, 1995)
Very useful all-round identification and how-to guide.

Tarrant, David A.
Canadian Gardens (Whitecap, 1999)
David visits twenty spectacular and inspiring gardens from the Gulf Islands to Nova Scotia. Great photos.

Tarrant, David A.
Pacific Gardening Guide (Whitecap, 1990)
A year-round garden care guide for West Coast gardening. Includes ideal plants, organic methods of soil enrichment, pest control and a calendar.

Tarrant, David A.
A Year in Your Garden (Whitecap, 1989)
A month-by-month guide to gardening in BC. Year round and total gardening information from Tarrant's much-missed column in the *Vancouver Sun*.

Valleau, John M.
Heritage Perennials Perennial Gardening Guide (Valleybrook International Ventures Inc., 1988)
A great colour guide by the folks at Heritage Perennials, a grower in Abbotsford.

Wales, Paddy
Journeys Through the Garden: Inspiration for Gardeners in BC and the Pacific Northwest (Whitecap Books, 1998)
Wales, a well-known photogapher and writer, has combined her skills to produce a book that is both beautiful and useful.

Whitner, Jan Kowalczewski
Northwest Garden Style: Ideas, Designs, and Methods for the Creative Gardener
(Sasquatch Books, 1996)
Features 22 gardens, including some from BC.

Whitson, editor, *et al*
Weeds of the West (University of Wyoming and the Western Society of Weed Science, 1991)
Good colour pictures as well as descriptions.

Whysall, Steve
100 Best Plants for the Coastal Garden (Whitecap Books, 1998)
The *Vancouver Sun*'s gardening editor expounds on his favourites, and why he chose them.

Willis, A.R.
The Pacific Gardener (Whitecap, 1995)
A classic. Full of charts, drawings and simple pruning information (although pro-pesticides). First published in 1964, now in its 14th printing.

Gardening Pamphlets and Handbooks

March, Deborah
"Pest or Guest: A Guide to Alternative Pest Control in the Home" (Society Promoting Environmental Conservation, or SPEC, 1985)

"A Gardeners Guide to Pest Prevention and Control in the Home Garden" (Ministry of Agriculture and Food, 1995)

Natural History Handbook Series to the Flora and Fauna of BC (BC Provincial Museum)

GARDENING MEDIA

Television

A bonus of the increased interest in gardening is the increase in quality visuals for the couch-potato gardener. TV shows can be entertaining, educational and particularly welcome in the dead of winter as you pine for warm soil between your fingers. Every season grows a new crop of shows, and shows move around. Check your local listings for days and times.

Here's a listing of the current shows with the local hosts' names. The shows are listed by network.

CBC
Canadian Gardener with David
   Tarrant

CHEK TV
Get Up & Grow with Gord Nickel

Discovery Channel
Canadian Gardener with David
   Tarrant

Home and Garden TV
Breaking Ground
Burke's Backyard
Canadian Gardener with David
   Tarrant
Designer's Landscape
Gardener's Diary
Gardener's Journal
Garden Architecture
Gardening by the Yard
Great Indoors
Grow It!
Indoor Gardener
Rebecca's Garden
Surprise Gardener
Victory Garden
Way to Grow
Winter Gardening

Knowledge Network
At Home with Herbs with Renae
   Morriseau
The Seasonal Gardener with Brian
   Minter
Guerrilla Gardener with Grahame
   Beakhust
Earth's Garden with Ken Beattie

Life Network
Gardening
Mrs. Greenthumbs

Rogers Cable
Garden Time with Marlene Gurvich

WTN
Earth's Garden with Ken Beattie
The Herbal Primer with Ken Beattie
   and Arvel Gray
Small Space Gardening with Dagmar
   Hungerford and Paul Grant

VISION
Gardens of the World

Radio

CBC Radio 1
host: Brian Minter
time: Every 2nd Thursday, 1 to 2 p.m.

CHMB RADIO AM 1320
host: Penny Choy (in Cantonese)
time: Monday, 10:30 a.m.

CHQM-FM 103.5
host: John Hadley
time: Sunday, 9 to 10 a.m.

CISL 650
host: Mark Cullen
time: Sunday, 7 to 8 p.m.

CKNW 98
host: Wim Vander Zalm
time: Sunday, 11a.m. to noon

CKST AM 1040
host: Betty Murray
time: Friday, 11:00 a.m. to noon

STAR FM
host: Brian Minter
time: Saturdays 8 to 9 a.m.

Magazines

Build & Green
Free at libraries, garden centres etc.
2922 West 6th Ave., Van. BC, V6K
1X3 • 730-1940
website: www.buildngreen.com

Canadian Gardening
Local newsstands
fax: 905-475-9246
e-mail: letters@canadiangardening.com
website: www.ab.sympatico.ca/mags/
cangardening/

Coastal Grower
toll-free: 1-800-816-0747; fax: 360-1709
e-mail: grower@islandnet.com
website: www.coastalgrower.com/

Gardens West
toll-free: 1-800-263-1088; fax: 604-879-5110
e-mail: grow@gardenswest.com
website: www.gardenswest.com/

Gardening Life
phone: (416) 593-6310; fax: (416) 591-1630
e-mail: home@inforamp.net

Harrowsmith Country Life
toll-free: 1-800-387-0581
e-mail: hsmith@inforamp.net

Plant and Garden
phone: (905) 856-4178
e-mail: p&gmag@lanzen.net

Newspapers

The following newspapers run regular gardening columns or sections.

Vancouver Sun
editor: Steve Whysall, New Homes Section (Thursdays and Saturdays)
writer: Susan Balcom, Home and Garden Writer (Thursdays)

The Province
writer: Helen Chestnut (Sundays)
writer: Kerry Moore (Sundays: March to September expanded coverage)

Bowen Breeze
writer: Sue Rickett

Burnaby News
writer: Brian Minter

Burnaby Now
writer: Ann Risdon

Coquitlam Now
writer: Ann Risdon

Courier
section: Home & Garden Supplement in Spring

The Echo
writer: Ann Marrison

Langley Times
writer: Barry Peters

Ming Pao Daily News
writer: Iris Yim

North Shore News
writer: Roy Jonsson

Peace Arch News
writer: Lisa Rutledge

Richmond Review
writer: Barry Peters

Surrey Leader
writer: Barry Peters

Surrey Now
writer: Ann Marsden

The Undercurrent
writer: Vivamus

The Voice
writer: Brian Minter

INTERNET RESOURCES

On the Venn Diagram of folks who love to garden and folks on the Internet, there is a huge overlap. It's no wonder. Passions rule on the Internet, which was clearly invented for gardeners. Known as the "virtual allotment plot," you can ask questions, buy cool tools, post your favourite photos and swap seeds, ideas and resources. Plus, the weather, seasons, zones and borders do not restrict cyber-potting. If you don't have your own computer and Internet account, most Lower Mainland public libraries have terminals you can use. As well, there are many "cyber cafés" around town where you can rent time to check out some of these sites. Try it – you'll be amazed.

Here's the dirt on gardening on the Internet.

Favourite Gardening Newsgroups

These bulletin boards feature discussion groups and advice swapping one the widest variety of topics, and with the most diverse participants possible from all over the world.

rec.gardens (the most popular and most general!)
rec.gardens.edible
rec.gardens.orchids
rec.gardens.roses
uk.rec.gardening
rec.food.preserving
rec.ponds
aus.gardens
alt.agriculture.fruit
alt.agriculture.misc
alt.bonsai
alt.landscape.architecture
alt.sustainable,agriculture
alt.folklore.herbs
sci.agriculture
sci.agriculture.beekeeping
sci.bio.botany

Just the FAQs

The archive for rec.gardens includes the motherlode of FAQs (Frequently Asked Questions) where you can find compiled information on everything including compost-making, deer repellant plants, and fava-beans. http://sunsite.unc.edu/london/

E-mail Lists

As well as newsgroups and web pages, a feature of the Internet is the ability to subscribe to a topical list which deposits the discussion into your e-mail slot. For a massive list of mailing lists go to: http://www.liszt.com

Type in the key word "garden." You will find you can subscribe to over 40 mailing lists covering everything from alpines and bromeliads to square foot gardening to fans of irises.

Websites

Here are a couple of national treasures – and a lot of good regional sites.

BC Fruit Testers Association
website: http://www.islandnet.com/~bcfta/

BC Ministry of the Environment
website: http://www.env.gov.bc.ca
This site has loads of information on air, water, land and climate issues. Of particular interest is the integrated pest management section.

Canadian Botanical Conservation Network
website: http://www.rbg.ca/cbcn
The Canadian Botanical Conservation Network maintains a directory of Canadian Gardens & Arboreta (http://www.rbg.ca/cbcn/gardens.html) as well as lots of information on endangered plants in Canada and invasive alien plants.

City Farmer
website: http://www.cityfarmer.org/
City Farmer, based in Vancouver, is a non-profit society promoting food production and environmental conservation in urban areas. Their website has worldwide links to information on urban issues like composting, community and school garden projects, rooftop gardens and wartime victory gardens. The site includes some great essays, like "Diary of a Compost Hotline Operator" (see excerpt in Chapter 1 of this book).

Farm Folk/City Folk
website: http://www.ffcf.bc.ca/

Gardening BC
http://www.gardeningbc.com/index/
This is a resource list.

Get Set to Garden
website: http://www.gardeningbc.com/
Get Set to Garden is BC-based. It has lots of links to local commercial gardening supplies.

Hedgerows Garden Tapestry
website: http://www.hedgerows.com/
Locally, Hedgerows Garden Tapestry is a fantastic resource for information about events at the UBC Botanical Garden and VanDusen Botanical Garden. Created by Mala Gunadasa-Rohling as a volunteer effort at publicizing UBC and VanDusen, this website came on-line in May 1996. It holds listings of clubs around town, a garden calendar of upcoming events, local gardening TV listings, commercial services, a question-and-answer chat forum and more all the time. Mala Gunadasa-Rohling is also web creator for David Tarrant's Canadian Gardener Website.

Hortus West Magazine
website: http://www.hortuswest.com/
This is a monthly reference magazine for locating western North America's native plants and seeds.

I-can Garden
website: http://www.ICanGarden.com
Master Gardener Donna Dawson of St. Albert, Alberta has taken on the world for her information-sharing clinic. "I-can Garden" bills itself as "The Canadian Internet Gardening Resource" and it is as thorough as you could possibly imagine. This site will take you to hundreds of Canadian gardening sites, catalogues, clubs and societies, Canadian public gardens, notices of gardening events around the country and a global seed-sharing area. There is an area for information on Canadian Radio and TV programs about gardening, and there are some excellent articles.

Minter Gardens
website: http://www.minter.org/
Great weekly tips section.

Northwest Gardening
website: http://www.nwgardening.com
This site is a Seattle-based wealth of information for gardeners with weather like ours.

Pacific Northwest Native Wildlife Gardening
website: http://www.teleport.com/~allyn/natives/

Plantlovers.com

website: http://www.plantlovers.com/
This is Pam Erikson's (of Erikson's Daylilies in Langley) newest project. It is a database of North American nurseries, plants, events, accessories etc.

Slugs and Salal

website: http://www.slugsandsalal.com
Victoria-based, this site is updated weekly and loaded with info. on growing plants in this region, events throughout the Pacific Northwest. Includes "monthly gardening task lists, clubs and organizations, discussion groups, inspiring picture profiles of gardens and shows, features on deer-proofing, using seaweed and of course battling slugs." Also includes columns by Helen Chestnut.

Trees of the Pacific Northwest

website: http://www.orst.edu/instruct/for241/
Trees of the Pacific Northwest is an excellent on-line tutor.

UBC Botanical Garden

website: http://www.hedgerows.com/UBCBotGdn/index.htm

Urban Garden

website: http://www.urbangarden.com/
This is a beautiful monthly photo journal of a Vancouver container garden with hints and plant lists.

VanDusen Botanical Garden

website: www.vandusen.org

The Virtual Gardener

website: http://www.gardenmag.com/
The Virtual Gardener is an excellent on-line magazine out of Victoria. It is published by Clyde Snobelen, an instructor in Horticulture at Camosun College in Victoria and a partner in a landscape design company in Victoria. The magazine is filled with features, tips, readers' comments, book excerpts and classifieds.

Botany and Taxonomy Websites

Angiosperm Anatomy

website: http://www.botany.uwc.ac.za/sci_ed/std8/anatomy/
This website is from a Grade 8 botany class and has terrific diagrams.

Flora of North America

website: http://www.fna.org/index1.html

Glossary Of Taxonomic Terms Commonly Employed in the Identification of Woody Plants
website: http://bluehen.ags.udel.edu/gopher-data2/.botanic_garden/.glossary.txt

Internet Directory for Botany
website: http://herb.biol.uregina.ca/liu/bio/botany.shtml
This is the University of Regina's compilation of over 1000 links to international sites of interest to anyone with botanical inclinations.

Zone Map of Canada
website: http://www.icangarden.com/zone.htm

Master Gardener Websites

The Saskatchewan Master Gardener Program
website: http://www.ag.usask.ca/cofa/departments/hort/hortinfo/misc/master.html

Texas Agricultural Extension Services
website: http://www.hal-pc.org/~trobb/mastgar.html
Hosts a massive collection of links to Master Gardener programs throughout North America.

VanDusen Botanical Garden's Master Gardeners
website: www.vandusen.org
These master gardeners are just starting a web page

Pesticide-Alternative Websites

Garden Web
website: http://www.gardenweb.com/

Integrated Pest Management
website: http://pupux1.env.gov.bc.ca/~ipmis/ipmis.html

Biological Control (A Guide to Natural Enemies in North America)
website: http://www.nysaes.cornell.edu/ent/biocontrol/index.html

Plant Information Websites

AgriWeb
website: http://www.agr.ca/agriweb/awhome-e.htm
An enormous bilingual federal government project to promote remote access to Canadian agriculture and agri-food information resources on the Internet.

Garden Guides
website: http://www.gardenguides.com/
Includes a vast number of colour photographs of flowers, vegetables and herbs in a huge database of useful information.

Internet Directory of Botany
website: http://www.helsinki.fi/kmus/bothort.html
From the Botanical Museum at the Finnish Museum of Natural History in Helsinki, comes an information-dense resource with loads of links.

The Invasive Plants of Canada Project
website: http://infoweb.magi.com/~ehaber/referenc.html
The source for info. on Canadian weeds.

WebGarden
website: http://www.hcs.ohio-state.edu/webgarden.html
Ohio State University's Virtual Horticulture Department is loaded with on-line courses, a plant materials database, and tips galore for commercial nurseries and home gardeners. There is also a database of more than 5,000 links to horticultural factsheets from the United States and Canada.

Specialty Sites

Canadian Orchid Sites
website: http://www.ccn.cs.dal.ca/Recreation/OrchidSNS/wcanada.html

Firegirl
website: http://www.firegirl.com/home.html
For those hot for chili peppers.

Friends of the Daylilies Home Page
website: http://www.primenet.com/~tjfehr/daylily.html

The Internet Bonsai Club
website: http://www.geocities.com/Tokyo/Garden/6895/

The Museum of Garden History in London
website: http://www.compulink.co.uk/~museumgh/

The Rhododendron Page
website: http://haven.ios.com/~mckenzie/rhodo05.html

The Rose Page
website: http://www.mc.edu/~nettles/rofaq/rofaq-top.html

Worldwide Links

The Digital Librarian
website: http://www.servtech.com/~mvail/gardening.html
An excellent collection of best of the web for gardening.

Garden.com
website: http://www.garden.com
Glorious colour photos in the enormous plant database, magazines and online shop. Great plant finder feature.

Garden Net
website: http://www.gardennet.com/
This is another massive site and home of *The Ardent Gardener*, a weekly on-line gardening publication and Flora's Best, an online garden shop.

The Garden Gate
website: http://www.prairienet.org/ag/garden/
Log on for another world of links to books, magazines, seed catalogues (American), advice and gardening software reviews. The link "Down the Garden Path" takes you to botanic gardens around the world, including the Kew Gardens at the Royal Botanical Garden (http://www.rbgkew.org.uk).

USDA Home Gardening
website: www.usda.gov/news/garden.htm
Part of the United States Department of Agriculture Information Series.

Contributors

Lolita Aaron is smitten by her passion for gardens. She is pregnant with gardens, and yearns to give birth to them immaculately. She hopes to make it her life work, without taking herself too seriously.

The BC Landscape and Nursery Association has over 450 members working in nursery, landscape, retail, education, supply, service and government organizations in the landscape horticultural industry.

Art Bomke, P.Ag. is an Associate Professor UBC Faculty of Agricultural Sciences and Jean Schwartz, B.Sc. (Agriculture) is a Horticultural Consultant.

Odessa Bromley works at Southside Perennial Gardens.

Ron Clancy is a Master Gardener who was educated as a chemist, works as a librarian and thrives as an urban farmer in deepest Dunbar.

In her leisure time, **Terri Clark** is an avid home gardener. She has organized the VanDusen Private Garden Tour since its inception in 1987.

For the last 42 years, **Dana Cromie** has spent most of his spare time gardening for himself and his friends in Vancouver.

Spring Gillard works for City Farmer as Compost Hotline Operator/Educator at the Vancouver Compost Demonstration Garden. When she's not answering compost crisis calls, she writes and produces videos.

Joette Heuft is an architect and a VanDusen volunteer Master Gardener.

Jennifer Jones is a garden designer in North Vancouver with a passion for English perennial borders and rockeries. Her company is called J.J. Jones Garden Design.

Roy Jonsson, a well-known garden speaker, teaches for the North Shore Continuing Education Department and VanDusen's Master Gardeners program, writes the garden column for the *North Shore News* and does residential and commercial consulting.

Claire Kennedy is a Vancouver garden designer.

Ann Kent is a horticulturist and garden designer who enjoys the restoration of older gardens. She specializes in pruning ornamental and fruit trees. A Master Gardener, she is also a popular gardening instructor at local community centres.

Michael Levenston is the Executive Director of City Farmer, Canada's Office of Urban Agriculture.

Bruce Macdonald is the director of the UBC Botanical Garden. In 1997 he won the prestigious Gold Veitch Memorial Medal from England's Royal Horticultural Society for advancing and improving the "science and practice of horticulture." He is the first Canadian to receive this medal since its inception in 1922.

Rachel Mackenzie and **Mary Allen** are two of the original Fireside FOGS.

Steve McQueen, a "Pot Lucker" has a jam-packed garden in Beach Grove. She is the VanDusen Garden Plant Sale Chair for 1999.

Paul Montpellier is the City of Vancouver's arborist.

Aimee Murrell is the Chairman of the VanDusen Garden Seed Collectors.

Angela Murrills is a journalist and Food Editor at the *Georgia Straight*, and author of *Food City: Vancouver*.

Mike Nassichuk is a Master Gardener and biologist who lives and gardens in the rainforest of North Vancouver.

Moura Quayle is a landscape architect and UBC's Dean of the Faculty of Agricultural Sciences (programs for ecosystem, community and human health).

Shelagh Smith designs and implements horticultural therapy programs and teaches part-time at Langara College. Her business is called Heart & Soil Horticultural Therapy.

David Tarrant is the Education Coordinator at UBC Botanical Garden and host of CBC-TV's "Canadian Gardener".

The Universal Garden Society Steering Committee is a collective of Vancouver residents with a total of 64 years of living near VGH. Between them, they have 209 years of gardening activity and a wide range of educational, volunteer and occupational experiences. They are happily single/married/divorced/widowed with 15 great/grand/children.

Edward van Veenendaal is a self-employed Naturescape consultant with over 20 years' experience as a horticulturist. He has a lifelong fascination with nature.

Derry Walsh is an amateur gardener living in Aldergrove on five acres, with an interest in grafting dwarf apple trees (heritage and modern), growing apple trees under plastic, and raising bees (native and bumble) and llamas.

Elisabeth Whitelaw is a landscape architect. In 1983, she compiled Vancouver's Heritage Tree Inventory.

INDEX

About the Authors

Marg Meikle is a keen gardener. She is also a freelance researcher, writer and broadcaster who is best known as CBC radio's "Answer Lady." Marg contributes articles to numerous magazines, has been a syndicated Internet columnist and has written several books, including *Dear Answer Lady* (Douglas & McIntyre), *Bumbering Around Vancouver* (Douglas & McIntyre) and *Dog City: Vancouver* (Polestar). She lives in Kitsilano, BC with her husband Noel, their son Mac and Rosie the Border Collie.

Dannie McArthur is the executive producer of CBC-TV's "Booked on Saturday Night." She has lived and travelled in many parts of the world, admiring other people's gardens. In her spare time, she gardens in her own patch of land on Bowen Island, BC.

Please let Marg and Dannie know about any omissions, additions, deletions or comments for the next edition of *Garden City: Vancouver*. Write to them at:

Polestar Book Publishers
PO Box 5238 Station B
Victoria, BC V8R 6N4

Or contact Marg directly:
voice mail: 734-CITY (3489)
fax: 736-7052
e-mail: mmeikle@home.com

THE CITY SERIES
Indispensable Guides to Your Favourite Activities in Your Favourite Cities

These comprehensive guides present a dynamic way of experiencing favourite cities and popular urban activities. Here is indispensable and intriguing information for real people who live, work and play in and around major Canadian urban centres. Follow your dog's lead with *Dog City*; grow a green thumb with *Garden City*; dine out on *Food City*.
The City Series: Discovering new worlds in your own backyard.
Ask for: *Food City: Vancouver* and *Dog City: Vancouver*
Watch for: *Garden City: Toronto*

DOG CITY: VANCOUVER
The Definitive Guide for Dog Owners in Vancouver and the Lower Mainland
Marg Meikle, with an introduction by **Stanley Coren**, author of *The Intelligence of Dogs*

> "Pick a topic and chances are that Meikle's covered it. She has sections on everything from walks to pet liability insurance; from dog photography to recipes for dog food ... As good a guide as you're going to get to living with a dog." — *Vancouver Sun*

Explore the world of the urban canine! Journalist and dog owner Meikle has the inside scoop on finding, caring for and enjoying life with your dog in Vancouver and the Lower Mainland. From purebred pooches to Heinz-57 pups, breed kennels to animal shelters, personalized food bowls to dancing with dogs, obedience training to classroom canines, pet ambulances to dog portraits — this comprehensive guide has it all. Plus: trivia, quotes, a primer on dog-owner etiquette and advice on what to do with doo!
1-896095-38-0 • $18.95 • b&w photos and illustrations throughout

FOOD CITY: VANCOUVER
The Delectable Guide to Finding and Enjoying Good Food
in Vancouver and the Lower Mainland
Angela Murrills, with an introduction by **James Barber**, the Urban Peasant

> "Impressive research, lots of hits and no errors..."
> — Jurgen Gothe in the *Vancouver Sun*

Angela Murrills, resident food expert at the Georgia Straight, has compiled a delectable guide to comestible Vancouver. Test your tastebuds as Murrills embarks on a mouthwatering trek through the city's rich culinary life. You'll discover everything from kitchen supplies to profiles of master chefs to annual festivals to tips on where to dine and much, much more. Look no further for: restaurant listings and a guide to take-out; specialty ingredients and organic food suppliers; juice bars, coffee bars and food-and-wine clubs; kitchenware, cooking classes and recipe sources; markets, festivals and annual food events.
1-896095-47-X • $18.95 • b&w photos and drawings throughout

BRIGHT LIGHTS FROM POLESTAR BOOK PUBLISHERS

Polestar Book Publishers takes pride in creating books that enrich our understanding of the world. We support independent voices that illuminate our history, stretch the imagination and engage our sympathies.

Non-Fiction

Between Gardens: Observations on Gardening, Friendship and Disability
Dorothy Field and Carol Chudley Graham
1-896095-55-0 • $24.95 CDN/$19.95 USA • full-colour artwork throughout
With great insight and keen observation, this book documents a year in the life of two gardeners on Vancouver Island. It speaks about living in the moment – tossing seeds, working the soil and reaping what the land loves to grow. With beautiful photographs and artwork throughout.

From Farm to Feast:
Recipes and Stories from Saltspring and the Southern Gulf Islands
Gail Richards and Kevin Snook
1-896095-43-7 • $29.95 CDN/$24.95 USA • full-colour photos throughout
Here is the most valuable kind of cookbook: one that renews our relationship with healthy food while revelling in the delights of fine cuisine.

The Garden Letters
Elspeth Bradbury & Judy Maddocks
1-896095-06-2 • $19.95 CDN/$15.95 USA • illustrations throughout
"...lively anecdotes and humorous writings about the labours of life and gardening."
— *The Guardian* Weekend

The Real Garden Road Trip
Elspeth Bradbury & Judy Maddocks
1-896095-35-6 • $24.95 CDN/$19.95 USA • photographs throughout
Longtime friends Elspeth and Judy trek cross-country to find "real gardens and real gardeners."

Fiction

West by Northwest
David Stouck & Myler Wilkinson, eds.
1-896095-41-0 • $18.95 CDN/$16.95 USA
A brilliant collection of short fiction that celebrates the unique landscape and culture of BC. Includes stories by Bill Reid, Ethel Wilson, Wayson Choy, George Bowering, Evelyn Lau, Shani Mootoo and others.

Fresh Tracks: Writing the Western Landscape
Pamela Banting, ed.
1-896095-42-9 • $21.95 CDN/$18.95 USA
"A diverse gathering of over 40 writers, this is an entertaining and thoughtful exploration of how the western landscape influences all aspects of human life and creativity."
— *Quill and Quire*